Expert Systems
for
Business
and Management

Expert Systems
for
Business
and Management

Jay Liebowitz, Editor

YOURDON PRESS
PRENTICE HALL BUILDING
ENGLEWOOD CLIFFS, N.J. 07632

Library of Congress Cataloging-in-Publication Data

Expert systems for business and management / edited by Jay Liebowitz.
    p.   cm.
    ISBN 0–13–296468–6
    1. Expert systems (Computer science) 2. Decision support systems.
I. Liebowitz, Jay.
QA76.76.E95E9765   1990
658′.05633—dc20   89–22797
                                          CIP

Editorial/production supervision: Tally Morgan
Cover design: Bruce Kenselaar
Manufacturing buyer: R. Sintel

This book can be made available to businesses
and organizations at a special discount when
ordered in large quantities. For more information
contact:

Prentice-Hall, Inc.
Special Sales and Markets
College Division
Englewood Cliffs, N.J. 07632

Printed in the United States of America
10 9 8 7 6 5 4 3 2 1

Prentice-Hall International (UK) Limited, *London*
Prentice-Hall of Australia Pty. Limited, *Sydney*
Prentice-Hall of Canada Inc., *Toronto*
Prentice-Hall Hispanoamericana, S.A., *Mexico*
Prentice-Hall of India Private Limited, *New Delhi*
Prentice-Hall of Japan, Inc., *Tokyo*
Simon & Schuster Asia Pte. Ltd., *Singapore*
Editora Prentice-Hall do Brasil, Ltda., *Rio de Janeiro*

To the wonderful Liebowitz's and Zeide's

To those ''champions'' in organizations who encourage Expert Systems technology and applications, where appropriate.

Contents

Jay Liebowitz, Dept. of Management Science, George Washington University, Washington, D.C. 20052

Thomas J. Beckman, Artificial Intelligence Lab, Internal Revenue Service, 1201 E Street, Room 604, Washington, D.C. 20224

Chapter 3 MODELING AND REASONING: INTEGRATING DECISION SUPPORT WITH EXPERT SYSTEMS, 51

David King, AI Applications, Execucom Systems Corporation, 9442 Capital of Texas Highway North, Arboretum Plaza One, Austin, TX 78759

Chapter 4 EXPERT SYSTEMS AND DECISION SUPPORT SYSTEMS IN AUDITING, 77

Daniel E. O'Leary and Paul Watkins, School of Accounting, University of Southern California, Los Angeles, CA 90089–1421

Chapter 5 ANSWERS: AN EXPERT SYSTEM FOR FINANCIAL ANALYSIS, 101

Edward Blocher, Department of Accounting, Graduate School of Business, University of North Carolina, Carroll Hall CB #3490, Chapel Hill, NC 27599–3490

Chapter 6   THE FINANCIAL STATEMENT ANALYZER, 127

Chun Ka Mui, Carolyn F. Hassel and Lisa C. Curtis, Arthur Andersen & Co., 69 West Washington Street, Chicago, IL 60602

Chapter 7   THE DEVELOPMENT OF AN EXPERT SYSTEM THAT ESTIMATES CASUALTY INSURANCE LOSS RESERVES, 143

Betty C. Horn, Department of Accounting, George Mason University, Fairfax, VA 22030

Chapter 8 EXPERT SYSTEMS IN HEALTH INSURANCE: CASE STUDIES AT BLUE CROSS OF WESTERN PENNSYLVANIA, 167

David J. Gorney, Rawson Technologies, Inc., 727 Charles Street, Wellsburg, WV 26070

Chapter 9 EXPERT SYSTEMS IN SALES AND MARKETING, 181

Louis L. Odette, Applied Expert Systems, Inc., Five Cambridge Center, Cambridge, MA 02142 and L. J. Berkman, Advantage Systems, Inc., 950 Winter Street, Suite 2100, Waltham, MA 02154

Chapter 13 CESA: AN EXPERT SYSTEM PROTOTYPE FOR AIDING U.S. DEPARTMENT OF DEFENSE RESEARCH CONTRACTING, 281

Jay Liebowitz, Dept. of Management Science, George Washington University, Washington, D.C. 20052
Laura C. Davis and Wilson F. Harris, Navy Center for Applied Research in Artificial Intelligence, Naval Research Laboratory, Code 5510, Washington, D.C. 20375

Preface

Expert systems designed for business and management applications are rapidly increasing in number and diversity throughout the world. Expert systems are being integrated into existing "traditional" computer technology that enhances the utility of both expert and conventional systems. Most of the major corporations are experimenting with and using expert systems to help them with their operations, planning, and decision making. Expert systems are even being mass marketed to provide, for example, advice on income tax preparation or even medical advice on children's health problems. Companies are beginning to adopt expert system technology and are including expert systems as one possible tool in their decision-making toolkit.

In terms of business functional areas, expert systems have been and are continuing to be built for such applications as finance, accounting, marketing, contracting, construction management, strategic management, and others. This book provides a good sample of some of the business expert systems being developed and/or used in corporations, universities, and government. The book presents case studies of business expert systems, describing prototypes, field-tested systems, and delivered, commercially used full-production systems and insights into the development of these business expert systems. Many of the leading experts in these areas have contributed chapters for this book.

This is one of the first books specifically devoted to expert system applications in business and management. The growing number of conferences worldwide on this subject suggests the importance of this technology in business. This book will be useful for practitioners, both managers and knowledge engineers, interested in expert systems and artificial intelligence. The book will also serve as a primary or supplementary text for a university course on expert systems, especially a course offered through the business school.

I thank the authors for their significant contributions to the book, and I also acknowledge Ed Moura, Paul Becker, Noreen Regina, Tally Morgan, the competent Prentice-Hall staff, reviewers and authors for their help in producing a book on such a timely and important topic.

Happy reading!

Washington, DC   Jay Liebowitz D.Sc.

Expert Systems
for
Business
and Management

1

Introducing Expert Systems into the Firm

Jay Liebowitz

INTRODUCTION

Expert systems are quickly gaining credibility and usage in many organizations worldwide. Over the years, expert systems have been developed and used in a variety of domains, ranging from medical diagnosis to tax planning to telecommunications fault isolation and diagnosis [1, 2]. Within recent years, expert systems have been built and implemented for business applications. Since 1981, commercial interests started to become prevalent in the expert systems area, and soon thereafter, various companies specializing in expert systems products and consulting emerged. At a slightly later time, businesses began to learn and experiment with expert systems technology in order to build up an in-house capability for this advancing technology. With companies beginning to embrace this technology, a wide selection of business applications began to be used for expert system development. Business expert systems have been constructed and used for financial planning, tax planning, marketing, computer configuration, fault isolation and diagnosis, and many other applications. Today, there are probably about 2,000 expert systems [3] being used for business and nonbusiness applications. There are several thousand other expert systems being developed and field tested. Dupont alone has developed about 200 expert systems.

This chapter describes various approaches for firms to introduce expert systems into their organizations. Various businesses will be used as case studies to illustrate these approaches.

WHO IS USING EXPERT SYSTEMS FOR THEIR BUSINESS?

Many corporations are developing and using expert systems for selected, well-specified business applications. Computer companies such as Digital Equipment Corporation (DEC) are using expert systems to help configure computer systems. Digital Equipment Corporation is also utilizing expert systems to act as a salesman's assistant and to help perform scheduling functions. Aerospace firms such as Boeing and Lockheed have developed expert systems for navigation control, planning and scheduling functions, fault diagnosis, and training functions. Boeing has even developed a workstation called Aquinas to help perform knowledge acquisition and knowledge base development. Oil companies such as Schlumberger-Doll and Amoco have developed expert systems to help with mineral exploration and identification of faults in the oil-refining process. Airline companies have used expert systems for assigning planes to gates at selected major airports. Telecommunications firms are using expert systems on a daily basis to identify telephone cable and switch maintenance problems and to provide on-line assistance to network analysts and operators. Trucking companies are using expert systems for resource allocation and scheduling functions. Financial institutions and investment firms use some expert systems for providing financial and estate planning advice. Insurance companies are using expert systems for assisting underwriters in questioning clients on life insurance.

The military has been a major funder of expert system projects. Contractors to the government such as Mitre, Bolt, Beranek and Newman, and Planning Research Corporation are developing expert systems for mission-planning functions, resource allocation, multisensor integration functions, classification, interpretation, and data analysis.

Besides individual companies getting involved with expert systems on an ad hoc basis, there are also major programs worldwide that are encouraging the development of expert systems and other artificial intelligence (AI) applications. In the United States, the Strategic Computing Program has encouraged the development of expert systems for military use, such as the Pilot's Associate. There is also a consortium of U.S. companies, called MCC, which is channeling research and development funds into building advanced computer technologies, including expert systems. In Japan, the Fifth Generation Computer Program is underway to build expert systems and AI hardware. In Europe, two consortia called ESPRIT and EUREKA have been formed, and many expert system projects are being developed and implemented.

As shown, there is a significant interest for companies to build expert systems. We now take a look at why they are building them.

WHY ARE COMPANIES BUILDING EXPERT SYSTEMS?

There are various key reasons why companies are constructing expert systems. One major reason is to develop the corporate memory of the firm. Before experts retire or quit the company, expert systems may be used to capture the knowledge and experiential learnings of experts in well-specified areas. By capturing their successes and failures, other people in the firm performing the same tasks might learn from the experiences and knowledge of others. A second reason for using expert systems is to improve the company's productivity and return on investment. Dupont, for example, estimates that the average development cost of their typical expert system was $25,000. However, the amount of money that this expert system saves Dupont is about $100,000. Similarly, DEC's XCON, used for configuring their VAX computer systems, saves DEC about $40 million a year, even though it costs DEC about $2.5 million annually to maintain XCON. A third reason why businesses are using expert systems is to provide a means of obtaining advice if the expertise is scarce, expensive, or unavailable. If an expert system acted at the level of human expert performance and it was well validated, then perhaps the expert system could act as the surrogate expert if the expert cannot be used for whatever reason. A fourth major reason why companies might use expert systems is to help under time and pressure constraints, when one might not be able to think clearly and consider all the alternatives and factors in making a decision. With an expert system, its questioning strategy might help the individual to logically and comprehensively make a decision. The last important reason for businesses to construct and use expert systems is to give a good profile of the company in the public's eye. If a company is involved in advancing technologies, like expert systems, then it creates a public image of the firm being a state-of-the-art company.

Knowing why expert systems are being used by companies, we can discuss ways in which to introduce expert systems into the firm. These will be examined in the next few sections.

HOW TO INTRODUCE EXPERT SYSTEMS INTO THE FIRM

In order to develop an expert systems capability for the firm, there are various approaches for introducing expert systems into the company. Each approach has its advantages and limitations, but all of the following methods have been used by various companies. Each of these methods will be discussed in turn.

Approach 1: Develop an In-house Capability for Expert Systems

Many companies prefer to promote expert systems technology from within. Simply put, instead of having to rely on expensive consultants or subcontractors to develop expert systems for the firm, the firm decides to make a commitment to the technology and develop its own in-house expert systems group. Some companies may want to send some selected employees to training courses, seminars, tutorials, or conferences to learn about expert systems. Additionally, low-priced expert system shells for the microcomputer could be bought to allow potential knowledge engineers and experts to experiment with some expert system applications. Dupont, in fact, used this approach where the experts directly built expert systems in their respective areas through using expert system shells. Of course, in order to first learn about this technology, consultants or training specialists from expert system shell vendors may need to be hired to introduce the technology to the eventual in-house company expert systems group.

The company may decide on having a centralized or distributed expert systems group within the company [4, 5]. A centralized group may provide greater strength and a central focus within the firm. A distributed group, on the other hand, might allow greater technology transfer within the company as different departments would have an expert systems specialist. The expert systems specialist could in turn disperse the technology within his or her respective department to promote its application and use.

Developing an in-house expert systems group has its advantages and limitations. One main advantage is that the company would not have to rely on others for building and implementing expert systems. Also, there might be a savings in expert system development costs by having an in-house group instead of paying high-priced consultants. Additionally, an in-house group might be able to better promote the technology within the firm than by hiring outsiders. Of course, there are some limitations with this approach. An in-house expert systems group might take a while to build in order to have the necessary expertise. Also, the company is taking a greater risk by committing to an in-house expert systems group instead of using consultants or subcontractors when the need arises.

In spite of these limitations, many corporations elect to use an in-house group for introducing expert systems into their firm. Two groups, the U.S. Internal Revenue Service and Boeing Computer Services, both used this strategy. These situations will be described next.

The U.S. Internal Revenue Service knowledge-based systems group. Several years ago, the U.S. Internal Revenue Service (IRS) was looking into advancing technologies that would help its operations. Expert systems was one technology that was of interest to the IRS, particularly since expert systems used for tax planning, like Taxadvisor, had early success. The IRS paid for some consultants and training specialists in the expert systems area to come to the IRS and present some lectures and training courses in expert systems. After obtaining some initial indoctrination into expert systems and their potential, the IRS decided to develop an in-house knowledge-based systems group. Of course, this would not preclude the IRS from using outside groups like Arthur Andersen & Co. for developing some expert systems. But with an in-house group, some expert systems could be developed using talent within the IRS, and an in-house group would give the IRS greater control and knowledge over expert system projects.

In order to develop this in-house group, the IRS decided to make a commitment to expert systems. They carefully selected a group of IRS agents who had an interest in and potential for expert systems. Then, after selecting this group, the IRS decided to send these agents to the better universities specializing in AI in order to enroll them full time in master's programs. Of course, each agent was asked to sign a form that would commit the agent to work a certain number of years at the IRS upon successful completion of the master's program. This group of agents, who went to universities like MIT and the University of Pennsylvania, would then form the nucleus of the Knowledge-Based Systems Group at the IRS. Since the first group of agents for the Knowledge-Based Systems Group, there has been one other group of agents (another group started in the fall of 1989) sent for full-time graduate study in AI at leading AI universities.

The IRS made a strong commitment to develop an in-house expert systems group. Other government agencies have also formed groups or centers specializing in AI. The Navy Center for Applied Research in Artificial Intelligence at the Naval Research Laboratory is one such center whose charter involves developing AI applications for mostly Navy situations.

Besides the government, companies have also used the strategy of developing an in-house expert systems group. For example, ICF has an advanced computer systems group working on expert systems applications. American Management Systems has an in-house AI group. Another company that was one of the first to develop an in-house expert systems group is Boeing Computer Services.

Boeing Computer Services' advanced technologies group. As part of its Advanced Technologies Group, Boeing decided to explore expert systems technology as an aid in performing its business. Boeing, like the IRS, first had to educate its employees in the Advanced Technologies Group on expert systems. Boeing spent a fair amount of resources to bring in consultants and training specialists in expert systems to help educate its Advanced Technologies Group on expert systems. Boeing also sent some of these group members to tutorials and AI conferences to further learn about expert systems and the state of the art.

After this initial investment in training the group members on expert systems and AI, the Advanced Technologies Group bought the necessary hardware and expert system shells to begin developing in-house expert system applications. These efforts subsequently led to developing the Expertise Transfer System (ETS), an aid for acquiring knowledge based on the repertory grid technique. Later ETS evolved into Aquinas, a workstation of expert system tools to help an individual develop expert systems.

Boeing had decided early that an in-house capability for expert systems development was a prudent and effective strategy. Later, companies in the same industry as Boeing, like Lockheed, also became involved with expert systems for some of their space-related work. Lockheed worked closely with Inference Corporation to develop some of its initial expert systems.

Besides using an in-house approach for introducing expert systems into the firm, another approach is for a company to affiliate itself with a university or a company specializing in expert systems/AI. This approach is discussed next.

Approach 2: Affiliate with a University or a Company Specializing in Expert Systems/AI

Another approach that some companies use for introducing expert systems into their organizations is to affiliate with a university or a company specializing in expert systems/AI. By doing this, the company forms a close alliance with a good

AI university or expert system company. This allows the company to transfer the technology in an efficient manner, and it also allows the pooling of resources. Graduate students could be used to work on company expert system projects through company-sponsored research at the university. Similarly, knowledge engineers at an expert systems company could bring the uninitiated knowledge engineers of the company up to speed in expert systems technology and methodologies. Additionally, the company's overhead may not be as high by affiliating with an AI-type university or company as it might be by having an in-house expert systems group.

Even though these advantages exist under this strategy, there are some possible limitations with this approach. First, the company may feel that it is "locked in" to a set philosophy when it becomes affiliated with a university or another company. It may be difficult to break the ties or introduce other creative ideas when a strong affiliation occurs. Second, the company may want to obtain other insights from other parties relating to the expert systems work. Again, the affiliated university or company may feel threatened and may resist other parties and comments. Last, the company becomes somewhat dependent on the affiliated university or company.

The next section discusses DEC's relationship with Carnegie-Mellon University (CMU). Digital Equipment Corporation's situation exemplifies the second strategy of introducing expert systems into the firm.

The DEC–CMU alliance.   Digital Equipment Corporation has a strong affiliation with CMU, one of the leading universities in AI. Executives of DEC felt that they would have a joint collaboration with CMU if it looked like expert systems could help DEC in its operations. Around 1979, CMU was developing an expert systems prototype called R1 that would be used to configure VAX computer systems. Carnegie-Mellon had developed a small prototype system and asked DEC for its commitment to and support of the project, stating that it would support the project and eventually take it over if R1 met the accuracy rate determined by DEC and if the CMU professors could help DEC fully develop the system. The R1 team at CMU expanded the knowledge base by adding more component descriptions and more knowledge about computer configuration. Then R1 was validated and tested, and it met DEC's acceptance rate. Through the DEC–CMU collaboration, R1 eventually grew into an expert system consisting of several thousands of rules. Now called XCON, R1 is being used on a daily basis by DEC, and it saves DEC millions of dollars each year. It does, however, take a team of about 15 persons to maintain XCON.

Since the DEC–CMU collaboration of XCON, joint efforts have developed other expert systems used by DEC. The system XSEL is used by DEC salespersons to assist them in computer sales, and a scheduling expert system is also used by DEC for some of their work. Digital Equipment Corporation has its own expert systems group but gets close advice from CMU professors.

Another strategy for introducing expert systems into the firm is to merge, acquire, or become a major stockholder in an AI company. This strategy is discussed next.

Approach 3: Merge, Acquire, or Become a Major Stockholder in an AI Company

There is an old adage that applies to this third approach: "If you can't beat them, join them." In this case, a company might develop an expert systems capability by merging with or acquiring an AI company or by becoming a major stockholder in an AI company. This strategy is not uncommon in private industry. Mergers and acquisitions are taking place daily in order for a company to become stronger or more diversified. They are also occurring so that companies can quickly "pick up" a specialty, like in expert systems, that they would like to possess. With this approach, companies save in start-up time in possessing an expert systems capability. Another advantage of this approach is that the company is getting an experienced core of expert system specialists and does not have to spend much time in building up a cadre of expert system specialists. Of course, limitations of this strategy also exist, such as the need for a large layout of funds to be used to merge with or acquire another company. Additionally, it might take some time for the newly acquired company employees to become adjusted and familiar with the parent company's practices and goals.

In spite of these possible limitations, this approach is used in business as exemplified in the case of General Motors and Teknowledge.

General Motors (GM) and Teknowledge.   General Motors used the strategy of becoming a significant stockholder in one of the first AI companies, Teknowledge. General Motors might have used this strategy initially for investment purposes, but it turned out to be much more than that. Teknowledge was formed in about 1980–1981 by leading Stanford University AI professors. Teknowledge was involved principally in expert system consulting, namely, developing and customizing expert systems. Teknowledge also became involved in selling their expert system shells, M.1 and S.1, for expert system development. One of the first major expert systems that Teknowledge developed was an application for GM since GM was a major stockholder in the company. Teknowledge developed a car engine diagnosis system for GM cars to help car mechanics identify faults and correct them.

Since GM owned stock in Teknowledge, it was able to persuade Teknowledge to develop an expert system for its use. By having an interest in Teknowledge, GM essentially had a team of experts at its side for developing and advising in expert systems. It should be noted that during 1988 Teknowledge decided to concentrate on its expert systems consulting and services as opposed to aggressively selling its expert system products M.1 and S.1. Also, Teknowledge has been acquired by American Cimflex.

The next section looks at a fourth strategy for introducing expert systems into the firm.

Approach 4: Hiring Consultants or Subcontractors When the Need Arises

The last major approach that a company could use to introduce expert systems into the firm is to hire consultants or subcontractors on an as needed basis. If a company does not want in-house capability for expert systems development, then the company could subcontract out the expert systems work. By doing so, the company becomes very dependent on the subcontractors and may not have the management and knowledge to properly monitor the work of the subcontractors. Additionally, the company becomes reliant upon the availability of the subcontractor or consultant in order to get the work done. Of course, there are some advantages to this approach. First, the company does not have to carry the large overhead of people and hardware needed for an expert systems group. Second, the subcontractors' main line of work may be expert systems, so they could provide more expertise that the company may not have. Very often, this strategy is used by both large and small businesses. A contract might call for an expert systems project that handles Bayesian statistics for dealing with uncertainty. The contractor who is aware of the contract might be proficient in expert systems building but may not have the necessary background in Bayesian statistics. Thus, the contractor might hire a consultant or subcontractor who has proficiency in Bayesian statistics as applied to expert systems. Similarly, a consultant who is a university professor might be hired to advise on the methods used for a particular expert systems project. Or a consultant who is an expert in the verification and validation of expert systems might be hired to handle the testing of an expert system as part of an expert systems project.

This approach and the others previously mentioned are common strategies for introducing expert systems into a firm.

WHAT IS NEEDED AT THE MICROLEVEL

Now that we know strategies for introducing expert systems into the firm from a macrolevel, we can explore on a microlevel how to investigate expert systems technology to those for the first time. In the following sections, we look at who is needed to develop expert systems, what characteristics or skills are needed, how does the expert systems project team get those skills, and how does the team proceed once those skills are acquired.

Who Is Needed

In order to develop expert systems, the expert systems project team should consist of (1) a knowledge engineer, (2) a programmer, (3) a project manager, (4) an expert, and (5) a "champion" supporter of the project from top management.

The knowledge engineer is responsible for scoping out the problem and selecting an appropriate task for expert systems development. The task usually involves symbolic processing, takes a few minutes to a few hours to solve, has experts who can perform the task and are willing to work with the expert systems development team, does not involve much commonsense reasoning, and is performed frequently. Once the knowledge engineer identifies the appropriate task for expert systems development, his or her next role involves the acquisition of knowledge from the expert. The knowledge engineer then determines the best way of representing the acquired knowledge and looks at expert systems shells and appropriate AI or conventional languages for encoding the knowledge. The knowledge engineer does not necessarily perform the actual programming step. The knowledge engineer tests and evaluates the expert system and iteratively proceeds through these steps until the expert system performs at the client's desired level.

The programmer on the expert systems team is most involved with the actual encoding of the knowledge in the expert system. If an expert system shell is used, the programmer would encode the knowledge base and perhaps develop programs for improving the shell's existing user interface (i.e., dialogue structure). If an expert system shell is not used, then the programmer needs to develop the dialogue structure, inference engine (i.e., control structure), and the knowledge base of the expert system. The programmer also is involved in the testing phase in order to help check the verification and validation of the expert system.

The project manager is the team leader of the expert systems development team. The project manager is responsible for keeping the expert systems project on track in terms of time and cost constraints. The project manager also makes sure that deliverables and milestones are met, in accordance with the statement of work or proposal. The project manager is the spokesperson for the project and tries to promote its application.

Probably the most important team player in an expert systems development project is the expert. The expert is the individual whose knowledge will be captured in the expert system in order to build up the corporate memory of the firm. The expert must be articulate and willing to participate in the expert systems project. The expert must commit a substantial portion of his or her time to be involved with the various phases of the expert systems development life cycle. The expert should be enthusiastic about the project, and the expert system would hopefully free up some of the expert's time so that the expert could do other things that he or she never had time to do.

The last key player of the expert systems team is the champion of the project from top management. Usually someone from the higher echelons in the company is a "backer" of the project and a stimulator of employing new technologies in the firm. Perhaps this individual is the vice president of MIS (Management Information Systems) or the vice president of the Advanced Technologies Group in the company. Typically, the blessings of this individual are needed in order to get the moral and financial support for the expert systems project. This individual plays a marketing role as well as a financial role by promoting the expert systems project to other top management officers.

With these five players, a complete expert systems team is formed. However, it is not strictly necessary to have all five players on the team. For example, many expert systems are developed on a microcomputer by having just the expert key in his or her knowledge using an expert system shell. This might eliminate or lessen the need and role of the knowledge engineer or AI programmer. But for larger expert systems, the five players are typically used to make up the expert systems development team.

The next section looks at the skills needed by each of these key players.

What Skills Are Needed?

In order to have a successful team, there are various skills generally required of the knowledge engineer, programmer, project manager, and expert. We shall not discuss the backer in top management but only say that this individual should have enough clout to provide the moral and financial commitments to developing the expert system.

The knowledge engineer needs a strong combination of good interpersonal communications skills and technical skills. The knowledge engineer needs to have the ability to get along well with the expert and to successfully acquire the knowledge from the expert. Besides these communications skills, the knowledge engineer must know the techniques needed to be able to elicit the knowledge from the expert. Also, the knowledge engineer must know the knowledge engineering steps in order to build and test an expert system. These technical skills are crucial elements in the success of the project.

The programmer needs to have technical skills in programming in AI and conventional languages. A knowledge of LISP and/or Prolog provides the programmer with ability to program for symbolic processing. Additionally, the programmer should know conventional programming languages like C, FORTRAN, and/or Ada. The programmer should also be familiar with rule-based languages like OPS5 and should also feel comfortable working with various mainframe and microcomputer-based expert system shells.

The project manager should be technically trained with proven management skills. The project manager should have appropriate AI training and should have extensive experience in developing expert systems. The project manager should have the ability to interact well with his team members and users of the expert system. He should also have the confidence of his team members and top management in order to develop a successful expert system.

The expert should be enthusiastic about the expert systems project and should be able to spend the necessary time during the expert system's development. The expert should be articulate and understandable to the knowledge engineer. Of course, this means that the knowledge engineer needs to be familiar and comfortable with the expert system domain in order to understand and converse with the expert. The expert should be cooperative and should be recognized as an expert by his or her peers. It is also helpful to have a "backup expert" in case something happens with the "designated expert." In any case, other experts will be needed in the testing stages of the expert system.

The next section looks at how these skills can be obtained.

How Does the Expert Systems Team Get These Skills?

There are several ways to obtain training in expert systems and AI. One way is to take formal education courses in expert systems at universities or colleges. Some universities offer tracks, majors, and/or degrees in expert systems or applied AI. Individuals interested in expert systems might want to go for a graduate degree in expert systems/AI. A second way to obtain training in expert systems is to take short courses on expert systems on-site at the company or through a continuing engineering education group. Many expert systems vendors offer short courses in expert systems on-site at the company or at the vendor's location. Likewise, continuing engineering education groups offer short courses around the world in expert systems. Many of these courses are through a university's continuing education program. A third way to learn about expert systems is to attend tutorials, seminars, and conferences in AI. Many tutorials on expert systems are given at major conferences specializing in AI, such as the American Association for Artificial Intelligence conference and the International Joint Conference on AI. Also, there are various seminars and conferences throughout the year that focus on expert systems technology and applications. Persons interested in expert systems should go to those that are relevant to their interests. Last, many individuals can become familiar with expert systems by experimenting and using expert system shells and by reading various AI newsletters, journals, magazines, and books.

Of course, an individual interested in expert systems should do a combination of these approaches. Once some of this knowledge is obtained and a project team is formulated, the next step is knowing how to proceed to build an expert system.

Approach for Building Expert Systems

Once the expert systems team is composed, the next step is actually building the expert system. A three-stage method could be used [6]:

Step	Time
1. Build a demonstration prototype. This serves as a vehicle to demonstrate its effectiveness to senior management and convince them of the feasibility and value of the expert system. Also, it shows the ability of the project team to deal effectively with this new technology.	3–6 months
2. Build the full prototype that incorporates both breadth and depth across the problem domain but is not in a "deliverable" form for daily use.	6 months to 1 year
3. Build the delivered system, usable on a day-to-day production basis. This includes documentation on how to use and update the expert system.	18 months to 2 years

In building an expert system, an iterative, rapid prototyping method is used. Successive iterations of prototypes are developed until the final prototype is refined well enough to meet the intended scope and use of the system. In order to construct these prototypes, the problem task is first selected. Then after the task for expert system's development is appropriately scoped out, a cycling of the following steps is made: knowledge acquisition, knowledge representation, knowledge encoding, and knowledge testing and evaluation [1, 2]. The knowledge in the expert system is refined on an incremental basis until the system meets its intended goals. Refinement of the user interface is also important in order for the expert system to be accepted by the users. As with any software project, training and good documentation must be provided by the developers to the users in order to ensure a smooth transition and implementation. It is also vital to incorporate the users' feedback into the expert system and to obtain the expert's support so that the expert feels that the system is his or her "baby."

CONCLUSIONS

In the coming years, businesses will continue to develop and integrate expert systems into their existing systems and daily operations. Expert systems will serve as vehicles to build up the corporate memory of the firm and to improve the productivity, effectiveness, and efficiency of selected business operations. From a macrolevel, there are various strategies that companies can use to introduce expert systems into the firm. Businesses will have to select the best approach for their specific situation according to their strategic goals and objectives. Once an appropriate strategy is chosen, the firm can look at the microlevel in addressing how to get the right combination of people, money, hardware, software, and other resources to properly build expert systems. With an earnest effort in developing these macro- and microlevel approaches, the company will be well on its way to better facing its competition in the near future.

REFERENCES

1. Liebowitz, J., *Introduction to Expert Systems*, Mitchell, Watsonville, CA, 1988.
2. Liebowitz, J. (ed.), *Expert System Applications to Telecommunications*, Wiley, New York, 1988.
3. Feigenbaum, E., P. McCorduck, and P. Nii, *The Rise of the Expert Company*, Time-Life, Alexandria, VA, 1988.
4. Liebowitz, J. and D. A. DeSalvo (eds.), *Structuring Expert Systems: Domain, Design, and Development*, Yourdon/Prentice-Hall, Englewood Cliffs, NJ, 1989.
5. DeSalvo, D. A. and J. Liebowitz (eds.), *Managing AI and Expert Systems*, Prentice-Hall, Englewood Cliffs, NJ, 1990.
6. Cupello, J. M. and D. Mishelevich, "Managing Prototype Knowledge/Expert System Projects," *Communications of the ACM*, Vol. 31, No. 5, Association for Computing Machinery, New York, pp. 534–541, 1988.

2

An Expert System in Taxation: The Taxpayer Service Assistant

Thomas J. Beckman

INTRODUCTION

The Internal Revenue Service (IRS) employs several thousand assistors to answer telephone inquiries from taxpayers. The Taxpayer Service Assistant (TSA) is an expert system that enables IRS telephone assistors to provide advice to taxpayers on tax law topics. This chapter focuses on the design and development of the TSA. The conclusions drawn and lessons learned thus far are tentative because the TSA is just entering the implementation phase. In addition, the expert systems approach is compared to another design approach, text retrieval, that is also under development.

The section on task background sets the context from which opportunities to use expert systems technology arise. The assistor task is described in detail as it is now performed. Then the parameters of the overall task scope are outlined, as contrasted with the rest of the chapter that more narrowly focuses on the development of the TSA itself.

The section on conceptual design issues analyzes opportunities for applying expert system technology to the assistor task. The merits of three methodologies used in selecting task domains are examined. Next, four general design approaches are outlined. The section concludes with a discussion of some of the cognitive issues faced by assistors.

The section on defining the task narrows the dimensions of the assistor task so that the feasibility prototype can be constructed. The methodology used in choosing the specific tax topic is examined in some detail. Then, methods of acquiring formal knowledge and eliciting informal knowledge are discussed, followed by a determination of what roles the TSA should play. Lastly, the objectives for the TSA feasibility prototype are laid out.

The section on issues in constructing the system shows the evolution of the application's development. The development of various expert system features are analyzed, including reasoning methods, knowledge representation, uncertainty, user interface, explanation, and training. Finally, the section concludes with a discussion of how hardware and software were selected.

The section on system implementation is necessarily incomplete. The formal test of the TSA has just begun. Over the past few months, the system has been evaluated and modified through a series of demonstrations. Local domain experts are currently pretesting the system for errors and enhancements.

In the next section, the progress of another design approach that attempts to improve the assistor task is examined. The differing capabilities of the two approaches are discussed and contrasted as well as their respective difficulties in design and implementation. The author also looks at how organizational settings have influenced the design and development of the projects.

The final two sections cover conclusions and what future directions are planned for the TSA. Tentative conclusions are drawn about aspects of the project such as project selection methods, user interface, project support, equipment, and cost–benefit ratios. Finally, five stages of future development are outlined and eight objectives are proposed for future project work.

TASK BACKGROUND

Description of the Existing Task

Taxpayer service assistors are the IRS personnel who respond to telephone inquiries from taxpayers. Frontline assistors are the first persons with whom taxpayers speak when they call toll-free telephone assistance sites. Frontline assistors first identify and refer calls that are not related to taxpayer service issues and then categorize the remaining calls into account, procedural, or technical areas. The TSA addresses only the latter, technical questions on tax law.

Frontline assistors are employees with limited experience who answer frequently asked questions on a variety of simple tax topics. Initially, they receive four weeks of classroom training and two weeks of on-the-job training. Even after this intensive training, frontline assistors are not expected to answer questions from memory; rather, they are expected to know where to find answers in IRS publications. Assistors consult IRS publications to locate text or confirm answers on about half of the calls they receive [1]. Surprisingly, although frontline assistors are generalists who may encounter questions on over 130 different tax topics, they are able to answer 84% of taxpayer questions without referral.

When frontline assistors identify calls on topics in which they have not been trained, they refer taxpayers to more experienced assistors, that is, technical backups and specialists [1]. Technical backups are assistors who have completed all phases of assistor training and have at least one year of experience; taxpayer service specialists are local domain experts who have completed specialist training and possess considerably more experience. To answer these more difficult inquiries, technical backups and specialists often refer to sources such as IRS publications, IRS letter rulings, and the CCH Standard Federal Tax Reporter.

During the filing season, calls are referred directly by telephone when possible; during other times of the year, referrals are often written. Written referrals frequently need clarification, requiring technical backups or specialists to contact taxpayers for further details. Some questions are too difficult even for specialists to answer. In these cases, written inquiries are referred to either functional specialists in the field such as IRS agents or the IRS national office for letter rulings by IRS tax attorneys.

Quality review staffs at toll-free telephone sites monitor telephone calls to evaluate assistors on the courtesy, accuracy, and completeness of their responses. In addition, at the IRS national office, an Integrated Test Call staff designs questions on selected tax topics, administers them anonymously to assistors at toll-free sites, and evaluates assistor answers to provide another, more uniform measure of assistor effectiveness. Furthermore, questions are also devised at toll-free sites to uncover topics with high error rates. Remedial training is provided on tax topics with consistently high error rates.

Task Scope

There are 5,000 potential users of the TSA spread geographically across the United States in 34 toll-free telephone sites. These users include a permanent staff of 2,500 assistors and 500 specialists and a seasonal staff of an additional 2,000 assistors [2]. The number of year-round assistors at each site varies from about 20 to over 250. Additional potential users of the TSA are returns processing functions within IRS service centers and collection and examination personnel.

During fiscal year (FY) 1986, assistors responded to 38.2 million telephone inquiries [3]. Of these calls, 18 million (47%) were technical questions on tax law. Of these tax law questions, 2.9 million (16%) were referred either by telephone or in writing. In addition to telephone inquiries, 8.1 million taxpayers requested assistance in person; of these, 3.6 million (44%) were questions on tax law. There were also 241,000 written requests and 137,800 foreign inquiries on tax law issues. Altogether, there were about 22 million inquiries on technical tax issues in FY 1986.

The breadth and complexity of the assistor task can be gauged by examining the taxonomy for tax topics, the number of parameters associated with each topic, and the total amount of printed material on the subject. Questions can fall into one of 139 general tax topic categories [4]. Even simple tax topics require assistors to remember up to 10 key pieces of information; more difficult topics can often exceed 50 parameters. Any inquiry may require research into one of 159 IRS publications or into one of 10 volumes (totaling over 15,000 pages) of the CCH Standard Federal Tax Reporter.

The relative difficulty of calls can be inferred from production rates. Frontline telephone assistors answer about 12 calls per hour, whereas technical backups answer phone referrals at a rate of about 10 calls per hour. Specialists answer written referrals at a rate of 2.5 cases per hour [1].

The level of assistor expertise can be inferred from error rates. According to a recent General Accounting Office (GAO) study [3], frontline assistor performance in answering tax law inquiries prepared by GAO was disappointing: 63% were correct and complete, 15% were correct but incomplete, and 22% were incorrect. Responses by technical backups were much better: 86% were correct and complete, and only 14% were incorrect. Specialists' responses were over 95% correct and complete.

CONCEPTUAL DESIGN ISSUES

Methods for Selecting a Promising Task

Various authors, for example, Davis [5], Prerau [6], and Grady [7], have developed criteria to estimate the potential for success in applying expert systems technology to a task. From these checklists and his own experience, the author has compiled a checklist of selection criteria in the categories of task, potential payoffs, resource costs, expert, end user, decision maker, and designer. Table 1 shows an evaluation of the TSA using these criteria.

Another approach involves classifying prospective tasks into generic expert system tasks that are known to be successful. Again, various lists have been elucidated: Waterman [8], Martin [9], and Chandrasekaran [10]. The author has adopted a taxonomy (see Table 2) that closely follows Martin. However, the author draws two distinctions: Most tasks, and often even subtasks, are comprised of multiple generic tasks and nearly all tasks involve classification.

A third approach, developed by the author, decomposes the target task into subtasks and then determines the feasibility of applying expert system techniques to each of the subtasks. This approach is covered in the following two sections.

Task Decomposition

The task of answering taxpayer inquiries is not as simple as it initially appears. Instead of the two most obvious subtasks of listening to and answering questions, assistors actually perform the following subtasks:

1. Understand and clarify the taxpayer's question.
2. Classify question.
3. Refer question.
4. Access tax information from tax publications.
5. Recall tax information from memory.

TABLE 1. Evaluating the Assistor Task Using Selection Criteria

Desirable task characteristics:

Pass 1.	Task is primarily cognitive because it deals with decision making.
Pass 2.	Task consists primarily of symbolic knowledge and reasoning.
Pass 3.	Task is complex, requiring extensive training.
Pass 4.	Task uses heuristics and a knowledge taxonomy.
Pass 5.	Task involves chains of reasoning on multiple levels of knowledge.
Pass 6.	Task cannot be solved using conventional computing methods.
Pass 7.	Task is similar to existing expert systems (diagnostic).
Pass 8.	Task often must be solved with incomplete facts.
Pass 9.	Task often requires explanation and justification of advice.
Pass 10.	Task does not require temporal or spatial knowledge.
Pass 11.	Task knowledge is confined to a narrow domain and is stable.
Pass 12.	Incremental progress is possible; task can be subdivided.
Fail 13.	Task is at a stage of knowledge formalization that uses heuristics and classification, not search or algorithms.
Variable 14.	Task requires little or no common sense or general world knowledge.
Fail 15.	Data and case studies are available.
Fail 16.	Data and case studies are on magnetic media.

Desirable expert characteristics:

Pass 17.	Recognized experts exist.
Pass 18.	Expert performance is provably better than that of amateurs.
Pass 19.	Task is routinely taught to neophytes.
Fail 20.	Expert is accessible for extended periods, is cooperative, and communicates well.

Desirable end-user characteristics:

Pass 21.	End users have a strong felt need for help the system provides.
Pass 22.	End users want to be involved during the design and development of the system.
Pass 23.	End users do not have unrealistically high expectations.
Pass 24.	Most end users are novices and therefore will benefit most from a more mundane system.

Desirable management characteristics:

Pass 25.	Field management is supportive and enthusiastic about the system.
Fail 26.	Senior management is willing to commit significant resources to develop and deploy the system.
Fail 27.	Use of the system will not be politically sensitive.
Pass 28.	The system requires only minimal changes to existing procedures.
Fail 29.	Management understands that estimates for resources and deadlines are very difficult to estimate and probably will not be met.
Fail 30.	Management realizes that the system will make mistakes and may perform no better than a moderately proficient user.

Desirable designer characteristics:

Pass 31.	Designer knows how to use a shell appropriate for the system.
Fail 32.	Designer is knowledgeable or an expert in the domain.
Fail 33.	Designer has used the chosen shell before.

Desirable cost–benefit characteristics:

Pass 34.	Resulting system would have high payoff.
Pass 35.	Expertise is perishable or in short supply.
Pass 36.	System can be developed using commercial shells; little customized coding is needed.
Pass 37.	System can be phased in. Partial completion is still useful.
Fail 38.	Cost per user is low when compared with the benefits.

TABLE 2. Matching the TSA to Generic Expert System Tasks

1. Analysis
    a. Classification: TSA categorizes dependents into categories of claimable, not claimable, and incomplete/unknown
    b. Diagnosis
    c. Debugging/treatment
    d. Interpretation
    e. Monitoring
    f. Prediction: TSA is rudimentary predictor of consequences from an input set of data, with "unknown" as only measure of uncertainty
2. Synthesis
    a. Planning: TSA can perform "what-if" analyses but not true planning
    b. Design
    c. Simulation
3. Hybrid
    a. Instruction: student can run precoded prototypical examples or explore system responses and explanations based on user inputs; TSA can also teach structure of domain knowledge
    b. Control
    c. Repair
    d. Intelligent data base
    e. Interface: system interface exposes structure of domain knowledge

6. Match tax law information to the taxpayer's situation.
7. Answer question.
8. Explain answer.
9. Ensure that answer is understood.
10. Provide general information.
11. Refer taxpayer to appropriate IRS publications and order publications.

Not all subtasks are performed during any one taxpayer inquiry, and some subtasks are performed more than once.

Another form of task decomposition revolves around providing specific versus general answers. When possible, assistors provide specific answers. However, there are several conditions under which general answers are given: Taxpayers request general information, taxpayers' knowledge is not sufficient to understand the answer, or taxpayers lack specific data needed to provide a specific answer. When one of these conditions occurs, the assistor tries to educate the caller and, if possible, give a general answer. If there is too much information to relate, the assistor refers the taxpayer to appropriate IRS publications and orders them for the taxpayer.

Applying Artificial Intelligence Techniques to Subtasks

Some processes within the assistor task appear less promising than others for application of artificial intelligence (AI) technology. First, there are subtasks that are less promising because they are active research areas without mature existing applications such as:

1. Understand and clarify questions and ensure that taxpayers understand the answers—requires sophisticated knowledge of language, discourse, and intentions.

2. Refer questions—requires that the system know the boundaries of its own knowledge or that of its user and that it can model the domain and the understanding of the user.

3. Answer questions and explain answers—easy if canned text is used; otherwise, flexible text generation requires semantic understanding of concepts, not just syntactically correct forms.

4. Sophisticated match of tax law information to the taxpayer's situation—requires analogical reasoning.

Second, the author's knowledge of natural-language understanding and generation is limited. Therefore, subtasks such as understanding and clarifying questions, researching and referencing tax information from text, and generating text are not viable at present.

Finally, there are subtasks that are quite feasible given the state of expert system technology and the designer's capabilities. Classifying taxpayer questions into tax topic categories would make an excellent embedded application within a tax retrieval data base. Another possible application would be a smart front end to translate constrained natural-language inputs into correct and efficient text retrieval queries. The TSA combines referencing tax information, analyzing and matching tax law information to the taxpayer's situation, and answering questions and building explanations using somewhat flexible canned text.

Promising Design Alternatives

Based on the analyses in the preceding sections, several promising design alternatives appear feasible. The most obvious approach requires little new technology: Change the assistors from generalists into specialists. Each assistor could specialize in a cluster of, say, 10 related topics. Since most toll-free telephone sites have over 50 assistors, cross-training and adequate topic coverage would not be a problem. The only new technology needed would be an automatic call-routing mechanism keyed to various topic areas.

However, this approach entails changes that would alter the job classification and pay scale for assistors as well as the organizational structure. It also would place a greater burden on management to ensure that sufficient numbers of assistors were adequately crosstrained and would be available to cover all topics at all times. However, the improvement in quality and efficiency of taxpayer service would more than justify the increased burden on management.

In addition to the specialization strategy, there are four alternatives that use either conventional or AI-based technologies: text retrieval, expert systems, and two hybrid approaches.

Text retrieval.   The text retrieval approach selects relevant text from existing commercial tax law data bases. Assistors select text by using menus and/or keyboards to form logical combinations that access data bases containing the tax law, IRS regulations and publications, and other tax reference guides. This approach and the expert system approach are discussed in detail in the section that compares the expert system and text retrieval approaches.

Expert system.   The second approach, the one embodied in the TSA, is to use expert systems technology to restructure tax law text into a form that is more directly usable by assistors. In this case, tax law knowledge is restructured into an animated decision tree. The assistor is guided through a series of questions to obtain information needed by the system in order to reach an answer. In addition, an explanation facility justifies the system's answer. Furthermore, at any point during processing the system can tell the assistor its current status and in general terms, what data are still required in order to reach an answer.

Hybrid: expert system using text retrieval for explanations.   Another approach is to embed the text retrieval module within the expert system. In this approach, when rules in the expert system fire and draw conclusions, commands with keywords are generated from the expert system and sent to the text retrieval module to locate and retrieve text that supports these conclusions. The retrieved text is then stored and later displayed by the expert system. If explanations are needed that quote actual IRS publications, then this appears to be a good solution since any changes to the explanations are updated automatically in the data base. However, text retrieval is unnecessary even for explanations.

Hybrid: natural-language front end to text retrieval.   Another hybrid approach involves embedding a natural-language front end within a text retrieval system, again using existing commercial tax law data bases. However, rather than accessing text by entering keywords in logical combinations, a front-end natural language parser would interpret assistor requests made in constrained English inputs and transform them into keyword or query formats acceptable to the data base. Also, an embedded expert system could determine whether the request was likely to retrieve the relevant text desired and, if not, assist the user in refining the request. This approach has the advantage of allowing novices to retrieve text with minimal training in text retrieval while optimizing their efforts by using the strategy found in the expert system. However, this approach creates a difficult AI problem of natural language and discourse understanding and does not solve the basic problem of converting passive descriptive text into an active decision form.

Cognitive Issues in the Assistor Task

Assistors are in the unusual position of having their knowledge tested on a daily basis. To be successful, they must find solutions to three basic cognitive problems: managing task complexity, making knowledge usable, and learning shortcuts and strategies. An additional cognitive issue involves how to train assistors; namely, what is the most effective way to teach the assistor task?

First, assistors must learn to cope with and manage the complexity of their domain. The domain of answering technical tax questions encompasses enormous quantities of data, relationships, and constraints. Complexity also exists, in part, because assistors are trained as generalists, receiving inquiries on a diverse array of tax topics. Consequently, assistors cannot possibly answer questions on many tax topics directly from memory or from reasoning; the amount of knowledge required is just too vast. At present, assistors settle for knowing where to find the relevant information and then converting this text into a usable form.

Second, written knowledge in the form of text must be converted to a form that can be used by the assistor. Information found in IRS publications and other reference sources is in a passive form—descriptive text. As is, this text cannot be used directly to answer taxpayer inquiries. Therefore, assistors must understand and reformulate this formal written knowledge into active forms, such as decision trees or algorithms (see Figure 1, p. 24).

Third, much of the knowledge needed to answer taxpayer inquiries is not found in written materials. Instead, this so-called informal knowledge is often found in the form of heuristics, also known as rules of thumb. To achieve expert performance levels, assistors must learn heuristic shortcuts for which often there is no teacher except experience.

Heuristics may also take the form of strategy: knowing the best sequence of questioning that, in asking for data, will most quickly reach an answer. Expert assistors first try to ask questions that maximally narrow and constrain the search space. In other words, questions are asked in an order that is most likely to terminate the session as quickly as possible, either by disqualifying taxpayers or by qualifying them through the most likely set of conditions. For example, from the dependency test shown in Figure 2 (p. 25), it is usually most efficient to first ask questions about the gross income or support tests, rather than about the other three tests. However, if the taxpayer has a foreign accent, then it might be best to first ask questions about the citizenship test. Unfortunately, assistors sometimes learn unwarranted shortcuts, such as assuming that the lack of a foreign accent means that the taxpayer must be a U.S. citizen.

However, true expertise involves more than just solving these three basic cognitive problems; it also involves abilities such as reasoning by analogy, forming significant conclusions from subtle distinctions, recognizing limitations at problem boundaries, and formulating and validating new hypotheses and theories. This expertise, whether it was initially learned consciously or not, is quickly "compiled" into the expert practitioner's subconscious mind for efficiency's sake.

A final cognitive issue involves learning. Just how humans learn is not well understood. Minsky [11] proposes that humans only learn things that are close to what they already know or to which they can form analogies. This theory anticipates that training new assistors is difficult and time consuming because typically they do not already possess knowledge in the domains of tax law, tax administration, or accounting. Thus, an entirely new model or framework of knowledge must be created in the assistor. Two related problems concern the limits of the human mind: how much it can learn within a given time span and what it can remember and reason about at any given time. Hence, current training methods emphasize knowing where to find the relevant information needed to formulate answers rather than knowing how to answer questions directly.

DEFINING THE TASK

Choice of the Specific Tax Topic

Many factors were evaluated during the process of topic selection, such as impact on the quality of service provided, topic complexity, ease of developing system capabilities, system validation, and measures of system performance. Criteria from Table 1 were also used on a more detailed level to aid in selecting specific tax topics. In addition, potential topics were evaluated from analyses of report data [4] and from a questionnaire [1]. These efforts turned up two tax topics that were considered most promising: the dependency test and depreciation.

The most important criterion to be met is that the topic chosen should have a substantial impact on improving the quality of assistor responses (Table 1, criterion 34). Therefore, tax topics were analyzed by volume and error rates to determine which tax topics were associated with the largest volume of errors. Due to limited travel funds, it was important that the chosen topic have a sufficiently large volume of calls so that the system could be adequately tested at just one site. Report data [4] revealed that even questions on the most frequently asked topics amount to only 2% of total call volume; and many of the higher volume topics have low IRS measured error rates of between 3 and 7%. However, the dependency test is one of the few exceptions, with a volume of 1.2% of total calls and an error rate of 12%.

Early in the TSA's development, the author had planned on selecting a complex topic normally worked by specialists. The TSA was to serve as an assistant to specialists, allowing them to answer hard questions without research. It was also thought that this would best show off the capabilities of an expert system. The depreciation topic seemed like a good choice for specialists.

However, most assistors, specialists, and managers recommended choosing a tax topic that was simpler than depreciation. Topics that specialists normally answer have low error rates, not because the topics are easy but because specialists are domain experts. Therefore, topics such as the dependency test, in which novice assistors are trained, should be chosen to achieve the largest gains in quality. However, even this simple topic is much more complex than was initially thought. In fact, because it is a basic topic, assistors often answer from memory rather than looking up the answer, resulting in a higher error rate than might be expected.

Tax topics should be chosen that are predominantly symbolic in nature, minimize numeric calculations, and involve decision making (Table 1, criteria 1 and 2). The dependency test well meets these criteria; assistors deal primarily with symbolic information, use decision trees, and are instructed not to perform calculations for taxpayers because of the excessive time involved. Several topics were eliminated for this reason.

Knowledge for tax topics should be stable and confined to narrow domains (Table 1, criterion 11). The tax law, while not frozen, is for the most part a relatively stable, static body of knowledge. By choosing tax topics such as the dependency test, impacts from tax law changes are minimized. The dependency test appears to be an area of the tax code that is stable and represents a very narrow slice of knowledge. A related criterion is that topics should have clear and unambiguous interpretations under the tax code. The topic's clarity allowed other design issues to be more easily exposed—such as certainty measures, user interface format, and levels of assumed knowledge of users—that otherwise might have been obscured behind the complexity of implementing a more difficult topic.

Good domain topics require use of heuristics and judgment in arriving at answers (Table 1, criterion 4). Surprisingly, in performing the assistor task, not many tax topics actually possess this feature. Because assistors learn only the IRS interpretation of the tax law and not alternative views of tax courts, tax attorneys, and accountants, heuristics play only a minor role in most tax topics. However, there are a few topics, such as depreciation, that possess heuristics independent of tax law interpretations.

However, depreciation turned out to require more real-world knowledge for classifying objects than seemed wise in a prototype. Thus, it was decided that heuristics were not needed to add to the already substantial issues that arose during development of the system. Therefore, for all of the preceding reasons, the dependency test was selected as the initial "sliver of knowledge."

Knowledge Acquisition and Elicitation

The process of knowledge elicitation was atypical. The initial demonstration prototype was constructed entirely from formal IRS publications. Domain experts were not involved until late in the development process. Specialists who critiqued decision trees and evaluated the system also exposed overlooked points of the tax law, restructured the representation of domain knowledge, and improved how the system asked questions and their order.

Once the domain topic was chosen, the next step in system development was to locate sources of knowledge. First, formal, explicit knowledge was extracted from written materials, specifically IRS publication 501, "Exemptions and Standard Deduction." Approximately half of this publication deals with the dependency test. Thus far, this has been the only formal source of knowledge used in developing the system. Because the topic chosen was so clear-cut, other formal sources of tax law knowledge such as CCH Standard Federal Tax Reporter, IRS letter rulings, or IRS training manuals were not needed.

Publication 501 was first analyzed for relevant parameters and their allowed values and their relationships as dependent or independent variables. In the dependency test, the decision tree contains both AND nodes (all parameters must be true) and OR nodes (only one option need be true). There are four levels in the decision tree hierarchy, over 95 parameters, and over 160 sets of relationships.

Another part of the knowledge elicitation process involved constructing a decision tree that would later be translated into rules within an expert system. This

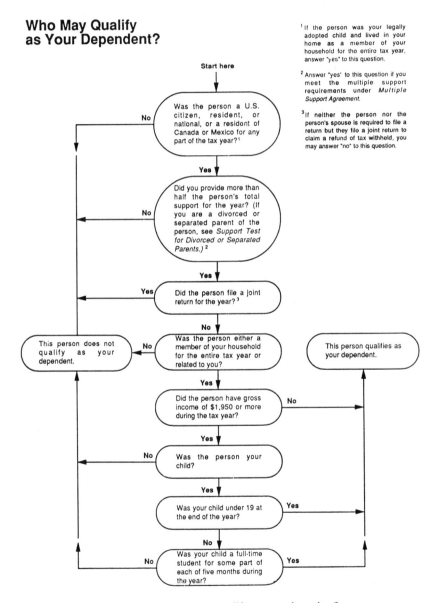

Figure 1   Who may qualify as your dependent?

method guides the assistor through a topic in an ordered fashion until a decision is reached. In fact, this is a frequently used tool in AI knowledge elicitation and resembles formal structured design methods from conventional data processing.

Publication 501 already contains a rudimentary decision tree (see Figure 1). However, the ordering and structuring of that decision tree was rather different than the one that was ultimately constructed. Initially, the tree used excluded the more complex parts of the support test, the multiple and divorced options. Figure 2 shows the hierarchical structure of the five dependency tests and the major options and expands a further level of detail for the support test.

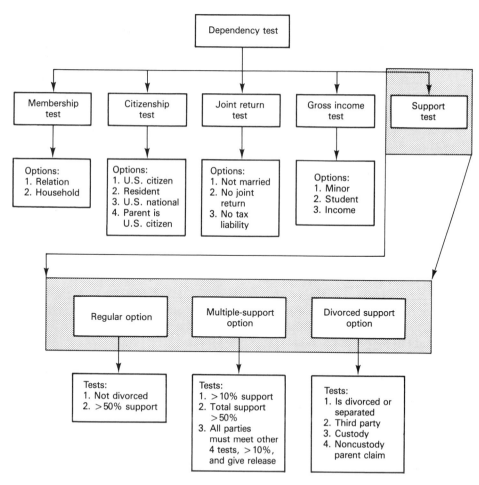

Figure 2 Detailed structure of domain knowledge.

User Expertise and Expert System Roles

The expertise of the typical user is crucial in determining the roles played by the system and the level of abstraction at which knowledge is to be represented. An expert system can play one of several roles: agent or decision maker, advisor, assistant, or tutor [12]. Each of these roles places different demands on expert system design. For example, an agent system must embody all relevant knowledge and some commonsense knowledge or it will not be relied upon. An advisor for experts need only provide answers from minimal inputs using jargon; explanations are probably not needed or desired. However, novice assistors might prefer a wordy assistant or tutor that provides lengthy explanations, defines terms if requested, and displays decisions made by the system during the questioning process. Novices might also prefer to see a graphical representation of the structure of the domain knowledge.

The TSA was initially envisioned as an assistant to experienced assistors. The design changed substantially when its role was modified to be an assistant for novices. The TSA shifts answering of complex but straightforward topics normally answered by specialists to less experienced assistors. In this role, the system not only serves as an advisor or assistant to novices, but also acts as an agent by replacing specialists. In fact, the dependency test has sections on multiple support and divorced/separated support that previously were referred to specialists to answer; these sections are now answered by frontline assistors. Specialists can now concentrate on answering questions that truly require their expertise.

The TSA also plays the role of a crude tutor. Students receive remedial training by exploring the system's knowledge base in its normal operational mode; students receive more formal training by running prototypical examples provided as part of the TSA. This is explained in greater depth in the section on training.

Objectives for the TSA Prototype

Objectives were based on the nature of the task, the needs of the users, constraints imposed by the state of AI technology, and limitations of the designer's expertise. These objectives set forth the basic capabilities desired in the design for the feasibility prototype:

1. Provide expertise that enables frontline assistors to answer technical tax questions directly without accessing research materials or referring inquiries to specialists.
2. Explain the system's reasoning both during and after the consultation session.
3. Justify the system's advice at the end of the session.
4. Send a hard copy of consultation sessions to taxpayers upon request.
5. Aid in training assistors through use of prototypical examples and exploratory learning.

ASPECTS OF CONSTRUCTING THE TSA

Reasoning Methods

A basic design decision involves choosing between forward and backward reasoning. In this task environment, most questions involve validating a single taxpayer hypothesis ("Can I deduct my dog?") rather than generating and evaluating multiple hypotheses ("What sort of deductions can a traveling salesman take?"). Therefore, a backward-chaining inferencing mechanism would seem preferable due to the smaller-sized tree traversed.

However, even with the theoretical advantages of backward chaining, the task domain itself imposes more important constraints on inferencing. It turns out that taxpayer inquiries better resemble unstructured conversations, or taxpayers telling stories [1], rather than structured interchanges in which the assistor controls the order of questions asked and data received. Backward chaining forces a sequence of questions that may not correspond to the order in which data are received from taxpayers. Only forward chaining provides this needed flexibility.

The user interface provided with most backward-chaining shells is quite limited. In preliminary demonstrations, assistors appear to prefer the display of several related pieces of data at one time on a screen, including a summary of the system's current status, rather than display of only one question at a time. This preference also favors forward-chaining shells because most backward-chaining shells follow the MYCIN model in which only one question can be answered at a time.

From the standpoint of efficiency, assistors want to ask questions in a sequence that minimizes the time spent per call. This is further complicated by the fact that some questions require much longer to answer than others. For example, in the dependency test, taxpayers are more likely not to qualify for the exemption because of the amount of support provided to the dependent rather than whether the dependent is a U.S. citizen, but it may take much longer to complete the support test.

Using prompts in forward-chaining systems yields two advantages: flexibility and optimization. Prompts suggest the best sequence in which to ask questions based on answers received thus far rather than forcing the sequence of questioning. This not only improves assistor performance but also serves as a training aid.

Knowledge Representation

The author learned much about the structure of domain knowledge through discussions with a manager at the test site [13]. One outgrowth of these discussions is that tax topics are structured into decision taxonomies comprised of "tests" and "options." For many tax topics, all tests within a tax topic must be passed in order for the topic to be passed. However, only one option need be passed in order to pass a test. In the dependency test, the decision tree contains both tests (AND nodes, all parameters must be true) and options (OR nodes, only one parameter set need be true). See Figure 2 for details.

Initially, an object-oriented approach was chosen for knowledge representation that was supported by GoldWorks, an expert system development tool. There were several reasons for this choice. First, the hierarchical, well-organized structure of the tax law lends itself to a frame lattice rather nicely. Next, the author believed that problems of scaling up could be more easily dealt with using an object-oriented approach. Finally, by modularizing and structuring the domain knowledge, programming codes could be shared and reused in other IRS expert system applications.

However, implementing the system using a strictly object-oriented approach had its problems, the most serious being demons. Creating demons is like writing unstructured rules in a forward-chaining system that sometimes fire unpredictably. Without the chronological trace provided by a rule-based shell, it quickly became difficult to discern the effects of demons and to debug the system. Also, with demons, no mechanism exists to control the order in which they fire; with a rule-based system, the inference engine controls rule firing through conflict resolution, sponsors, agendas, and other built-in mechanisms. As a result, demons were used sparingly, mostly for initializing parameters.

Because of the difficulties encountered in implementing the object-oriented approach, frames and rules were ultimately used to represent knowledge in the TSA. Even though there are four levels in the knowledge taxonomy for the dependency test, a flat frame structure proved easier to implement, especially since inheritance was not needed. In the TSA, rules are used for a number of purposes, such as to draw conclusions, add text for later explanation, prompt users, control screen display, and build explanations.

Although rules can be written through the GoldWorks system interface without writing any LISP code, the author found it easier to learn the syntax and write rules in LISP. Also, when rules are written in LISP, LISP code can be executed within rule consequents, and variable values bound within the same rule are evaluated. To expedite writing rules, rule clauses can be written as pattern triples: the familiar MYCIN triple "(attribute, object, value)" becomes "(slot-name frame-instance slot-value)." GoldWorks maintains logical consistency between asserted pattern triples and existing related slots. All rule clauses and assertions in working memory are represented as patterns in LISP list form. GoldWorks provides a powerful pattern matcher that accepts lists of any number of elements and even processes embedded lists.

The dependency test has over 95 slots representing parameters and over 160 rules dealing with relationships between parameters. In addition, a like number of corresponding slots in screen window frame instances are needed for display of these parameters, and about 25 rules are used to control screen displays. Another 20 rules prompt assistors as to which question to ask next. The explanation facility consists of 35 slots, 6 rules, and roughly 100 lines of custom code. Implementing just the dependency test required roughly 240 rules and 225 slots. This illustrates the relative complexity and compactness found in descriptive text. The text corresponding to this topic comprises just four pages in IRS publication 501, and also included 36 examples.

Uncertainty

There are several aspects to uncertainty in the domain of tax law advice that are rather different than those found in other areas of knowledge. The assistor's advice is based on the IRS interpretation of the tax law. This greatly simplifies the representation of uncertainty. Although this interpretation is usually consistent, there are occasional points of conflict, and areas exist for which no formal interpretation can be given. In any event, it is important that advice given be consistent and explainable.

Another problem area resides with data provided by the taxpayer. If data needed to provide a definitive answer are unknown, uncertain, or inconsistent, the TSA can respond with a conditional answer indicating which pieces of data are still needed to complete the session and their legal range of values (not yet implemented).

At present, when taxpayers do not have needed pieces of information readily at hand, assistors give general answers and offer to mail out relevant IRS publications to taxpayers. In these situations, taxpayers are forced to determine the correct answer by themselves at a later time when both the publication and data are available. A typical example that arises in the dependency test are assistor requests for income and support data, items that many taxpayers do not have at hand when they call.

A final issue involves measures of certainty. In the dependency test topic, providing an "unknown" value for most parameters was not only desirable but also essential. Entering "unknown" as a value permits the system to continue collecting data, drawing conclusions, and providing contingent answers that are as accurate and complete as possible.

However, for topics such as depreciation, categorizing objects into classes is inherently probabilistic. Many taxpayers might find numerical probabilities or certainty factors unacceptable as an answer. Answers posed in English might take the form of "it is certain that" or "it is possible that." For questions on depreciation, it is likely that multiple possible answers might exist, presenting a dilemma to the designer: accuracy versus clarity, comprehension, and confidence.

User Interface

How pieces of information and their relationships are displayed can be crucial to user acceptance. Successful design of the user interface depends on the typical user's level of expertise and the roles to be played by the system. Experienced assistors may prefer a display of the relevant parameters and their legal range of values. On the other hand, novice assistors might prefer a more verbose guided question-and-answer format with the ability to define terms.

The TSA is designed to operate as an assistant or advisor system for use by novices. Thus, it is important that all actions taken by the system are displayed.

Screen 1. **Work screen with Membership, Citizenship, and Joint Return Tests**

* Screens Clear Entries Examples Show Explanation

```
* Dependency Tests Status *════════════════════════════════════
  Pass Dependency          2. Citizenship  PASS   4. Gross Income
  1. Membership   PASS      3. Joint Return PASS   5. Support
```

```
* 1. Membership Test *═══════════════     * 2. Citizenship Test *═══════════
    Is person related?      YES            U.S. Citizen?          NO
  1A. Relationship Option FAIL             Resident?              OTHER
    Direct blood?                          U.S. National?              YES
    Indirect blood?                        Parent U.S. Citizen?
    By marriage?                           Foreign Student?
    Legally adopted child?  FOSTER
  1B. Household Option PASS               * 3. Joint Return Test *═══════════
    In Household Entire Yr? NO              Person Married?        NO
    Type of Absence?        VACATION        Filed Joint Return?
    Household Employee?     NO              Tax liability if either
                                           spouse filed separately?
```

Screen 2. **Work Screen with Gross Income Test and Regular Support Option**

* Screens Clear entries Show Explanation

```
* Dependency Tests Status *════════════════════════════════════
  Pass Dependency PASS      2. Citizenship  PASS   4. Gross Income PASS
  1. Membership   PASS      3. Joint Return PASS   5. Support      PASS
```

```
* 4. Gross Income Test *═══════════      * 5. Support Test *═══════════════
  4A. Child Minor Option PASS             5A. Regular Support Option FAIL
    Child under 19?      YES                 Provide 100% of Support? NO
  4B. Child Student Option                  Dep. Expenses -- Do Calc YES
    Student Status?                         + Lodging($)          3000
    >= 5 Mos. Full-Time?                    + Household           1200
    Type of school?                         + All Other            240
  4C. Gross Income Option                   = Total Exp  4440  Unk Exp
    Tax Year?                               Claimant Support in % 27
    < Threshold Amount                      + Lodging($)          1000
    + Gross Income?                         + Household            200
    - Allowable Expenses?                   + All Other             0
    Excludable Types                        - Not allwd 0    Type NONE
    - Excludable Income?                    = Total Supp 1200  Unk Exp
```

Based on your answers, you may claim the person as your dependent.

Screen 3. **Work Screen with Multiple and Divorced Support Options**

* Screens Clear entries Show Explanation

```
* 5B. Multiple Support Option *══════     * 5C. Divorced/Separated Support Option *
  5B. Multiple Support Option  PASS        5C. Divorced Support Option   FAIL
    Others Provide Support? YES              Div/Sep Parent? NO      Qual? NO
  Qualified Support by Other Parties       Third Party Support Test
    First Other Qual. Party PASS             Is Third Party Support?
    a. Passed Other 4 tests     YES          Third Party Custody >= 6 Mo?
    b. Total             $500                 Total         -    % Support
    c. 11%  d. Have 2120     YES           Custody Test
    Second Other Qual. Party PASS            Is there a Written Decree?
    a. Passed Other 4 tests     YES          Latest Decree Gives Custody?
    b. Total             $1300               Physical Custody > Spouse?
    c. 29%  d. Have 2120     YES           Noncustodial Parent Claims
    Third Other Qual. Party FAIL             Granted Dep to Non-Cust Spouse?
    a. Passed Other 4 tests     YES          Pre-85 Decree to Non-Cust-Sps?
    b. Total             $250                 Amt of Support?        $1200
    c. 6 %  d. Have 2120     YES             Decree Gives Sole Use of Home?
  Ttl Qual Party Support $3000               Paid Child's Medical Expenses?
  % By Qual Parties 68 Do Calc YES
```

Screen 4. Explanation Screen for Taxpayers

```
*  Screens  Clear entries  Show Explanation
─────────────────────────────────────────────────────────────────────
┌─────────────────────────────────────────────────────────────────────┐
│* EXPLANATION OF CONSULTATION SESSION *═══════════════════════════════│
│ IRS Office:              IRS Assistor:  Assistor         Date:       │
│ ADVICE:  In order to claim your dependent as an exemption, you must pass│
│ all five dependency tests.  Based on the information you have given us,│
│ you MAY claim the person as your dependent.                          │
│ EXPLANATION:  You have passed all five dependency tests as follows:  │
│ The Relationship Test was met because the person is your CHILD.      │
│ The Citizenship Test was met because the person is a U.S. citizen.   │
│ The Joint Return Test was met because the person was not married.    │
│ The Gross Income Test was met because the child was under 19 years old.│
│ The Multiple Support Option was met because you paid for 27 % of support,│
│ more than the 10% threshold, and total qualified support of 68 %     │
│ was greater than the 50% threshold.                                  │
│                                                                     │
│                                                                     │
│                                                                     │
│                                                                     │
└─────────────────────────────────────────────────────────────────────┘
```

Screen 5. Explanation Screen for Assistors

```
*  Screens  Clear entries  Show Explanation
─────────────────────────────────────────────────────────────────────
┌─────────────────────────────────────────────────────────────────────┐
│* EXPLANATION OF CONSULTATION SESSION *═══════════════════════════════│
│ IRS Office:              IRS Assistor:  Assistor          Date:      │
│ TEST/OPTION   RESULT   PASSING VALUE     TAXPAYER VALUE              │
│ Dependency    PASS                                                  │
│ Membership    PASS                                                  │
│  Relation     Pass     Direct Blood      CHILD                      │
│ Citizenship   PASS     U.S. Citizen      U.S. Citizen               │
│ Joint Return  PASS     Not married       Not married                │
│ Gross Income  PASS                                                  │
│  Minor Opt    Pass     Child <19 years old                         │
│ Support Test  PASS                                                  │
│  Regular Opt  Fail     >50%              27 %                        │
│  Multiple     Pass     >10%, Ttl Qual >50% Claimant = 27 %, Ttl Qual = 68 %│
│  Divorced     Fail     Divorced/Separated  Not Divorced or Separated │
│                                                                     │
│                                                                     │
└─────────────────────────────────────────────────────────────────────┘
```

Figure 3 Example of passing the dependency test with a minor child as dependent who passed the multiple-support option but not the regular support or divorced support options.

Otherwise, the system's "reasoning process" is opaque, and users will be more tentative in trusting system results. Actions taken and conclusions drawn by the system resulting from user actions are displayed in the form of comments at the bottom of the screen (see bottom of Screen 2 in Figure 3). As much as possible, the system's actions are explicitly represented as comments. From these comments, assistors can discern the effects and consequences of entering new data or changing existing data known to the system.

Because the TSA is designed for use by novice assistors, the tax knowledge in the system is targeted at a much lower level of abstraction than would be the case for a system used by specialists. Much more knowledge about the domain is made explicit in a greater degree of detail, and less jargon is used. At present, the TSA arrives at operational meanings of terms by making detailed decisions. However, assistors should be able to request more detailed information from the system. More detailed knowledge such as the meaning of terms or the meaning of questions that ask for data will be displayed as popup windows. This feature has not yet been implemented.

A manager at the test site [13] made the observation that learning and usage would be facilitated if the structure of the domain knowledge could be made more explicit. Not only can tax topics be arranged in a hierarchical structure, but also so can the details of a given topic. At present, the TSA provides some evidence of the structure of the dependency test topic through a status summary and organization of domain knowledge into tests and options. For example, two status lines near the top of the screen show progress made thus far: which tests are passed, failed, or unknown and which tests are not yet answered (see Screen 1 in Figures 3–4). Figure 2 shows the formal structure of knowledge for the dependency test; the screens in Figures 3–5 show how this structure is implemented in the TSA.

In addition to comments describing what actions the system has taken and what the current status of the system is, novice assistors also need suggestions as to what to do next. Although prompts may not be needed by domain experts, prompts should not get in their way. Prompts displayed at the bottom of the screen help novices decide what action is best to take next. These prompts represent heuristics developed by specialists to minimize the length of each call. However, in the TSA, following the advice of prompts is optional; assistors are free to choose their own course of action or one directed by the taxpayer.

Explanation

The TSA provides two types of explanation, one for taxpayers and another for assistors (see Screens 4 and 5 in Figures 3–5). Taxpayers receive a less detailed explanation consisting of one narrative sentence for each test completed; assistors receive a more detailed explanation consisting of one line of data in an abbreviated tabular format for each test and option completed. Each line of data consists of the option or test name, the allowable values, and the values given by the taxpayer.

The author tried three different approaches in developing an explanation facility. First, the explanation facility that comes with GoldWorks was tried; it did not work. Even after receiving assistance and code from Gold Hill, the approach of tracing back through the rule tree after an answer had been reached was much too complex. Rules that possessed "or" clauses on several levels required tracing backward through multiple paths, clearly a bad idea. The author next attempted to build explanations by using demons. However, it was impossible to control the sequence of execution of demons and rule retractions when using the GoldWorks logical dependency feature.

Finally, the author tried a more intuitively attractive approach—capturing pieces of explanations directly as rules fire in forward-chaining mode. Whenever rules fire that make decisions for tests or options, corresponding text found in consequent clauses is asserted into frame slots. Each explanation slot stores strings of text related to a specific option or test. By using the logical dependency feature provided with GoldWorks, whenever a parameter value is changed in the antecedent of a previously fired rule, all assertions in the consequent of that rule are retracted, thus deleting corresponding text from those slots. Therefore, whenever an explanation is requested, it is built directly from existing string slot fragments.

Another advantage of this approach is the ease with which contingent answers can be built. A recent addition to the TSA is the ability to give simplistic contingent

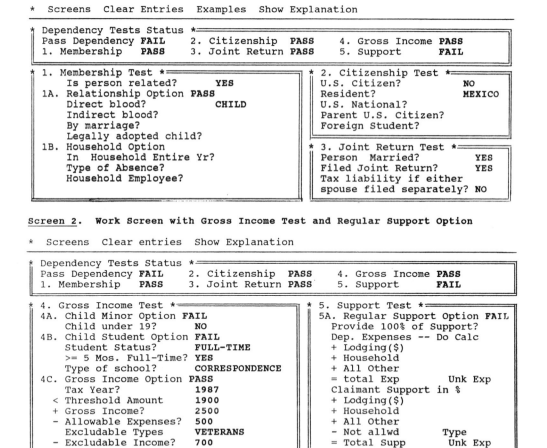

Figure 4 An example of failing the dependency test because the divorced spouse claiming the exemption did not pass the noncustodial spouse test.

Screen 3. **Work Screen with Multiple and Divorced Support Options**

* Screens Clear entries Show Explanation

```
* 5B. Multiple Support Option *═══╗   * 5C. Divorced/Separated Support Option *╗
  5B. Multiple Support Option  FAIL    5C. Divorced Support Option  FAIL
  Others Provide Support?               Div/Sep Parent? DIVORCED  Qual? YES
Qualified Support by Other Parties    Third Party Support Test  PASS
  First Other Qual. Party               Is Third Party Support?        NO
  a. Passed Other 4 tests               Third Party Custody >= 6 Mo?
  b. Total                              Total    -    % Support
  c.    % d. Have 2120                Custody Test  FAIL
  Second Other Qual. Party              Is there a Written Decree?     YES
  a. Passed Other 4 tests               Latest Decree Gives Custody?   NO
  b. Total                              Physical Custody > Spouse?
  c.    % d. Have 2120              Noncustodial Parent Claims Test  FAIL
  Third Other Qual. Party               Granted Dep to Non-Cust Spouse? NO
  a. Passed Other 4 tests               Pre-85 Decree to Non-Cust-Sps? YES
  b. Total                              Amt of Support?             $500
  c.    % d. Have 2120                Decree Gives Sole Use of Home?
Ttl Qual Party Support                Paid Child's Medical Expenses?
% By Qual Parties     Do Calc
```

Screen 4. **Explanation Screen for Taxpayers**

* Screens Clear entries Show Explanation

```
* EXPLANATION OF CONSULTATION SESSION *═══
IRS Office:              IRS Assistor: Assistor        Date:
ADVICE:  In order to claim your dependent as an exemption, you must pass
all five dependency tests.  Based on the information you have given us,
you may NOT claim the person as your dependent.
EXPLANATION:  You have failed one of the following dependency tests:
The Relationship Option was met because the person is your CHILD.
The Citizenship Test was met because the person is a resident of MEXICO.
The Joint Return Test was met because the person was married, filed
a joint return, but had no tax liability.
The Gross Income Test was met because gross income of $2500  less allowable
expenses of $500   and less excludable income of $700
was less than threshold of $1900.
The Divorced Support Option was failed because although a third party
provided less than 50% of support, and you have a pre-1985 grant for the
non-custodial exemption, you provided $500   of support, < $600 minimum.
```

Figure 4 *(continued)*

Screen 5. Explanation Screen for Assistors

* Screens   Clear entries   Show Explanation

```
* EXPLANATION OF CONSULTATION SESSION *════════════════════════════
  IRS Office:                  IRS Assistor:   Assistor        Date:
  TEST/OPTION     RESULT     PASSING VALUE       TAXPAYER VALUE
  Dependency      FAIL
  Membership      PASS
    Relation      Pass       Direct Blood       CHILD
  Citizenship     PASS       Valid Resident     Resident of MEXICO
  Joint Return    PASS       Married, Filed Jointly, had no Tax Liability
  Gross Income    PASS
    Minor Opt     Fail       Child 19 or more years old
    Student Opt   Fail       Child Full-time Student attending CORRESPONDENCE
    Income Opt    Pass       < $1900            Inc $2500 - Exp $500 - Excl $700
  Support Test    FAIL
    Regular Opt   Fail       3rd parth <50%, pre-85 grant, <$600 support
    Multiple      Fail       3rd parth <50%, pre-85 grant, <$600 support
    Divorced      Fail       3rd parth <50%, pre-85 grant, <$600 support
```

Figure 4 (*continued*)

Screen 1. Work screen with Membership, Citizenship, and Joint Return Tests

* Screens   Clear Entries   Examples   Show Explanation

```
* Dependency Tests Status *═══════════════════════════════════════
  Pass Dependency PASS    2. Citizenship  PASS    4. Gross Income PASS
  1. Membership    PASS   3. Joint Return PASS    5. Support      PASS
```

```
* 1. Membership Test *══════════          * 2. Citizenship Test *══════
     Is person related?     YES           U.S. Citizen?          YES
  1A. Relationship Option PASS             Resident?
      Direct blood?       CHILD            U.S. National?
      Indirect blood?                      Parent U.S. Citizen?
      By marriage?                         Foreign Student?
      Legally adopted child?
  1B. Household Option                    * 3. Joint Return Test *══════
      In Household Entire Yr?              Person Married?          NO
      Type of Absence?                     Filed Joint Return?
      Household Employee?                  Tax liability if either
                                           spouse filed separately?
```

Figure 5 Example of dependency test that is incomplete because taxpayer did not have information regarding gross income and support tests at hand. As a result, a contingent answer is given along with sources to use in answering the missing tests. (There are no entries for Screens 2 and 3.)

Screen 4. Explanation Screen for Taxpayers

* Screens Clear entries Show Explanation

```
* EXPLANATION OF CONSULTATION SESSION *═══════════════════
  IRS Office:                IRS Assistor: Assistor        Date:
  ADVICE:  In order to claim your dependent as an exemption, you must pass
  all five dependency tests.  Based on the information you have given us,
  you may NOT at present claim the person as your dependent because
  insufficient data exists for a conclusion.
  EXPLANATION:  You have answered the following tests:
  The Household Option was met because the person is a member of your
  household, was not an employee, and VACATION is a valid temporary
  absence.
  The Citizenship Test was met because the person is a U.S. national.
  The Joint Return Test was met because the person was not married.
  CONTINGENCY:  You must answer and pass the following test(s)
  before you can claim the person as your dependent:
  Gross Income Test      Reference:  Pub 17, Pages 22-23; Pub 501, Page 6
  Support Test           Reference:  Pub 17, Pages 23-26; Pub 501, Pages 6-9
```

Screen 5. Explanation Screen for Assistors

* Screens Clear entries Show Explanation

```
* EXPLANATION OF CONSULTATION SESSION *═══════════════════
  IRS Office:                    IRS Assistor:  Assistor        Date:
  TEST/OPTION    RESULT    PASSING VALUE        TAXPAYER VALUE
  Dependency
  Membership     PASS
    Relation     Fail      Legally Adopted      Foster or not legal
  Citizenship    PASS      U.S. National        U.S. National
  Joint Return   PASS      Not Married          Not Married
  Gross Income
  Support Test
  CONTINGENCY:   You must answer and pass the following test(s)
  before you can claim the person as your dependent:
  Gross Income Test      Reference:  Pub 17, Pages 22-23; Pub 501, Page 6
  Support Test           Reference:  Pub 17, Pages 23-26; Pub 501, Pages 6-9
```

Figure 5 *(continued)*

explanations when data are either missing and/or unknown. Of course, if any test is failed, then no contingent answer is needed. For all tests that are unanswered or have an unknown as an answer, references are made to the relevant IRS publication (see Screens 4 and 5 in Figure 5), and the options and their allowable values are displayed (not yet implemented).

Training

Even after an initial four weeks of classroom training, the experience of a filing season's questions, and four additional weeks of training on more complex tax issues, assistors often either answer technical questions incorrectly or needlessly refer questions to specialists. The extent of novice assistor training and frequency of assistor errors and omissions illustrate how difficult it is to improve their knowledge and expertise. This presents a very difficult problem not only to human teachers but also to the development of intelligent tutoring systems. To date, intelligent tutoring systems have not been very successful.

Conventional methods such as extensive classroom training, checklists, role-playing, and on-line quality review are used to improve the quality of assistor interactions with taxpayers. While these approaches have met with some success, they have not solved the training problem. Currently, the Taxpayer Service Organization is testing the use of written algorithms in answering questions on specific tax topics, and initial results are encouraging. Of course, expert systems automate this algorithm decision process as well as provide explanations.

At present, the TSA facilitates training in several ways. First, the system contains examples to illustrate how typical calls can be answered. Second, the system can be used in an exploratory mode. Students can enter values for parameters and watch the consequences in actions that the TSA takes. When values are changed, assistors can observe which data elements are dependent on others. Students also can examine two types of explanations that justify the system's answer. Most learning will occur as students explore the system and observe system actions, comments, prompts, and explanations.

Choice of Hardware and Software

The strategy pursued in selecting equipment for developing and testing the feasibility prototype emphasized practicality and expediency. Rather than design custom software, a commercial expert system shell was selected to promote rapid prototyping and development. Due to the large number of potential users, ultimately the cost per user will determine whether the system is deployed. At the time, another consideration was the limited funds available for system development and feasibility testing. In addition, it was important that the TSA could be demonstrated and tested at a remote site. Finally, in order to speed system development and testing and anticipate future developments in the marketplace, the TSA uses the same hardware and software for both development and deployment. For these reasons, only shells that ran on microcomputers were considered.

Initially, Texas Instrument's PC Plus expert system shell running on a PC XT clone was chosen for development, primarily because of immediate availability of both hardware and software. However, two months into system development, it was determined that PC Plus lacked the needed functionality and flexibility.

The choice of software has driven the selection of supporting hardware. Consequently, when the prototype was redesigned using Gold Hill's GoldWorks shell, the minimum hardware required was a Compaq 286 with a 5-Mbyte extended memory board. Currently, the TSA is being developed on a Compaq 386/20 with 8 Mbytes of extended memory. Use of a mouse greatly improves the speed of operating the system as well as user acceptance.

SYSTEM IMPLEMENTATION

Introducing the TSA into the Existing Work Environment

When introducing a new application such as the TSA, it is essential that the project receive the endorsement and support of top management. In this regard, the involvement and support of TSA executives at the test site have been excellent. Not only have assistors and managers been made available for questionnaires, system briefings, and demonstrations, but also the project coordinator who was selected, Robert Marsetta, has contributed his considerable skills as a psychologist, learning theorist, and organizational behaviorist to ensure the success of the TSA. Without this good fortune, the fate of this project would be far less certain.

It is also important that the disruption of existing assistor work flow be kept to a minimum. System acceptance could be greatly hindered if managers and assistors believed that the TSA would be too much trouble to learn and use or that it would waste precious assistor resources. There are two reasons why there will be little disruption. First, routing calls on specific tax topics is an established process. Second, for each call correctly referred, the assistor receives credit for a completed call, improving their call efficiency statistics.

There are several reasons why it is best that all calls on tax topics covered by the TSA be referred to assistors with the system. First, even tax topics with the highest volume of calls amount to little more than 2% of total calls. Therefore, in order to maximize system utilization and testing, referring calls is the only way to obtain sufficient call volume. Second, this process of referring calls parallels the existing process for both verbal and written referrals. Third, more accurate call monitoring and test measurement are possible.

The system test procedure works as follows:

1. When assistors with the system are not engaged with a call, calls on the dependency topic are referred directly to them to answer.
2. When assistors with the system are busy, up to two callers may be referred and placed on hold. Calls are answered in turn from the holding line.
3. When system assistors are busy and the holding line is full, frontline assistors write down taxpayer questions and phone numbers and route this information

to system assistors. When system assistors are subsequently free, they call taxpayers back in the order in which the referrals were received.

4. When system assistors are free and no referred calls are waiting, they answer calls on other tax topics just as frontline assistors normally do.

In the existing approach, questions that cannot be answered by technical backups over the phone are referred to specialists, later answered in writing, and then mailed to taxpayers. Verbal responses used in the TSA test seem preferable to written responses because taxpayers receive responses in minutes or hours rather than days later. Other advantages are that questions can be immediately clarified, additional facts can be given, and taxpayers can receive explanations of answers given.

Test Design

In order to better validate the system, a control group without the TSA will alternate with the system group in answering routed calls. This test design does have a flaw: Both groups are expected to improve their performance as a result of the learning effect from answering questions on only one tax topic. However, the alternative seems worse: If assistors do not refer calls, then the TSA would be used too infrequently to obtain statistically meaningful samples of calls for analysis.

Three skill levels of assistors will be used to test the system:

1. Novice assistors who have recently completed Phase I training.
2. Assistors with some experience who have completed Phase II training.
3. Experienced assistors (at least one year of experience) who have completed Phase III training.

Six assistors from each skill level will participate in the two-month test, three as system users and three in the control group. The test results should not only indicate at which skill levels the TSA should be aimed but also provide a more statistically valid sample. Specialists will not be part of the formal test. Not only are they a scarce resource, but also their error rate is negligible.

The use of the TSA as a training aid will also be tested. Initially, the TSA will be used during on-the-job training. Also, for those assistors in training who fail the test on the dependency module, the TSA will be used in place of written materials for remedial training. Test scores from retesting will be compared between the system group and a control group as a measure of value of the TSA as a training aid. Later, the system will be used in training workshops and continuing professional education modules.

Specialists at the test site have probed the TSA for several days in order to identify programming bugs, logic errors, interface deficiencies, common call sequences, optimizing the sequence of data gathering, and future enhancements. Numerous minor changes have been made thus far based on this procedure.

Sample Sessions

Three types of sample sessions are illustrated. Figure 3 shows the results of passing all tests. Figure 4 shows the results of failing the support test. Figure 5 shows the results of requesting an explanation when the session is incomplete.

TWO APPROACHES: EXPERT SYSTEM VERSUS TEXT RETRIEVAL

Currently, there are two projects under development at the IRS that attempt to improve performance on the assistor task. The TSA takes an expert system approach; the Automated Taxpayer Service System (ATSS) focuses on text retrieval. The TSA provides advice and explanations based on taxpayer responses to system questions entered by assistors; the ATSS locates and retrieves relevant pieces of text from a data base of IRS publications based on entering appropriate keyword combinations.

Text Retrieval Approach

The approach taken by ATSS augments the present way that the assistor task is done. Currently, assistors reference IRS publication(s) using tables of contents and indices to locate relevant portions of text. With a text retrieval system, text is accessed directly by entering keywords. When keywords match words in the text, all sections of text that match are retrieved and displayed. Keywords often are combined logically in order to restrict the number of text sections retrieved. Text is retrieved from data bases containing IRS publications, the tax law and its IRS interpretation, and later possibly other tax reference guides.

One advantage of this more conventional methodology is that tax law data bases and extensive off-the-shelf text retrieval packages are readily available from commercial sources. Also, vendors keep their tax data bases current through frequent updating. A further advantage is the relatively low cost per user of providing this capability. Finally, this approach requires no extensive software development for its use.

One disadvantage of the text retrieval approach is that users must learn how to use keywords and queries in order to access relevant text sections. Revenue Canada's experience [14], although positive, indicated that at least one week of classroom training and several weeks of usage were needed to reach proficiency. Assistors must also learn how to narrow the scope of retrieval so that only the most relevant sections of text are selected. An unexpected drawback of text retrieval systems is the limited amount of text that is visible on a screen at any one time as compared to printed media.

However, the most serious deficiencies of this approach go to the root of the assistor task. Namely, text retrieval methods still leave the assistor with the burden of reading, understanding, interpreting, and restructuring text into a knowledge form that can be used directly to answer taxpayer questions. In addition to arriving at accurate and complete answers, assistors must often provide explanations of their answers at a level that is understandable by taxpayers. Here, again, assistors must formulate cogent explanations from text; in most cases, simply reading relevant passages of text to taxpayers is not adequate because the reasons behind the advice and decisions given often are not self-evident.

Expert System Approach

The second approach, the one embodied in the TSA, restructures text from IRS publications and the tax law into an active form of knowledge using expert systems technology. The TSA implements algorithms and decision trees so that domain knowledge can be used directly to perform the assistor task. There are several advantages:

1. Data acquisition is focused; only parameters relevant to the taxpayer's situation are requested.
2. Knowledge is in a readily usable form.
3. Knowledge is better organized.
4. Knowledge is represented more explicitly.
5. Explanations show how decisions and advice were arrived at.
6. At any point in the session, the current state of the system can be explained along with parameters still needed to reach an answer.

Use of expert systems technology shifts the burden of knowing, remembering, and reasoning about details of technical tax law from the human mind to the expert system. The TSA eliminates the need to refer to IRS publications in answering taxpayer questions. The system can either supplant assistors' existing tax knowledge or, when topics are unknown to them, provide a comprehensive source of knowledge.

The TSA is expected to reduce referrals of taxpayer inquiries to specialists, allowing those specialists to concentrate their expertise on answering only the most difficult cases. Current policy, procedures, and training require less experienced assistors to refer questions outside their area of expected competence to specialists for resolution. Not only is this aggravating to taxpayers and employees alike, but also it is time consuming because questions must be restated and understood a second time. In addition, the author believes that using the TSA will reduce "answer shopping" (repeat calls on the same question by taxpayers looking for a more favorable answer) by providing more accurate, complete, consistent, and unambiguous advice. Furthermore, if printouts of consultation sessions were made available to taxpayers upon request, this might further reduce repeat calls.

Use of the TSA should result in several training benefits. Training costs may be reduced while increasing retention through use of the system in its exploratory mode. Additionally, when used as a tutor or as an assistant during daily work, assistors might incrementally increase their expertise about taxes. During the knowledge acquisition process, some expert knowledge was uncovered that formerly was implicit. The author believes that by continuing this process, new insights will be discovered and existing concepts and relationships will be clarified. Ultimately, more effective teaching methods should result.

However, there are disadvantages to this approach. The main disadvantage is that expert systems are hand crafted. Parameters, their relationships, and allowable values must be determined through a lengthy process of knowledge acquisition from printed materials and knowledge elicitation from experts. In addition, screen interfaces must be designed very carefully with the typical user in mind. Thus, the time required for development is quite significant, especially if the entire breadth of the tax code is to be represented.

A second drawback is that expert systems require considerably greater computing resources than text retrieval systems, resulting in a higher cost per user. However, this differential cost will likely moderate over time due to continuing cost efficiencies in both hardware and software. A final unresolved issue is determining the most effective configuration for system deployment. The optimal medium might be either distributed processing, stand-alone microprocessors, or some mix in between.

Organizational Environment

The Taxpayer Service Division (TPSD) was established with the mission of providing quality service and advice to taxpayers. It is one of four divisions under the Assistant Commissioner for Taxpayer Service and Returns Processing. In addition to providing tax information and specific assistance to taxpayers directly by IRS personnel, outreach programs on taxpayer education are administered and supported jointly by TPSD and volunteer organizations such as the American Association of Retired People.

A look at some selected milestones in TPSD history:

1971 TPSD was created.

1983 TPSD was not funded by the administration but as the division was being dismantled, funding was restored by Congress.

1985 The Office of ATSS was created.

1987 GAO study of TPSD [3] indicated problems with the quality of service in answering technical tax questions.

1988 Congress granted additional funding for more assistor positions and training but not for automation efforts.

1989 ATSS was funded for $2 million.

Traditionally, TPSD has relied on its personnel rather than on technology to provide improvements in service. Funding for staff positions is based on providing a certain (typically 80%) level of phone service. This means that roughly 20% of taxpayer callers will not reach an assistor on the first try. Although this method of staffing results in an efficient use of resources, it has engendered a short-term planning focus. Most automation efforts require a multiyear perspective as well as significant capital funding for development and deployment. Perhaps as much as any other factor, the current method of staffing may have slowed funding and other support for extended automation efforts.

The attempt to eliminate TPSD in fiscal year 1983 was the culmination of the Reagan administration's belief that if taxpayers want or need help, they should pay for it, and the IRS should not be in the business of providing such assistance. From this nadir, the TPSD organization has ascended in importance and is now under the Assistant Commissioner for Taxpayer Service and Returns Processing.

ATSS. The ATSS project office was organized in 1985 within TPSD to explore means of improving phone service to taxpayers through use of computer technology. At present, the ATSS staff has grown to eight. Most of the staff are former assistors who have extensive experience in various aspects of TPSD; the remainder have strong computer backgrounds with little or no taxpayer service domain knowledge.

The ATSS project, while less ambitious in its depth, is broader in scope than the TSA. The ATSS is focusing on implementing a computer system comprised of several tools. The main component of this system is a text retrieval module to aid assistors in performing research. Other components can access and change taxpayer accounts, access refund information, and retrieve images of tax forms from a data base.

AI Lab. In 1983, staff of then Assistant Commissioner for Planning, Finance and Research, John Wedick, conducted a study that indicated that AI technology might be applied profitably to tasks in the IRS. In 1984, in response to this study, Wedick created the IRS AI program. Prior to the AI program, the IRS did not possess any capability to develop AI applications in-house nor did it feel competent to contract work out to AI vendors.

Wedick's staff interviewed leading academic researchers and business practitioners to find the best methods of achieving an AI capability within the IRS. As a result, Wedick devised a program with two strategies for training IRS domain experts in AI technology. A one-year program was designed to develop AI project managers capable of overseeing vendor work and evaluating contract proposals for AI services. Four program participants were trained in project management and design at a leading research concern. A two-year course of study was designed to educate domain experts in AI techniques and create a cadre capable of developing extensive AI applications in-house. Nine two-year participants were schooled at one of three leading AI universities.

In 1985, Wedick created the AI Lab as a section within the Research Division, one of three divisions under his leadership. The Lab is currently staffed by 22 AI specialists. Thus far, two classes have completed the AI training program. A third class began training in the fall of 1989. Prior to receiving AI training, most of the program participants were domain experts from various functional areas within IRS. The remainder were computer programmers and systems analysts from the computer services function.

John Wedick, now one of two deputy commissioners, has provided continuing support for the AI Lab, ensuring its long-term viability. He has funded not only subsequent classes of trainees but also the procurement of equipment and software for the Lab. This support has, in part, created a work environment encouraging a host of AI applications. In contrast to the concentrated effort of the entire ATSS staff working on one project, the AI Lab has 18 on-going projects, most of them with only one AI specialist assigned. In addition, there are several student projects that in the future may become permanent projects.

Because expert systems technology is most effective only on certain classes of problems or tasks, only trained AI specialists are qualified to select the most promising projects. Hence, in many cases, AI Lab participants have had complete freedom in selecting projects. However, for some projects, this freedom has been double-edged. Support and participation by functions with the selected projects often have been disinterested at best until successful prototypes have been built and demonstrated. The TSA is an example of this phenomenon. Freedom in project selection as well as diversity of domain expertise have encouraged a variety of AI applications under development. However, early progress on the TSA was stunted because only one AI specialist was assigned.

TENTATIVE CONCLUSIONS

Project Selection Methods

Although the methodologies employed for selecting the TSA resulted in an entirely satisfactory task and tax topic for the initial prototype, there is no substitute for acquiring domain knowledge and expertise. Over the past two years, the author has become increasingly knowledgeable concerning the overall assistor task and the organizational environment that surrounds it. If the TSA had not been designed with these contexts in mind, the project's ultimate success would be far less certain.

The third selection method, decomposing the task and determining the feasibility of applying AI technology to each subtask, appears to be the most effective evaluation technique. The first method, evaluating tasks by comparing them with selection criteria from checklists, is helpful, but it is not sufficiently rigorous to ensure success. However, the selection criteria checklist approach is quite useful in choosing the most promising slices of domain knowledge. The second method, matching application tasks to generic expert system tasks, appears to have little merit other than in eliminating inappropriate tasks.

Knowledge Acquisition

Many inadequacies found thus far in the TSA can be traced to the author's failure to involve domain experts early on in the development of the system. In future work, specialists will develop and discuss cases that reveal important issues and key distinctions between similar cases and participate in structured interviews designed to uncover and model their reasoning processes. Other less unconventional methods from cognitive science, such as verbal protocols, also may be employed to aid in obtaining this implicit knowledge from domain experts. It is hoped that these methods will uncover terminology problems, misconceptions by the author, most likely scenarios, and optimal sequencing of questions. A set of case studies and prototypical questions are needed both for system validation and assistor training.

User Interface

Since the assistors are the target end users of the TSA, one might expect that they would be experts when it comes to deciding what sorts of display and interactive format are desirable. After conducting demonstrations and pretests, it appears that only experienced users have the background needed to evaluate the interface and make suggestions, although their needs and preferences will be different from those of novices. Early results indicate that screens should display a semantically relevant number of variables and related values. For example, on the dependency test, only one test or option might be displayed at a time. Compare this to the current interface in which all work screens display more than one test or option (see Screens 1–3 in Figures 3–5). Assistors liked the status lines that display the current state of progress so they are always aware of which tests remain to be answered.

Project Support

Ideally, executive support for developing an expert system application should exist from the start of a project. Even though this support was initially lacking, after analyzing numerous possible tasks within the IRS, the author was convinced of the exceptional potential of the TSA and proceeded with its design and development. Although TPSD field management in Boston realized the potential of the TSA and strongly supported it early on, national office executives did not recognize its value until the feasibility prototype was demonstrated. Over the past eight months, the author has demonstrated the TSA to over 10 IRS executives at the national office and in the field. Since then, support has steadily grown. Recently, with the support of top IRS executives, a task force of three AI specialists completed work on extending the number of tax topics covered from 3 to 55 using Level 5, a simpler expert system shell.

Software and Hardware

System designers should resist the temptation to force fit applications into available shells and toolkits. However, practical considerations will force a choice between developing custom shells and purchasing off-the-shelf tools. Several experienced practitioners [15] have expressed the belief that development of serious expert systems will inevitably involve building custom shells and interfaces. Based on limited experience with developing an explanation facility, the author is rapidly approaching the same conclusion.

There are several areas in which vendors could provide more functionality than is required by the Common LISP standard. Macros for input–output processes such as reading and writing files and printing would be quite helpful. Vendors should meet current spreadsheet standards for manipulating and displaying data (such as providing for right-justified numeric field inputs) and parsing and editing numbers with dollar signs, commas, and decimal points.

Expert system shells also need greater functionality than now exists. Shells should come with a complete explanation facility. Hooks for control of screens, menus, and cursor should be available to developers. A value of "unknown" should receive special treatment by the inference engine, just as "true" and "false" now are handled. Vendors should supply several forms of uncertainty handling rather than ignoring the implementation details of this feature. Another desirable piece of software would be an animated decision tree similar to but more developed than Gold Hill's Axle or Neuron Data's Nexpert. Finally, shells should provide a basic machine learning capability for optimizing parameter weights.

The author chose to develop the feasibility prototype using GoldWorks primarily because it offered more features than other PC-based shells. Both the rule and frame facilities provide excellent flexibility and extensive capabilities without being too difficult to learn or use. GoldWorks offers considerable control over inferencing through use of sponsors, agendas, and rule priorities. In addition to both forward and backward chaining, GoldWorks also supports goal-directed forward chaining. Although not used thus far in this application, an extensive pattern-matching facility is also provided. Gold Hill provided good support in resolving most problems, including review of the author's code.

When GoldWorks was selected, the author did not realize how desirable the features of forward chaining and later logical dependency would be. In the forward-chaining mode, use of the logical dependency feature (truth maintenance) proved most valuable. Not only did this feature keep knowledge consistent as data were changed, but also it allowed the easy construction of the flexible explanation facility used in the TSA.

One major disappointment in using GoldWorks was its lack of an explanation facility. Although a minimal explanation facility was provided, it was inadequate for all but the most basic needs. Some code was offered by Gold Hill as a solution, but it worked with rules of only the simplest structure. Unfortunately, other high-end shells provide equally dismal explanation facilities. Approximately two staff-months were spent in developing a flexible explanation facility. See the explanation section for details.

The author encountered several other deficiencies with GoldWorks. Unfortunately, the logical dependency feature does not work when antecedent clauses test for slots without values. This deficiency could be remedied by keeping a list of these slots without values and retracting related consequent assertions whenever values are asserted for any slots on the list. As is, rules must be rewritten to eliminate tests for missing assertions in order for the logical dependency feature to work properly. In the object-oriented mode, two irritations are the out-of-sequence firing of popup menus and screen display demons, and the cursor being thrown from the screen slot being worked following use of popup menus.

GoldWorks and the underlying Common LISP consumed over 4 Mbytes of extended memory, and TSA application code gobbed up another 3 Mbytes. Given these extreme memory demands, it is disappointing that Gold Hill does not provide for segmenting or code swapping to a hard disk. This constraint greatly limits use of GoldWorks for large applications, including the scaled-up version of the TSA.

Experience dictates slight changes in hardware requirements. Future hardware should be equipped with 15-inch color monitors, not 12-inch monochrome monitors. This allows more data to comfortably fit on a screen, and color can help sell a system. Also, at least one lap-top portable system should be purchased for demonstrations at remote sites.

System Costs

A major issue that must be addressed in the deployment phase is the installed system cost. Because there are 5,000 potential end users, system development costs are trivial when compared to total system deployment costs. However, due to the continuing rapid advances in computing power and technology, the author believes that longer term planning for system deployment is premature except in the most general terms.

As currently configured using GoldWorks, about 6 Mbytes of extended memory are needed to operate the TSA in run time mode. When additional tax topic modules are added, total extended memory requirements could quickly reach 8 Mbytes or more. An additional memory cost of over $2,000 per user would be incurred if GoldWorks were used for delivery.

There appear to be two generic solutions. In the first approach, GoldWorks would reside on a host machine with extensive memory and storage capacity at each toll-free site. Processing for the expert system would be shared between the host and smart terminals using a local area network. In the second approach, a custom shell would be written in C, Scheme, or some other compact language, and the system then delivered on stand-alone 286 or 386 microcomputers with 1 Mbyte of memory. Clearly, there are drawbacks to both approaches. In the first approach, response time may be too slow and networking costs too high; in the second approach, system administration, maintenance, and updating will be onerous.

Potential Benefits

There are many advantages both to the IRS and to taxpayers if the TSA is successful. Benefits to the IRS include improved quality of service, public image and assistor effectiveness, as well as higher productivity, reduced training levels, and increased compliance. Benefits to taxpayers include improved quality and promptness of service and reduced levels of frustration and confusion.

FUTURE DIRECTIONS

Scaling Up

Knowledge representation schema are not a significant concern when there are but few tax topics. However, representation issues take on additional importance as the knowledge base grows. When the TSA covers 50 tax topics, successfully managing its complexity will become critical. An object-oriented approach using a frame lattice hierarchy with inheritance, default values, demons, and handlers would make this task easier. Designers can manage the complexity inherent in scaling up by structuring knowledge into taxonomies, defining primitive objects and operations, guiding users through the system, anticipating user needs, and documenting code.

Future Development Strategies

The strategies to be used in developing later phases of the project may differ substantially from those used in the prototype. There are several stages of project work still required to reach a fully operational system. The first stage, the feasibility prototype, is described extensively in the preceding sections. In the second stage, the system's functional capabilities will be extended. This may require building a customized shell. The third stage expands the scope of the knowledge base to include many specialized topics. The fourth stage enhances the user interface and implements the TSA for operational use by several levels of assistors. A final stage might involve constructing a "bombproof" version of the system for direct taxpayer access either in person at IRS sites or by computer and modem at remote sites such as commercial data bases.

For the prototype, only one sliver of knowledge was developed. Another plan for future development would be to spread the implementation of tax topics across the remaining stages rather than expanding the breadth of knowledge primarily in one stage. Expanding the TSA's functional capabilities appears to be more difficult than expanding its breadth of knowledge. Capabilities such as intelligent tutoring, understanding natural-language inputs, machine learning to optimize ordering of questions, providing for error-resistant knowledge additions and modifications by specialists, and generating flexible text are all active research areas with few successful commercial applications. Therefore, some of these features will be explored only after a working version of the TSA with a breadth of tax topics has been implemented.

The following objectives will be pursued to varying degrees in later phases of the project:

1. Provide extensive tutoring and training of assistors on issues covered by the TSA. Teach novice assistors who are learning the material for the first time. Provide a refresher course for more experienced assistors.

2. Parse syntactically textual inputs with limited vocabularies. Understand limited natural-language inputs semantically.

3. Learn from experience to optimize the ordering of remaining data needed to be input to the system to reach a decision. The user would be prompted as to which data to ask for next. This would be implemented using genetic algorithms built on top of a rule-based system [16].

4. Allow specialists to modify the knowledge base without assistance by designing a front-end knowledge acquisition module that would perform validity and consistency checks on these modifications to ensure an accurate and complete knowledge base [17, 18].

5. Allow assistors to customize the interface to best suit their individual needs and style.

6. Provide interface and explanation facilities that accommodate multiple levels of knowledge of assistors and/or taxpayers.

7. Make the structure of knowledge visible by giving it graphical form as an animated flowchart or algorithm. If hierarchical decision trees were displayed graphically, indicating relationships between data, their taxonomy, and what data are still needed for a decision, then novice assistors might be able to learn how to create their own mental models of tax knowledge.

8. Facilitate knowledge acquisition among multiple experts [19].

REFERENCES

1. Beckman, T., "TSA Questionnaire," results of questionnaire, May 1987.
2. Internal Revenue Service, "National Summary Report," Taxpayer Service Management Information System, April 25, 1987.
3. General Accounting Office, "IRS' Efforts to Help Taxpayers During the 1987 Tax Filing Season," GAO Congressional Testimony, April 8, 1987.
4. Internal Revenue Service, "Quality Review Trend Analysis," Taxpayer Service National Report, May 6, 1987.
5. Davis, R., notes from MIT course on knowledge-based systems, Massachusetts Institute of Technology, Cambridge, MA, 1985.

6. Prerau, D. S., "Selection of an Appropriate Domain for an Expert System," *AI Magazine*, Summer 1985.

7. Grady, G., "A Survey of Expert System Selection Criteria." Internal Revenue Service, Washington, DC, unpublished paper, 1986.

8. Waterman, D. A., *A Guide to Expert Systems*, Addison-Wesley, Reading, MA, 1985.

9. Martin, N., notes from a Smart Systems Technology course, Washington, DC, 1984.

10. Reitman, W. (ed.), *Artificial Intelligence Applications for Business*, Ablex, Norwood, NJ, 1984.

11. Minsky, M., *The Society of Mind*, Simon & Schuster, New York, 1986.

12. Beckman, T., "Design of Knowledge-Based Systems," MIT Sloan School Doctoral Workshop, 1986.

13. Marsetta, R., personal communication, IRS, Boston, 1988.

14. Ahmed, A., personal communication, Revenue Canada, Ottawa, 1988.

15. Patil, R., Davis, R., and Martin, N., personal communication, M.I.T., Boston, 1986–1988.

16. Holland, J. H., Holyoak, K. J., Nisbett, R. E., and Thagard, P. R., *Induction: Processes of Inference, Learning, and Discovery*, MIT Press, Cambridge, MA, 1986.

17. Davis, R. and Lenat, D. B., *Knowledge-based Systems in Artificial Intelligence*, McGraw-Hill, New York, 1982.

18. Politakis, P. G., *Empirical Analysis for Expert Systems*, Pitman, Boston, 1985.

19. Trice, A., "Facilitating Consensus Knowledge Acquisition," doctoral thesis, Massachusetts Institute of Technology, Cambridge, MA, 1989.

3

Modeling and Reasoning: Integrating Decision Support with Expert Systems

David King

INTRODUCTION

Theoretically, a *decision support system* (DSS) is a software system designed to assist and support managers with semistructured decision-making tasks. A *semistructured* task is one that is ill-defined and involves uncertainties and complex relations among a number of variables. Examples of such tasks include deciding whether to build a new plant, to acquire another company, or to add a new offering to a product line. At the heart of a DSS is a language for constructing and manipulating models. In most cases a model is a set of equations and logic used to represent the (financial) activities of a business entity. A simple model depicting the profit variance of a corporation is shown in Figure 1. When the model is solved, it produces the results in Table 1.

A model can be manipulated in order to understand not only past performance but also the possible consequences of future activities. Through what-if, goal-seeking, impact, and sensitivity analysis, the user of a DSS can assess the effects of potential decisions, evaluate alternative courses of action, measure trade-offs among different situations, and allocate resources to meet objectives. For example, in the simple model in Figure 1 the user might question whether increases in price, decreases in cost, or increases in units sold will lead to larger increases in profits (what if). Or the user might want to determine the unit price that will render a specific profit (goal seeking). It is analyses of this sort that are the forte of DSSs.

While conventional DSSs provide a range of facilities for describing what has happened and what could happen, they lack facilities for automating a number of other tasks in the decision-making process. For instance, the results in Table 1 indicate that profits are below budget. This raises a number of questions:

- Why are profits below plan?
- Is this trend likely to continue?
- Are there other problems associated with the drop in profits?
- What can be done about the problems?

While DSSs provide the tools to explore these questions, they offer little automated support for explaining why events have occurred, projecting the implications of those events, and prescribing remedies where needed. Instead, the exploration is left to the skills and perseverance of the user.

Automated diagnosis and prescription are the purview of expert systems (ESs). Increasingly, ESs are being applied to the analysis of business and financial problems that have traditionally fallen under the wing of DSSs. As Shwartz (1988) puts it:

> The market for expert systems is one that, for the past decade, has been the province of *decision support systems*. The functional role of expert systems and traditional decision support systems is the same—to aid in decision-making.

A sample listing of some of the business and financial tasks to which ESs have been applied is shown in Table 2. While ESs provide the tools for automating diagnostic tasks, they suffer a number of problems that handicap their application in the realm of decision support.

Among the most important are:

- Much of the historical information on which decisions are based reside in data bases and model bases and not in knowledge bases.
- Expert system shells require more skill to use than a DSS. The typical user of a DSS often finds it easier to represent business activities with a set of equations or a spreadsheet than with the representation schemes provided by most ES shells (rules, frames, procedural logic, etc.).
- Expert system tools are designed to handle symbolic reasoning and lack some of the arithmetic capabilities required to deal with business and financial data. Particularly important are financial functions (e.g., internal rate of return and

Columns Actual, Budget, Variance
Units sold = 216, 232
Price per unit = 3.05, 2.97
Sales = Units sold * Price per unit
Costs per unit = 1.10, 1.06
Costs = Units sold * Costs per unit
Profit = Sales − Costs
Column Variance = Column Actual − Column Budget

Figure 1　Sample model of profit variance.

TABLE 1. Model Solution

	Actual	Budget	Variance
Units sold	216	232	−16
Price per unit	3.05	2.97	.08
Sales	658.8	689.0	−30.24
Costs per unit	1.10	1.06	.04
Costs	237.6	245.9	−8.320
Profit	421.2	443.1	−21.92

net present value) and functions for dealing with time series data (e.g., compound growth rates, time lag operators, and regression functions).

• In an ES the focus is on getting the "reasoning" right, while in a DSS the focus is on exploring the effects of changes in logic and data. This is why few ES shells provide the "simulation tools" found in a DSS. The feeling is that the average user does not understand the underlying logic well enough to alter the system.

In addressing these limitations, a number of researchers and practitioners (Turban and Watkins, 1986; Federowicz and Manheim, 1986; Schank and Reisbeck, 1981; Jarke and Vassiliou, 1984; Al-Zobaidie and Grimson, 1987; Kershberg, 1984; Schur, 1988) have suggested that the way to automate various decision-making tasks is to couple ES technology with conventional DSS and/or data base management system (DBMS) technology. Several names have been suggested for the combined technologies (Turban, 1988). The term *intelligent decision support system* (IDSS) will be used in this chapter.

While the implementation of an IDSS can proceed in a variety of ways, one of two approaches have been used in most commercial systems. Both approaches are depicted in Figure 2. In the first of these a (one-way) communication link is

TABLE 2. Expert System Applications in Finance

Applications
Financial statement analysis
Portfolio management
Insurance risk assessment
Interest rate swapping
Acquisitions and mergers
Stocks and bonds trading
Tax planning
Investment
Auditing
Banking services advice

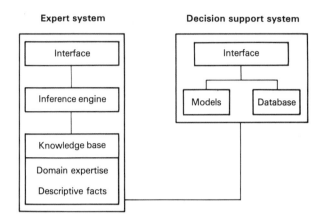

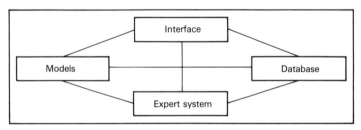

Figure 2   Coupling expert systems and decision support systems.

created between the systems. Here, the DSS or DBMS is treated as a source of data or facts describing the problem which the ES is being used to solve. Intellicorp's KEE Connection product, which enables users of the KEE shell to capture data from SQL data bases, is a good example of this approach. In the second approach, the facilities provided by an ES shell are incorporated into the DSS or DBMS in such a way that it becomes a subsystem of the larger product. Guru is an example of an integrated system that combines spreadsheet, data base, and ES shell components into a single product. Even though the systems are combined in this approach, the DSS and DBMS components are still viewed primarily as sources of data for the ES component. The problem with both of these approaches, however, is that they fail to really address all of the limitations noted in the preceding. In particular, the difficulties with the representational schemes, the focus on expertise, and the lack of facilities for exploring problems rather than producing specific solutions are still present.

As an alternative to these approaches, what if selected ES technologies and techniques were "embedded" directly in the various subsystems of the DSS. This is much like the approach used by Stonebraker (1986) in the experimental Postgres system, which couples ES capabilities with the Ingres DBMS. As Stonebraker contends, a DBMS possesses the necessary efficiency and features to handle large-scale data problems. The language used in a DBMS to create and manage data (e.g., SQL) can be easily understood by a large class of users. What a DBMS lacks is the ability to carry out deductive reasoning. From Stonebraker's perspective, it is easier to add deductive reasoning to a DBMS than it is to add data management facilities to an ES. The reasons for embedding ES and artificial intelligence (AI) capabilities in a DSS are similarly grounded. Like data bases, models are well understood by a large number of DSS users. Decision support systems already provide access to corporate data and possess the arithmetic functions necessary to represent a wide range of business and financial activities. What a DSS lacks, however, is the ability to (1) handle qualitative data and symbolic reasoning and (2) explain its results and reasoning. This latter characteristic is often cited as a crucial element distinguishing an "intelligent" system from other kinds of systems. In Schank's words (1981):

> An understanding system should be able to explain its own actions. . . . The only way to know if a machine is *intelligent* is to make it do what we expect a human to do in a similar situation and to explain how it did it. Furthermore, it must have some connection with how the task in question has actually been performed.

This chapter describes how a DSS can be wed with ES capabilities to handle qualitative reasoning and to explain its results. The discussion focuses on (1) some simple changes to the modeling language in Execucom's Interactive Financial Planning System (IFPS) that enable a model to represent a knowledge base and (2) a facility in IFPS for automatically generating English language explanations of the qualitative and quantitative results produced by a model. IFPS is a DSS used extensively in a number of corporations. It is taken to be representative of the larger class of DSSs. The chapter also discusses how ES technology can be used to "front-end" the operation of a DSS. In this way "intelligence" and "knowledge" can be used to automate and/or guide the simulation procedures used to explore the potential consequences of alternative courses of action.

EXPERT SYSTEMS AND PROBLEM SOLVING

To understand how a DSS model can be used to represent knowledge, a brief review of the problem-solving approach used in many ESs is necessary. The review is couched in the context of a simple problem that has been adapted from an example in Sterling and Shapiro's (1986) book on Prolog programming. The problem is

rule = rule1:
  set fin_scale to net_worth_to_assets*5
    +last_years_sales_growth
    + 5*gross_profits_on_sales
    + short_term_debt_to_sales*2;

rule = rule2:
  if
    currency_deposits >= requested_credit
  then
    set collateral to excellent;

rule = rule3:
  if
    currency_deposits >= .7* requested_credit;
    (currency_deposits + stocks) >= requested_credit;
  then
    set collateral to excellent;

rule = rule4:
  if
    (currency_deposits + stocks) >
      .6*requested_credit;
    (currency_deposits + stocks) <
      .7*requested_credit;
    (currency_deposits + stocks + mortgages) >=
      requested_credit;
  then
    set collateral to good;

rule = rule5:
  if
    (currency_deposits + stocks + mortgages) <
      requested_credit;
  then
    set collateral to moderate;

rule = rule6:
  if
    fin_scale <= −500;
  then
    set financial_rating to bad;

rule = rule7:
  if
    fin_scale > −500;
    fin_scale <= 150;
  then
    set financial_rating to medium;

rule = rule8:
  if
    fin_scale > 150;
    fin_scale <= 1000;
  then
    set financial_rating to good;

rule = rule9:
  if
    fin_scale > 1000;
  then
    set financial_rating to excellent;

rule = rule10:
  if
    collateral is excellent;
    ((financial_rating is excellent) or
    (financial_rating is good));
    ((expected_yield is reasonable) or
    (expected_yield is excellent));
  then
    set evaluation to give_credit;

rule = rule11:
  if
    collateral is good;
    financial_rating is good;
    ((expected_yield is reasonable) or
    (expected_yield is excellent));
  then
    set evaluation to consult_superiors;

rule = rule12:
  if
    collateral is moderate;

  if
    collateral is moderate;
    ((financial_rating is medium) or
    (financial_rating is bad));
  then
    set evaluation to deny_credit;

Figure 3 Rule-based system for loan evaluation.

paraphrased as follows: A loan officer is charged with the task of evaluating credit requests from small business ventures. The evaluations are to be classified into one of three categories: "Give Credit," "Consult a Superior" for more advice, and "Deny Credit." The evaluation is to be based on three factors: an assessment of the business' "collateral" in comparison to the amount of credit requested; a "financial rating" based on a weighted sum of the business's net worth to assets, last year's sales growth, gross profit on sales and short-term debt to sales; a qualitative rating of the bank's "expected yield" from the loan (where yield is classified by the loan officer as "poor," "reasonable," or "excellent").

A simple *rule-based* ES for automating the evaluation process is shown in Figure 3. Without going into too much detail, we note that rule 1 in the system establishes the definition for the weighted sum (fin_scale) used in determining the financial rating of the business. The remaining rules in the system utilize a standard if–then format for establishing the relationship between various antecedents and conclusions. For instance, rule 12 says that if the "collateral" is "moderate" and the "financial_rating" is either "medium" or "bad," then the "evaluation" is "Deny Credit."

A sample run of this particular system is shown in Figure 4a. As the output indicates, the system is running in a "backward-chaining" mode, which means that the user first establishes a "goal" or "hypothesis." Based on this goal or hypothesis, the system works down through the rule set to determine whether the goal or hypothesis is supported or invalidated by the underlying logic and data. For instance, in this example the loan officer is trying to determine the loan "evaluation." Based on this goal, the system first finds those rules whose conclusions contain the goal of interest and examines them one at a time in the order in which they appear in the system. In other words the system starts with rule 10 and tries to determine whether the "evaluation" is "give credit." This is done by examining in turn the validity of each of the antecedents in the rule. That is, the system tries to first establish whether the business's "collateral" is "excellent," next whether its "financial_rating" is "excellent" or "good," and finally whether the "expected_yield" is "reasonable" or "excellent." To determine whether the "collateral is excellent," it looks at rules 2 and 3; to determine whether the "financial_rating" is "good" or "excellent," it examines rules 8 and 9; and to determine whether the "expected_yield" is "reasonable" or "excellent," it asks the loan officer for his or her input because none of the rules in the system have this goal in their conclusions. If all of the antecedents are supported by the system, then the system will conclude that the "evaluation" is "give credit." However, if any of the antecedents are invalid, then the conclusion is invalid, and the system will move on to the next rule, which can be used to establish a value for the loan "evaluation" (in this case rule 11).

At the end of the process the user can ask the system to explain its conclusions. In this case, the user can ask the system to indicate "how" it decided that the value for "evaluation" was "give credit." The system response is shown in Figure 4b. This type of response is fairly typical of most rule-based ESs. In systems of

Please wait while the knowledge base is loaded.
Enter knowledge bases (one at a time), ⟨return⟩ at end.
What knowledge base? fin.kb
Command: (push return for list of goals)
  evaluation
  collateral
  financial_rating
  expected_yield
  requested_credit
  currency_deposits
  stocks
  mortgages
  net_worth_to_assets
  last_years_sales_growth
  gross_profits_on_sales
  short_term_debt_to_sales
  fin_scale
  quit
Command: (push return for list of goals) evaluation

How much does the client have in cash deposits? 50000
What is the amount of credit needed? 50000
What is the value of stocks that can be pledged? 9000
What is the value of the client mortgages? 12000
What is the ratio of net worth to assets? 40
How much did sales grow last year? 20
What is the ratio of gross profits to sales? 45
What is the ratio of short term debt to sales? 9
What is the expected yield: excellent, reasonable, poor? excellent

The value(s) concluded for evaluation are:
  give_credit, with confidence 1.00

                        (a)

Command: (push return for list of goals) explain evaluation
give_credit, with confidence 1.00
From rule rule10:
  Hypotheses:
    true (1.00):
      (collateral is "excellent" 0)
    true (1.00):
      ((financial_rating is "excellent" 0) or (financial_rating is "good" 0))
    true (1.00):
      ((expected_yield is "reasonable" 0) or (expected_yield is "excellent" 0))
  Conclusions:
    (set evaluation to "give_credit" 1) {confidence 1.00}
                    (b)

Figure 4   (a) Output from loan evaluation system. (b) Explanation of loan evaluation.

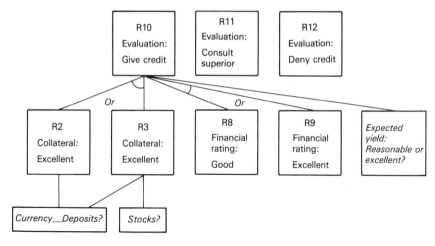

Figure 5   Goal tree (italics means ask user for data).

this sort, an explanation is an enumeration of the values of the antecedents in the rule used to establish the conclusion. If we conceptualize the system in terms of a goal or decision tree (as in Figure 5), then an explanation is seen as nothing more than an enumeration of the nodes one step down from the (goal) node being explained.

SIMILARITY OF EXPERT SYSTEMS AND DECISION SUPPORT SYSTEMS

There are strong structural similarities between a rule-based ES and the modeling subsystem in a DSS. These similarities are summarized in Table 3. As the figure suggests, an ES has a knowledge base consisting of a set of rules and a set of facts describing the problem of interest. Conclusions are drawn by an inference engine that uses the knowledge base of rules to reason about the problem description. At the end, the user can ask the system how it reached its conclusions. Alternatively, in a DSS a model can be thought of as a set of nonprocedural, algebraic rules (meaning that the equations can be entered in any order). The facts that the model

TABLE 3.   Similarities of Expert Systems and Decision Support Systems

	Expert Systems	Decision Support
	Facts	Data
	Rules	Equations
	Inference engine	Compiler/solver
	Explanation	???

uses are data constants specified in the model or read in from a data base. In order to reach a solution, the *compiler/solver* substitutes the data constants and uses a constraint-directed algorithm to solve for the unknowns in the algebraic equations. The compiler/solver works in much the same way that an inference engine with combined forward and backward chaining works. What is missing from the DSS is the ability to explain the model solution. However, because a model can be conceptualized as a (decision) tree, it is easy to envision a process of explanation similar to that found in many rule-based ESs.

USING MODELS TO BUILD EXPERT SYSTEMS

Most modeling systems support some form of if–then–else reasoning. What they lack, however, is the ability to deal with *text* or *string* values in a variable. For instance, to represent a rule like

IF fin_scale > 1000 THEN set financial_rating to excellent

the user would have to establish a dummy value (say, the number 3) to represent the text string ''excellent'' and in turn use this dummy value throughout the model. While this seems like a trivial problem, it can become quite substantial as the number of equations and if–then–else statements grows.

Obviously, the problem can be eliminated by letting variables take text strings as values. Take the following model as an example:

Columns Company1, Company2
Expected Yield = "Excellent", "Poor"
Evaluation = IF Expected Yield = "Excellent"
        THEN "Give Credit" ELSE "Deny Credit"

Here, the columns of the model represent the companies of interest. The expected yields for companies 1 and 2 are ''Excellent'' and ''Poor,'' respectively. If the model were solved, then ''Evaluation'' for company 1 would be ''Given Credit'' while ''Evaluation'' for company 2 would be ''Deny Credit.'' Using text strings, the ES found in Figure 3 can be represented with the model shown in Figure 6. When this particular model is solved, the data shown in Table 4 are produced.

There are a number of important points to make about the preceding model and its solution in comparison with the representation and results produced by the ES:

• The modeling syntax permits mathematical and quantitative relations to be represented in a more straightforward fashion. This is especially true for those situations where powerful functions can be substituted for more cumbersome

```
\ List of Clients
Columns Client1, Client2
\ Input Data
requested credit = 50000,7500
currency deposits = 50000,4500
stocks = 9000,10000
mortgages = 12000,20000
net worth to assets = 40,45
last year's sales growth = 20,25
gross profits on sales = 45,35
short term debt to sales = 9,10
\
fin scale = 5 * net worth to assets + last year's sales growth +'
          5 * gross profits on sales + 2 * short term debt to sales
\
expected yield = "excellent","reasonable"
\
collateral = if (currency_deposits .GE. requested credit) then "excellent" '
    else if (currency_deposits .GT. (.7 * requested credit)) .AND.'
      ((currency_deposits + stocks) .GE. requested credit)'
      then "excellent" '
    else if ((currency_deposits + stocks) .GT. (.6 * requested credit)) .AND.'
      ((currency_deposits + stocks) .LT. (.7 * requested credit)) .AND.'
      (currency_deposits + stocks + mortgages) .GE. requested_credit
      then "good" '
    else "moderate"
\
financial rating = step(fin scale,-1000,"bad",-500,"medium",'
      150,"good",1000,"excellent")
\
evaluation = RULE EVL(collateral,financial rating,expected yield)
```

RULE NAME: EVL

collateral	financial rating	expected yield	Output
excellent	excellent	reasonable	give credit
excellent	excellent	excellent	give credit
excellent	good	excellent	give credit
excellent	good	reasonable	give credit
good	good	reasonable	consult superiors
good	good	excellent	consult superiors
moderate	good	—	consult superiors
moderate	medium	—	deny credit
moderate	bad	—	deny credit

Figure 6 Model for loan evaluation.

TABLE 4. Solution to Loan Evaluation Model

	Client 1	Client 2
Requested credit	50,000	75,000
Currency deposits	50,000	45,000
Stocks	9,000	10,000
Mortgages	12,000	20,000
Net worth to assets	40	45
Last year's sales growth	20	25
Gross profits on sales	45	35
Short-term debt to sales	9	10
Financial scale	463	445
Expected yield	Excellent	Reasonable
Collateral	Excellent	Moderate
Financial rating	Good	Good
Evaluation	Give credit	Consult superiors

if–then–else comparisons. A case in point is the "Step" function used to determine the value for "financial_rating." Here a single function replaces the range checks used in rules 6–10 of the ES.

- In addition to text strings, this particular DSS (IFPS) also supports a new function called a "rule table," which is used as a substitute for a nested set of if–then–else statements that are often found in an ES representation. The rule table used with the model in Figure 6 is shown at the bottom of the figure. A rule table is nothing more than a look-up table that enables a user to specify the value of some *output* variable based on the values of a series of input variables. Here, the output variable is "Evaluation" while the input variables are "Collateral," "Financial Rating," and "Expected Yield." For any given column, the value of the output variable is found by matching the values of the input variables against the rows of the table. For company 1 (column 1), the input values are "excellent," "good," and "excellent," which match the values in row 3 of the table. In essence each row of the table can be considered an if–then statement so that row 3, for instance, is read as:

IF
    collateral = excellent and
    financial rating = good and
    expected yield = excellent
THEN
    evaluation = give credit

The power of a rule table is considerable because like any other function in a model the input values can themselves be functions.

- The model can handle a series of cases (here companies) or time periods without having to iterate with a *loop* structure. When the model is solved, the spreadsheet of results enables the user to easily compare the outcomes for all of the cases (entities or time periods). In the same vein, the solution also enables the user to easily see all of the facts and intermediate conclusions drawn by the system without having to construct a special report. It is important to note that while the constants in the preceding model are hard coded, it is possible to fill these values directly from a data base (e.g., DB2). In this way a *template* model can be constructed for comparing outcomes from a number of cases.

- Because the conclusions and facts are couched in terms of a model, it is easy to explore what happens when changes are made to the various facts or logic of the model. Using what–if questions, for instance, it is possible to examine the impact of reweighting the factors in the "financial scale" or the impact of tightening or loosening the ranges in the step function. By comparison, questions of this sort are often difficult to handle in an ES.

Clearly, with some simple changes to the modeling language, a DSS can be used to deal with a number of problems typically handled by *rule-based* ESs. However, even with the addition of text values and rule tables, most DSSs still cannot do the following:

- Represent uncertain reasoning.
- Explain its results.
- Activate a procedure from an if–then–else rule (all it can do is assign a value).

While it is a rather cumbersome process to add MYCIN-like *certainty factors* to the values produced by a model, it can be done in much the same way that it is done in a rule-based system. Similarly, *fuzzy logic* could be added to a model. Examples of the use of fuzzy logic in DSSs are provided in the literature (Negotia, 1985; Whalen et al., 1987). Because the application of uncertain reasoning to DSSs has been discussed elsewhere, it will not be considered in this chapter. Instead, the discussion will focus on the remaining limitations.

EXPLAINING MODELING RESULTS

A prototypical system for explaining the results produced by a DSS model is described elsewhere (King, 1986). This prototype was developed at Execucom in conjunction with researchers at the Intelligent Systems Laboratory of Carnegie-Mellon University (Kosy and Wise, 1984). The substance of this prototype is now included as part of the mainframe version of IFPS. In this version, users can ask *why* questions about modeling results and obtain a natural-language explanation pinpointing those variables most responsible for the results. Users can query the system either in natural language or with the aid of a natural-language menu. Recently, in a newer workstation prototype,

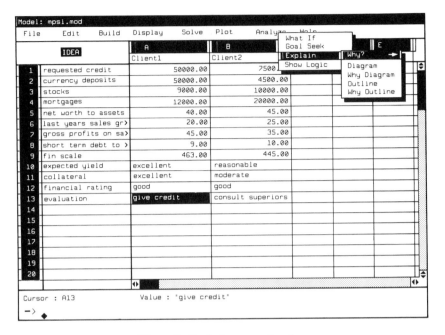

Figure 7 Producing an explanation.

the interface to the explanation facility has been changed and the types of questions and data that the facility can handle have been expanded. Instead of an English language interface, the newer prototype provides the user with the ability to simply point at one or more values in a solution (displayed as a spreadsheet) and select the question to be asked from an *explanation menu* (see Figure 7).

There are three basic types of questions that can be asked about modeling results, including:

- Why does a variable in a model take a particular value in a given column?
- What are the factors responsible for the change in a variable across two columns or the pattern of changes across three consecutive columns?
- Which components of a consolidated structure are responsible for the change in values of a variable in node at a higher level in the structure?

Each type of explanation is illustrated in what follows along with a brief description of the techniques used in generating the explanation.

WHY IS?

Figure 8 exemplifies the type of response that results when the user highlights a particular value (with the mouse) and asks the system to explain the value (i.e., selects "Explain → Why → Is" from the "Analyze" menu). Typically, the system

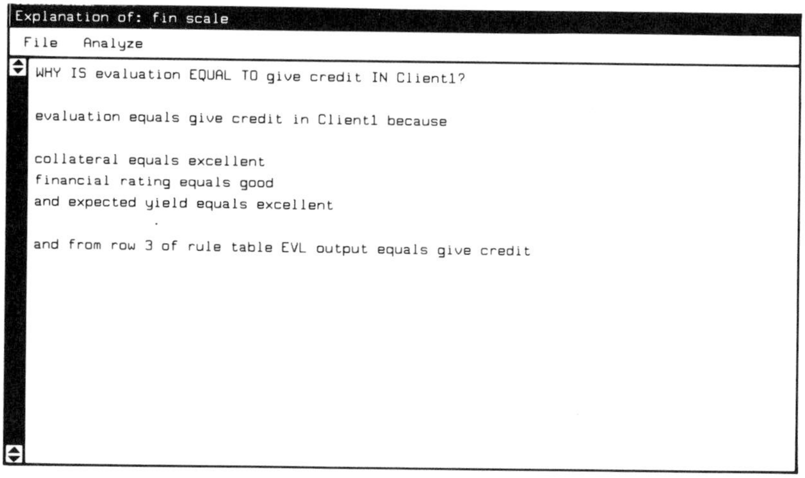

Figure 8   Modeling explanation of loan evaluation.

responds by specifying the equation used in computing the value and displaying the values of the input variables in the equation. For example, if the user were to point, in Figure 8, at "fin scale" and ask "Why is the value of fin scale equal to 463 in Company1?" the system would respond by displaying the equation for "fin scale" along with the values for the component parts of the equation in the specified column (e.g., by showing the value of "net worth to assets"). If the value of interest is based on an if–then test or on a *rule table*, then the system would respond by showing the clause of the expression or the row in the rule table that produced the value along with the values of the input variables. Figure 8, for instance, shows the response to the query "Why is Evaluation in Company1 equal to Give Credit?" Because "Evaluation" depends on a rule table, the system has answered by showing the values for the input variables to the rule table and the row matched by the values.

While the explanation for the value of a variable in a single column may seem rather trivial, it is essentially the same type of explanation provided in most rule-based ESs. That is, the ES simply specifies the rule used to derive the conclusion and the values of the various antecedents in the rule. In this case, the system is simply stating the equation (i.e., rule) involved in deriving the value of the variable of interest and the values of the input variables (i.e., antecedents) in the equation. In fact, this simple process is even more inclusive than the explanation given by an ES because, in most instances, an ES cannot explain numerical calculations.

CHANGES ACROSS COLUMNS

In addition to being able to explain the value of variable in a column, the prototype can also explain changes across two columns or three consecutive columns. The types of why questions that can be answered in this case include:

- Why did the value change from one column to the next?
- Why did the value go up or down across two columns?
- Why did the value stay the same across two columns?
- Why did the value peak, dip, go up or down so much, or go up or down so little across three columns?

Again, the question is asked by pointing at a value of interest and then selecting the question from the "Explain" menu. Here, the assumption is that comparisons are being made with the preceding column, with the two preceding columns, or with the columns on either side in the case of "peaks" and "dips." For a two-column comparison, the system will respond by indicating those variables in the defining equation that are responsible for the change in the value of the variable of interest. Without going into too much detail (because of the proprietary nature of the algorithms used), in the case of numeric expressions, the system is trying to find a subset of variables that can account for approximately 80% of the change. For instance, Figure 9 shows the explanation for the difference in "fin scales" for the two companies. Here, the primary reason for the difference is found in the values for "gross profits on sales." If the defining equation involves an if–then–else statement, then the system responds by indicating the difference in values for the input variables across the two columns and notes the clauses of the if–then–else responsible for the respective results. For example, an explanation of the differ-

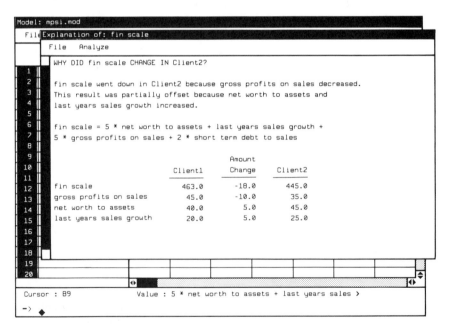

Figure 9   Explaining differences across columns.

ence in "collateral" between the two companies would specify their respective values for "requested credit," "currency deposits," and "mortgages" and would indicate that the values for company 1 satisfy the first clause of the if–then–else statement, while the values for company 2 satisfy the else clause. The strategy used in explaining changes across three columns is similar to the strategy used with two columns; although in this case the system begins by looking for input variables whose patterns of change are the same as the pattern of change in the dependent variable of interest (e.g., if we ask why a variable peaked, then the system will start by looking at the independent variables in the defining equation that also peaked).

Again, it is important to note that the explanations provided for two- and three-column comparisons follow the same logic as the explanations in an ES. That is, the focus is on a parent node in a goal or decision tree, and the explanation is produced by looking at the child nodes of that parent. In the case of a numeric expression, the parent node is the variable of interest, while the child nodes are the input variables. The difference, however, is that an explanation of a numeric result also provides some indication of the order of significance of the "causes." Of course, as later discussion will indicate, knowing the historical causes of a pattern does not necessarily mean that these are the most important factors in remedying a current or projected problem.

CONSOLIDATED RESULTS

Consolidated reports are the focal point for many of the decisions made by senior management and executives (Rockhart and DeLong, 1988). Consolidated reports tend to involve either

- exception reports showing the difference between actual and budgeted results for a number of variables at the corporate level, or
- cross-tabulations of a single variable across two or more factors where the factors can involve not only comparisons within a company but also between the company and its competitors or between the company and its industry.

Unlike the explanation of modeling results, the explanation of consolidated results is couched in terms of the contributions of the individual nodes making up the consolidated structure. Take, for example, a fast-food corporation consisting of two reporting divisions, "East" and "West." If consolidated results indicate that corporate profits are below plan, then an explanation of the variance from plan answers the question "Are corporate profits below plan because of low profits in the East or in the West?" In contrast, a modeling explanation would answer the question "Are profits below plan because of falling sales or rising expenses?" (i.e., an explanation of modeling results is stated in terms of the input variables in the equation). Of course, the two types of explanations can be used hand-in-hand.

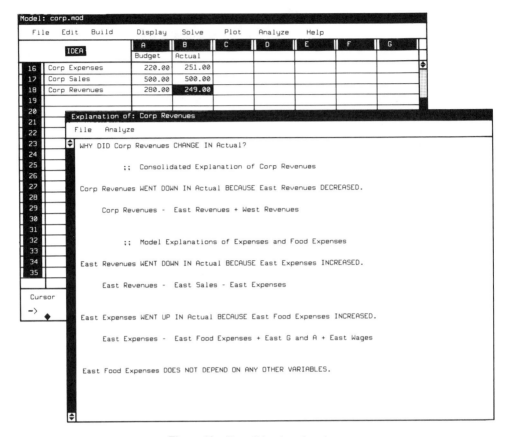

Figure 10 Consolidated explanation.

That is, once a consolidated explanation has pinpointed the important nodes in a structure, a modeling explanation can be used to understand the specific results in those nodes. Figure 10, for example, depicts this process. Here, the top of the explanation indicates that corporate profits are down because profits in the east are below plan (consolidated explanation). Further explanation reveals that profits in the east are below plan because expenses in the east are above plan (modeling explanation). Finally, we see that expenses in the east are above plan primarily because food expenses are above plan (again, a modeling explanation).

DATA BASE RESULTS

A recent article by Schur (1988) describes some of the important elements of an intelligent data base. One of these elements is the ability to explain aggregate summations and ratios generated from data in the data base. It is these aggregate summations and ratios that can serve as *key* indicators describing the success or failure of the company. For example, the query

> WHERE DIV IN('West', 'Southwest', 'Midwest')
> SELECT Div, SUM (Revenue), SUM(PlanRev)
> FROM Accounts

provides aggregate information about the ratio of actual revenues (Revenue) to planned revenues (PlanRev) for a series of divisions in a company. In Schur's terms, an intelligent data base would provide answers to questions like "Why were actual revenues above or below plan?"

The figures generated by the preceding query are similar to the consolidated figures produced by a model. The difference, however, is that there is no set of equations or specified structure describing the relations among the fields and values in a data base. Instead, the underlying model or structure is implicit. It is this implicit model or structure that can be used to explain data base results in much the same way that an explicit model or structure is used to explain consolidated results from a DSS.

As an illustration, data base results are presented in Figure 11. This figure

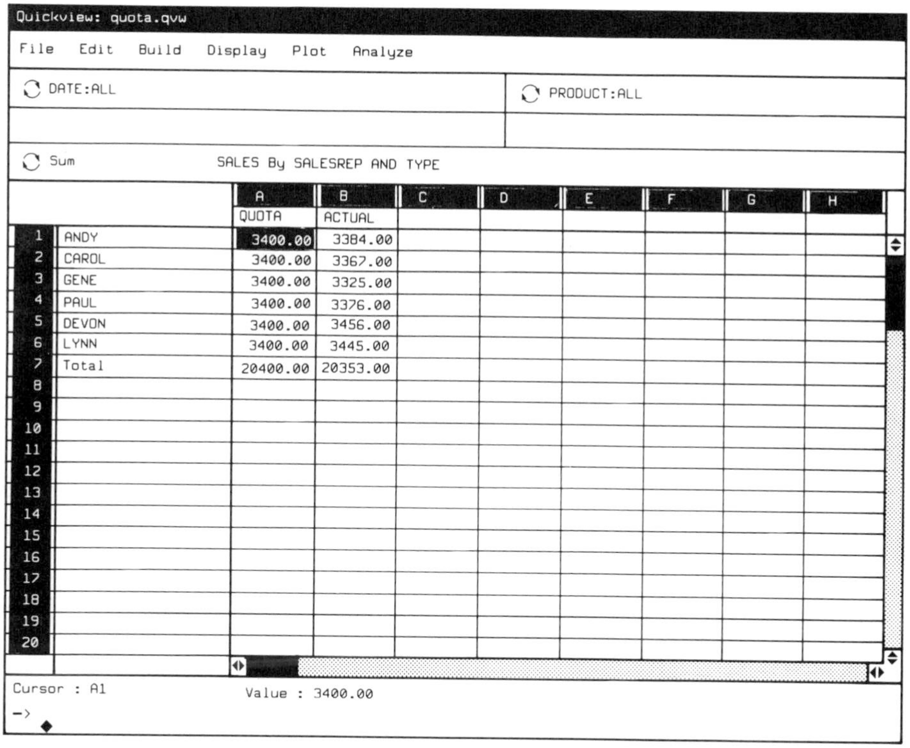

Figure 11 Cross-tabulation of data base results.

displays a cross-tabulation of actual and quota sales by sales person (SALESREP). The sales figures have been summed across all time periods (DATE) and all products (PRODUCT). The structure underlying these results can be conceptualized in a variety of ways. Two that come readily to mind are depicted in Figure 12. In both structures, the total represents total sales for the company as a whole. The nodes immediately underlying this total are the sales people. Thus, an explanation of "Why actual sales for the company are below quota?" is couched in terms of those sales people who are behind quota. When we look at the figures for an individual sales person, we see that the explanation of results depends on whether the underlying structure is considered to be DATEs or PRODUCTs. If it is considered to be DATEs, then the explanation will indicate which date (QTR1 or QTR2) contributed most to the variance between actual sales and quota. If it is considered to be PRODUCTs, then the explanation will specify which products (CALC, FURN, PAPER) contributed most to the variance.

In constructing an explanation of data base results, the prototype assumes that the overall row and column totals are explained by the figures displayed in the body of the table. That is, if the user asks why a particular total takes on a specific value, then the value is explained by simply displaying the row or column values making up the total. If the user asks why there is a difference in total values between

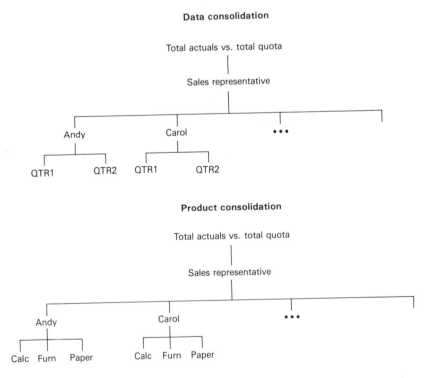

Figure 12 Hierarchical structure of data base results.

two rows or columns (e.g., why the total for actual is less than the total for quota), then only the most important rows or columns accounting for the difference are reported in the explanation. Again, it is the same strategy used in explaining model or consolidation results. If the user is interested in the values for a given row or column (e.g., why Andy's actual sales are less than her quota), then the explanation is given in terms of the *page* factors appearing in the table (here, they are DATE and PRODUCT). Instead of focusing on a particular page, the prototype produces a brief explanation for each of the pages. In this instance, the explanations appear in the form of *bullet* summaries. For example, the explanation of the variance between Andy's actual and quota sales would appear as

> Why did Andy's actuals go down from quota?
> Andy's actuals went down from quota because
> • actuals went down in QTR2
> • actuals went down in CALC

EXPLANATIONS AND REMEDIES

Care must be taken in interpreting the results of an explanation. Just because a factor was important in the past does not mean that it will be important in the future. For one thing the so-called cause of a historical pattern may be a variable over which we have little control (e.g., a rise in the tax rate that caused a drop in profits from one year to the next). For another thing, just because a variable was deemed unimportant in an explanation does not mean that it cannot have an impact in the future. If a company has experienced a drop in profits while maintaining constant prices, then clearly, prices could not have caused the change. Yet this does not mean that a change in prices will not have an effect over the next quarter. Indeed, other historical figures or "simulated" figures may indicate that lowering prices will stimulate demand or that increasing prices will cover the shortfall. Thus, there is no clear way to tell what the impact of one variable on another variable will be simply by looking at an explanation. At best, an explanation should be treated as just one piece of information to be considered before further analyses are performed.

USING AN ES TO FRONT-END A DSS

Taken together, the addition of text strings, rule tables, and explanations to the modeling subsystem of a DSS enables users to attack many of the substantive problems currently being addressed by rule-based ESs. In comparison to an ES, however, an IDSS with these added features provides:

• A simple representation scheme that requires little additional learning on the part of the user.

- Immediate access to existing models and data.
- An extensive array of built-in financial and arithmetic functions.
- Facilities for exploring the ramifications of changes in logic and facts.

In addition, a myriad of features (e.g., reporting) are likely to be found in a DSS that are missing from an ES.

On the other hand, the combination of the added features still omits crucial elements required to automate various decision-making and problem-solving tasks. It is up to the user to determine the contents of the models, the data to be explored, the analyses to be performed, and the interpretations to be made of the data and analyses. It is here that an ES can provide additional leverage. Instead of using the ES to simply analyze data from the DSS, the ES could serve as an intelligent front end to the DSS. In this case, the knowledge base of the ES would not contain domain-specific knowledge about a particular application (e.g., mergers and acquisitions and cash flow analysis) but, instead, would contain knowledge about how to use the DSS.

Various prototypes exist that already utilize an ES as a front end to a more conventional system. One of the best known of these is the Regression EXpert (REX) system (Gale, 1986). Regression EXpert advises a user in the analysis of regression problems. In the words of its developers:

> Rex guides the analysis by testing assumptions of regression, suggesting problem transformations when assumptions are violated, and justifying its suggestions when requested. It interprets intermediate and final results, and instructs the user in statistical concepts.

In essence, REX is an intelligent help system.

A similar approach can be used with DSSs except that the task is broader in scope and a little more difficult. It is broader because it involves an entire system, not just a procedure within a system. It is a little more difficult because the rules for determining which procedures to use and how to interpret the results are not as standardized in the DSS world as they are in the world of statistics.

One way to approach the task of front-ending a DSS with an ES is to eliminate the command language provided with the DSS and in its place put an ES shell. Most DSSs, DBMSs, spreadsheets, and even simple file systems provide users with a macro or command language that can be employed to build applications and automate various tasks. Instead of a command or macro language, however, an ES shell could be used to create a knowledge-based application for automating these tasks. The benefits of substituting an ES shell in place of these languages are the same benefits obtained when one uses an ES shell instead of a conventional programming tool to create any knowledge-based application. Briefly, in comparison to existing macro or command languages, an ES shell permits incremental additions to the knowledge base, provides much stronger pattern-matching capabilities, enables event- or data-driven processing as opposed to user-driven processing, and can explain its actions.

To investigate the utility of front-ending a DSS with an ES, a prototype, coupling IFPS with an ES shell (both CLIPS and a product called the Advisor have been used), was developed. Instead of replacing the command language, however, the two systems were coupled in such a way that rules generated from the shell were used to do the following automatically:

1. Generate a command file (i.e., program written IFPS command language).
2. Activate the DSS in such a way that it executes the command file.
3. Capture the output produced by the DSS after the command file has been run.
4. Determine whether it should generate and run additional command files based on the output.

A simple marketing problem can be used to illustrate the way in which the prototype works. In this problem, the marketing staff is faced with the task of deciding which, if any, products to eliminate from a product line. The decision to eliminate a product is to be based on the profitability of each of the products and on the potential impact of this decision on the projected profitability of the entire product line.

If the problem were solved solely with a DSS, the user might construct a model for calculating the profitability of a single product as well as the projected profitability of the entire product line after the product had been eliminated. To simplify the analysis, the user might then construct a command file that would solve the model for each of the products under consideration. Once this had been done, the user could then examine each of the solutions to determine which products to eliminate. If an ES were added to the process, the entire set of results for all products would likely be stored to a data file that could then be accessed by the ES. In this way, the ES could be used to make recommendations about which products to eliminate.

As an alternative approach, the user might construct two models; one for determining the profitability of the product and one for determining the effects of eliminating the product on the profitability of the entire product line. Next the user could write a set of rules in the ES shell that would run the first of these models for a given product, determine the profitability of the product from the model solution, run the second model only if the product turned out to be unprofitable, and finally, examine the results from the second model in order to recommend whether to eliminate the product or not. In the prototype the actual interaction between the ES shell and the DSS is a little more hands off. For each of the products being considered, the shell first writes a set of commands to a command file and then wakes up the DSS (with a system call) in such a way that the file is executed. Next, the DSS writes its results to a designated data file that is then read by the shell. Using the results in the data file, the shell determines whether or not to write another set of commands to run the second model. The second model is run in essentially the same fashion, and its results are returned in the same data file. In this instance, the ES is not only being used to make domain-specific judgments about the eventual product mix but is also being used to make judgments about which analyses to perform.

While the prototype is fairly rudimentary, it still possesses most of the advantages that accrue to an ES shell. That is, the knowledge base can be built incrementally. The system can be used to automate knowledge-intensive tasks (e.g., the task of determining which products to eliminate without having to examine the detailed results by hand). And the system can explain its actions, not only its judgments about domain-specific problems (e.g., Why did you recommend elimination of a particular product?) but also its decision to perform or, in the case of the Advisor version of the prototype, not perform specific tasks (e.g., Why didn't you run a particular model?).

CONCLUDING REMARKS

In the business and financial worlds, decision making requires the integration of data, models, and business expertise. Historically, these sources of information and knowledge have been the purview of three separate information-processing systems: DBMSs, DSSs, and most recently, ESs. The advent of ESs has brought renewed awareness of the need to handle these sources in uniform fashion. Much of the recent work aimed at integrating these systems has focused on the integration of ESs and DBMSs. Efforts aimed at merging ES technologies with DSS technologies are still in their infancy.

In the current generation of prototypes and commercially available IDSSs, integration involves little more than a *loose coupling* of the systems, where coupled system communication links are provided among the stand-alone components (Jarke and Vassiliou, 1984). The links typically provide the means for an ES to access and translate data provided by the DSS. In other words, in most IDSSs, the DSS component simply serves as an additional source of data that is used by the ES component during the inferencing process. As long as the task at hand is primarily "symbolic" in nature, a loosely coupled system may prove to be adequate. However, when the task involves a substantial amount of numerical computation and requires exploration of various alternatives, the strategy of relegating the DSS to a passive role is grossly inadequate. Clearly, many decision-making tasks in the business and financial worlds are of this sort. At the core of these tasks is a cycle that requires an analyst or a group of analysts to define the problems and opportunities of interest, determine the data to be investigated, determine the analyses to be performed, and make the appropriate interpretations and recommendations. Obviously, this requires a *tighter coupling* between the expert and decision support components, one that takes advantage of the numerical and exploratory capabilities of the DSS.

As we have seen in this chapter, with appropriate changes, the modeling language in a DSS can be used to represent the kinds of knowledge found in most rule-based ESs. The primary advantages of using a model instead of a rule-based system are twofold. First, the language used in building a model is easy to learn and (with appropriate changes) combines numerical capabilities with symbolic reasoning. Second, by couching knowledge in the form of a model, the user can take advantage of the simulation tools provided by the DSS. For instance, the what-if capabilities of a DSS enable any user, not just a knowledge engineer, to easily explore the impact of altering not only the facts but also the logic in the application. Of course, there are limitations to this method. Certain types of problems and entities cannot be represented by a model. There is no way, for instance, to represent a framelike structure with an equation. Similarly, there is no elegant way to attach a procedure to an equation. The only thing an equation can do is assign a value to a variable. In an ES, however, rules, frames, and logic are used not only to assign values but also to activate procedures.

Overcoming the preceding limitations requires not only an enhanced modeling language but also a system that tightly couples the strengths of both the DSS and the ES. One way to couple the systems is to replace the *command subsystem* in the DSS with an ES shell. Most DSSs provide facilities for creating applications that can be used to automate various processes. These facilities are known as the command subsystem. Like conventional programming tools, the command subsystem provides little means for representing the knowledge of the application builder, which is really of two kinds. First, a builder has expertise concerning an application domain. A portion of this knowledge can be represented directly in models. Second, a builder has knowledge of how to use the system. By replacing the command subsystem with an ES shell, we enable the application builder to use his or her knowledge to control the operation of the system. In essence the ES becomes an intelligent front end to the DSS.

Recently, Lee, Lark, and Hayes-Roth (1988) noted:

> Expert systems and, in general, knowledge systems, have emerged from fifteen years of research and development activities in applied artificial intelligence. . . . As experience has accumulated, it has become clear that most applications of this technology will not be as isolated, "expert" systems. Rather, the application of expertise (or more generally, knowledge) will occur in the larger context of "integrated" systems.

It is clear that the future of DSSs will follow this same route. Most applications built with DSSs will not occur in isolation but will be implemented with an integrated ES–DSS. The investigation of possible architectures for an IDSS has only just begun.

REFERENCES

AL-ZOBAIDIE, A. AND GRIMSON, J. (1987), "Expert Systems and Database Systems: How Can They Serve Each Other?" *Expert Systems*, February.

ERMAN, L., LARK, J. AND HAYES-ROTH, F. (1988), "ABE: An Environment for Engineering Intelligent Systems," IEEE Software, December, pp. 1758–1770.

FEDEROWICZ, J. AND MANHEIM, M. (1986), "A Framework for Assessing Decision Support and Expert Systems," *Transactions of Sixth International Conference on Decision Support Systems*, Washington, DC, pp. 116–127.

GALE, W. (1986), "REX Review," in *Artificial Intelligence and Statistics*, W. Gale (ed.), Addison-Wesley, Reading, MA.

JARKE, M. AND VASSILIOU, Y. (1984), "Coupling Expert Systems with Database Management Systems," in *Artificial Intelligence Applications for Business*, W. Reitman (ed.), Ablex, Norwood, NJ.

KERSHBERG, L. (1984), *Expert Database Systems, Proceedings of First International Conference on Expert Database Systems*, American Association for Artificial Intelligence, Kiawah Island, South Carolina, October.

KING, D. (1986), "ERGO: An Explanation Facility for Decision Support Systems," *Proceedings of the 6th International Workshop on Expert Systems and Their Applications*, Vol. II, EC2, Avignon, France, pp. 991–1011.

KOSY, D. AND WISE, B. (1984), "Self-Explanatory Financial Planning Models," *Proceedings of the American Association for Artificial Intelligence Conference*, American Association for Artificial Intelligence, Menlo Park, CA.

NEGOTIA, C. (1985), *Expert Systems and Fuzzy Systems*, Benjamin/Cummings, Menlo Park, CA.

ROCKHART, J. AND DELONG, D. (1988), *Executive Support Systems*, Dow Jones-Irwin, Homewood, IL.

SCHANK, R. AND REISBECK, C. (1981), *Inside Computer Understanding*, Lawrence Erlbaum, Hillsdale, NJ.

SCHUR, S. (1988), "Intelligent Databases," *Database Programming and Design*, June, pp. 46–55.

SHWARTZ, S. (1988), *Applied Natural Language Processing*, Petrocelli, Princeton, NJ.

STERLING, L. AND SHAPIRO, E. (1986), *The Art of Prolog*, MIT Press, Cambridge, MA.

STONEBRAKER, M. (1986), "Triggers and Inference in Database Systems," in *On Knowledge Base Management Systems*, M. Brodie and J. Mylopoulos (eds.), Springer-Verlag, New York.

TURBAN, E. (1988), *Decision Support and Expert Systems*, Macmillan, New York.

TURBAN, E. AND WATKINS, P. (1986), "Integrating Expert Systems and Decision Support Systems," *MIS Quarterly*, June.

WHALEN, T., SCHOTT, B., HALL, N., AND GANOE, F. (1987), "Fuzzy Knowledge in Rule-based Systems," in *Expert Systems for Business*, B. Silverman (ed.), Addison-Wesley, Reading, MA.

4

Expert Systems and Decision Support Systems in Auditing

Daniel E. O'Leary
Paul Watkins

INTRODUCTION

This chapter examines the current state of expert systems and decision support systems in auditing. In so doing we examine completed or prototype expert systems and decision support systems in four broad functional categories:

- Electronic data processing (EDP) auditing.
- External auditing.
- Governmental auditing.
- Internal auditing.

This chapter focuses on those auditing-based systems that have appeared in the literature or have been presented at a conference or of which the authors are currently aware. There may be some systems that have been developed and are in use but are not reported here. Generally, that would be because there has been little information on those systems in the literature.

This chapter does not provide a general overview of expert and decision support systems. Such treatments are available from a number of sources, including Hayes-Roth et al. [1].

In addition, this chapter does not discuss or try to differentiate between expert systems and decision support systems. Both types of systems support auditing decision making, and thus, both are included. The interested reader is referred to Turbin and Watkins [2] for such a discussion.

Previous Surveys

There have been a number of other surveys of accounting and audit-based expert systems and decision support systems in academic outlets, for example, Amer et al. [3], Bailey et al. [4], Bedard et al. [5], Borthick [6], Chandler [7], Dillard and Mutchler [8], Messier and Hansen [9], and O'Leary [10]. There have also been a number of surveys of audit-based expert systems in professional outlets, for example, Bailey et al. [11], Borthick and West [12], Elliot and Kielich [13], Flesher and Martin [14], and McKee [15]. However, these surveys generally have ignored intrusion detection-type systems, internal auditing, and governmental auditing. In addition, there has since been a structural change in the development of expert systems. The first reports of expert systems in auditing were almost entirely from academics. Now, it seems that many of the systems that are generating the most interest are systems developed for commercial purposes.

These commercial systems differ from systems developed by academics in a number of ways. First, they are not just developed to see if such a system can be developed. They generally are designed with the idea that they ultimately will be used. Second, commercial ventures usually entail the use of greater resources than can be mustered in most academic-based expert system developments. Third, in commercial efforts, the application is dominant. Methodology issues, design issues, and other research issues are the primary focus of many academic systems.

Organization of This Chapter

This chapter proceeds as follows. First, the auditing environment in which expert systems must respond is discussed. The following sections review audit-based expert systems in EDP auditing, external auditing in academic systems, external auditing in commercial systems, governmental auditing, and internal auditing. A brief summary of selected aspects of the validation and verification literature follows that encompasses the auditing of such systems. Then some of the limitations of auditing-based expert systems are analyzed followed by a discussion of sources for publication and a presentation of information relating to expert systems. The final section provides some summary remarks.

THE AUDIT ENVIRONMENT

The audit environment is a unique and highly complex decision-making environment. As a result, there are sources of error and inconsistency that are unique to that environment. Personal computers and other changes in technology have had and will continue to have an impact on the audit environment. In addition, the audit decision-making environment is process oriented and not results oriented. Finally, the audit process typically is a team process.

Complexity

The audit environment is highly complex. In a discussion of that complexity, Hansen and Messier [16] note that the audit problem of checking control weaknesses is a "nondeterministic polynomial" (NP) problem. This indicates that audit problems have a large number of solutions and that it is difficult to sort through those solutions in order to choose the best one. Such problems often are solved best by using heuristic approaches to find *good*, but not necessarily *optimal* solutions. In the case of audit problems, this generally means using the rules of thumb of experienced auditors. Since such rules of thumb can be included in expert systems, such systems offer an alternative and feasible solution methodology to auditing situations.

Sources of Error and Inconsistency

Holstrom [17] identifies 32 different sources of error and inconsistency. Holstrom [17, p. 1] states:

> Judgment *errors* occur when there is a departure from a generally accepted criterion. Judgment *inconsistencies* occur whenever there is a difference between judgments, given the same data set and objectives, regardless of whether a generally accepted criterion exists. An *error* in overall judgment occurs when the auditor issues an incorrect audit opinion. An *inconsistency* in overall audit judgments occurs when different auditors render significantly different audit opinions based upon an identical set of financial statements and an identical set of audit evidence. In the latter case, we could determine that an *inconsistency* has occurred, but we could not conclude which overall judgment is in *error* unless we know in fact whether the financial statements were materially mis-stated.

Research (e.g., Hogarth [18]) has shown that computer programs such as expert systems can be used to improve the consistency of human responses and mitigate errors. For example, as noted by Dillard and Mutchler [19, p. 17] "Utilization of the . . . [expert] system will lend consistency, thoroughness and verifiability to the audit opinion decision process."

Personal Computer Environment

One of the primary developments in computing is a shift toward a personal computer (PC) computing environment. Researchers (e.g., O'Leary [20]) noted that the change to the PC environment can have a major impact on auditing. First, the PC allows users to take computing power with them to various locations. As a result, expert systems can now be developed to support the auditor in the field. Second, since so much work is now done on PCs there is increased need to be able to audit in a PC environment. Thus, expert systems can be used to bring auditing knowledge to the auditor for the audit of PC-based systems.

Changing Technology

Holstrom et al. [21] identified "numerous trends that are likely to have a major impact on audit evidence, the audit process and the role of auditing in the next 10 to 15 years." They summarized the changes in information technology in four categories: office automation and transaction automation, data communications, computer hardware, and computer software.

Their initial results indicate an increased use of expert systems in auditing in the future as exemplified by some of the applications discussed later in this chapter. In addition, it is likely that expert systems will be used to mitigate some of the problems resulting from, for example, the move toward a paperless society. For as the *law of requisite variety* (e.g., Ashby [22]) notes, it takes equivocality to remove equivocality. Accordingly, as there are changes in complexity in those four categories, the systems needed to process information from those systems also must be more complex.

Process Oriented, Not Results Oriented

Many problems in auditing do not have feedback mechanisms that provide for the recognition of correct or incorrect responses (Kelly et al. [23]). As a result, instead of being results oriented, auditing is process oriented. The quality of the work is not judged by results, but by the record of the process as summarized in the work papers.

Expert systems can be used to promulgate a particular process and record work done in that process. Thus, they can provide uniform documentation of the process and act to defuse knowledge to the auditors.

Team Approach

Auditing typically either directly or indirectly involves a team approach. An audit team typically involves personnel from at least four levels in an audit firm, including a partner, manager, senior accountant, and staff accountant. Since audits employ a team approach and are embedded within the context of an organization, we can expect members of the audit team to carry with them in their decision making some *organizational* and *team baggage*. Behavior of individuals may be dependent on, for example, meeting the expectations of the partner on the job rather than on strict focus on the issues.

Expert systems and other artificial intelligence (AI) based systems can work to assist the individual auditor to mitigate the effect of some of that organizational baggage. On the other hand, group decision support and expert systems, which focus on assisting groups in their decision-making processes, have been ignored in accounting and auditing applications. This likely is because although the audit process involves a team, the individual activities typically are allocated to individuals rather than groups in a parallel and sequential processing of task information.

EDP AUDITING

Expert systems developed for EDP auditing take two primary formats. One approach is to develop an expert system to assist the auditor in auditing the EDP system. Another approach is to develop EDP-based systems that audit uses of a system in order to determine if there has been intrusion into the system.

Auditing General EDP Systems

There is really only one system that has been developed to assist in auditing general EDP systems. That system, EDP-XPERT, has been described in two primary papers (Hansen and Messier [24, 25] and Messier and Hansen [26]), which, respectively, describe the system and the validation of the system.

EDP-XPERT was one of the first auditing-based expert systems on which development efforts initiated. Early discussion of that system was given in Hansen and Messier [16] and Messier and Hansen [9]. EDP-XPERT was developed using the rule-based, expert system shell AL/X.

A sample rule from EDP-XPERT is as follows (Hansen and Messier [24]):

If   1)   Message Control Software is Complete and Sufficient and

     2)   Recovery Measures are Adequate and

     3)   Adequate Documentation is Generated to Form a Complete Audit Trail,

Then   There is strong suggestive evidence that controls over data loss are adequate.

This system demonstrates that rule-based expert systems can be used to aid the auditing of internal controls in EDP systems. However, as noted in a related inquiry, Biggs et al. [27] found that EDP auditors generally do not use if–then rules of this type. Alternatively, such rules may be constructed from knowledge acquired from those auditors.

Specific EDP-Based Applications

The MIS Training Institute has developed a number of "expert systems" to assist internal auditors. Currently, there are seven applications available, four of which are based on IBM systems. Those four systems focus on CICS (based on IBM's communications system), "System/36," "Expert Auditor System/38" (two IBM minicomputers), and IMS (IBM's data base environment). The remaining three systems are more general. Those systems are concerned with data center reviews, disaster recovery, and auditing microcomputers.

Each of the systems developed reflects at least three of the guidelines of a "good" expert system application (see O'Leary [10]), thus providing empirical support for those theoretical observations. In particular, each system is based on a set of audit concerns about highly specific environments; each of the systems is the concern of a large number of auditors; each system operates in a PC environment; each of the applications is in an area that requires a substantial amount of specific expertise. Each of the systems apparently makes use of a sequence of interrelated questions.

Intrusion Detection Systems

An important aspect of auditing EDP systems is ensuring their integrity. Expert systems have been designed to provide continuing, on-line *intrusion detection* protection of EDP systems. Such systems stay resident in the computer system, monitoring the behavior of system users.

Denning [28] has discussed such a system. That system is based on the hypothesis that exploitation of systems involves abnormal use of the system. Thus, by detecting abnormal use of the system, security violations can be detected. There are a number of examples of such violations, including the following (Denning [28]):

> *Attempted break-in:* Someone attemping to break in to the system likely would generate a large number of illegal passwords.
>
> *Successful break-in:* An illegimate user successfully breaking in to a system may have different location or connect time than the legimate user on whose account they have accessed the system.
>
> *Penetration by a legitimate user:* A legitimate user interested in penetrating the security of a system might execute programs different from or in a different order than would be expected.
>
> *Leakage by a legitimate user:* A legitimate user that attempts to leak unauthorized data might employ a remote printer not normally used at a time of the day that is also unusual.
>
> *Virus:* A virus may cause an increase in the storage used by executable files or an increase in the frequency of execution of files.

Typically, normal behavior is represented using profiles for each user or facility. Then behavior is compared to those profiles to determine if it is normal or abnormal.

A research area with substantial potential impact is making such systems more efficient and effective. This research requires the investigation of the efficiency of different intrusion detection strategies. Generally, this means determination of those variables that best signal intrusion and those means (e.g., statistical) that best determine the levels of those variables that indicate intrusion. Further, it is unclear what the impact of context (a given firm) is on both variable effectiveness and methods of investigation. In addition, it is unclear what is the organizational impact of such systems. For example, if intrusion detection systems are used, do human ''detectors'' continue to function or do users just say ''oh, the system does that.'' Initial inquiry at one firm has indicated that once a system is in place that examines activities for errors, it is assumed that the computer will investigate the possibility of all errors.

ACADEMIC-BASED EXTERNAL–INTERNAL AUDITING SYSTEMS

Projects of concern to internal and external auditors have received the most extensive attention. In this area there have been a number of applications, including:

Adequacy of allowance for bad debts: Chandler et al. [29], Dungan [30], Dungan and Chandler [31, 32], Braun [33].

Audit planning: Kelly [34, 35].

Going concern process: Biggs and Selfridge [36], Selfridge [37], Selfridge and Biggs [38, 39], Dillard and Mutchler [40, 41].

Internal controls: Meservy [42], Gal [43], Meservy et al. [44], Bailey et al. [45], Grudnitski [46].

Materiality: Steinbart [47, 48].

Risk assessment: Mock and Vertinsky [49, 50], Dhar et al. [51], Peters et al. [52].

Adequacy of Allowance for Bad Debts

The first audit-based expert system was developed by Dungan [30] (see also Dungan and Chandler [31, 32]) to analyze the problem of the adequacy of the allowance for bad debts for large commercial clients based on analyzing the accounts individually. The system, entitled AUDITOR, was developed using the rule-based expert system shell AL/X.

AUDITOR gives advice in the form of an estimate of the probability that a given account balance will prove to be uncollectable. That research study [30] had as ''its objective the creation of an expert system model of certain judgment processes of auditors.''

A second prototype expert system is currently being built by Braun [33]. In some respects it is an extension of AUDITOR (Chandler et al. [29]). However, the emphasis of the Braun [33] study is on the hospital industry. In addition, it considers the combination of analytical and judgmental variables.

As noted by Dillard and Mutchler [19], output from systems like the one described here could be used as input to other systems in order to take advantage of development efficiencies.

Audit Planning

Kelly [34, 35] developed a prototype model, ICE (Internal Control Evaluation), to aid in the audit-planning process. ICE featured a knowledge hierarchy of different levels. The first level included knowledge about the industry, economy, management, and audit history. The second level focused on the client environment, the organization, planning manuals, and accounting procedures. The third level focused on internal control functions in the purchasing process.

ICE was developed using LISP. Unlike most expert systems, ICE made use of both frames and rules.

Going Concern Process

The going concern problem is one of the most difficult facing auditors. As noted by the AICPA [53], "in order to render a going concern judgment, the auditor must (1) recognize that a problem exists, (2) understand the cause of the problem, (3) evaluate management's plans to address the problem, and (4) render a judgment on the basis of whether the problems are sufficiently serious and whether management plans are judged to succeed.

There have been at least two ongoing academic efforts to address the going concern problem. Both the work of Biggs and Selfridge and the work of Dillard and Mutchler can be traced in a series of papers describing the systems change over time.

Probably one of the most sophisticated accounting and auditing expert systems is GCX (Going Concern Expert), discussed in a sequence of papers by Biggs and Selfridge [36], Selfridge [37], and Selfridge and Biggs [38, 39]. GCX was programmed in MacScheme, a dialect of LISP, that runs on an Apple Macintosh II. GCX was tested on five years of data from a real-world company about which the auditors who were questioned had substantial knowledge.

The research questions addressed in the development of GCX included (Selfridge and Biggs [38, p. 2]):

What are the categories of expert knowledge and how are they represented?

What are the reasoning strategies of the expert auditors and how are they represented?

How is the knowledge and reasoning strategy organized in GCX?

In Biggs and Selfridge [36], the system included expert knowledge in measures of financial performance, business and the business environment, and management plans. GCX had 100 financial reasoning rules and 80 business and business environment events.

In Selfridge and Biggs [38], it was reported that there were six categories of knowledge, including events, interevent causality, company function (financial model and operations model), events/financial performance causality, measures of financial performance, and going concern problems. In that model there were 140 event frames and 215 entity frames.

The model summarized in that paper employs Schank's [54] MOPs (memory organization packets). For example, in the operations model there is a hierarchy of MOPs that employ successively more detailed descriptions of company operations.

In Selfridge and Biggs [39], that knowledge was extended to general financial knowledge and knowledge of actual events, normal events, company function, company markets, the industry, multiple business lines, changes over time, and other companies.

In each of the successive models the knowledge changes. As a result, the resultant auditor reasoning through that knowledge also must change. That is reflected in each of the papers.

In addition to addressing the issues specified by the authors, the sequence of papers that reflect the development of GCX allow insight into the growth and development of an expert system.

Dillard and Mutchler [19, 40, 41] also have done extensive work in the area of modeling the auditor's going concern opinion decision. Their system was developed on a DEC 2060 using a menu shell, XINFO. The system apparently employs approximately 450 decision frames or nodes in a decision tree. The intelligence in the system is in the decision structure and hierarchy.

The system contains "technical" knowledge about such things as basic accounting procedures, audit procedures, audit standards, and the business, economic, and legal environment in the context of a *task support system*. This knowledge is organized in a hierarchical branching structure with nodes representing primative and intermediate decisions. Technical knowledge was gathered in each of seven categories: operations, financial, market, management, industry, audit, and other.

The system uses a system architecture that interfaces the task support system with three other components: task action system, external interface system, and a guidance system. The task guidance system uses frames to provide suggestions and rules and methods for making decisions specified in the task support system. The task action system supports programs for data access, statistical analysis, and other additional tools that the auditor may wish to use. Finally, the external interface system allows for the generation of documentation and audit trails.

The system does not exactly mimic expert behavior. For example, the system employs numeric rating systems, but it is unlikely that auditors use this method in going concern problems.

Internal Controls

The first auditing-based system to implement AI techniques in the system was TICOM (The Internal Control Model) (Bailey et al. [45]), an analytic tool that aids the auditor in modeling the internal control system and querying the model in order to aid the auditor in evaluating the internal control system. TICOM was implemented in Pascal.

Recently, Bailey et al. [55] developed TICOM-IV also to assist the auditor in the design, analysis, and evaluation of internal controls. The system uses Prolog to represent knowledge about the internal control system.

Materiality

Steinbart [47, 48] developed an audit judgment model, AUDITPLANNER, for the assessment of materiality. AUDITPLANNER uses six different sets of inputs to aid in the materiality decision: prior year's materiality levels, financial characteristics of the client, nonfinancial characteristics of the client, future plans of the client, nature of the audit engagement, and intended uses of the client's financial statements.

The system was built for use in a number of profit and not-for-profit firms. The test clients included manufacturing firms, trucking firms, supermarkets, a school district, and a boy scout council.

AUDITPLANNER was built using the rule-based expert system shell EMYCIN. The system did not include the use of certainty factors.

Risk Assessment

There is a substantial literature on risk assessment (e.g., Mock and Vertinsky [50]). However, there are a number of problems where it is difficult to quantify risk. As a result, Dhar et al. [p. 51] describe "the problem of risk assessment as knowledge-based, where knowledge about the client's history, recent events specific to the firm or industry, and knowledge about the internals of a firm are crucial in shaping the auditor's judgment about risks associated with accounts, and hence the audit plan." This interpretation is further enhanced by the general finding (Mock and Vertinsky [49, p. 1]) that people are "not 'good intuitive statisticians' and therefore the craft of 'risk assessment' is fraught with risks."

There has been at least one paper on the use of risk assessment in auditing decision support systems (Mock and Vertinsky [49]) and at least two papers on the use of expert systems in assessing risk (Dhar et al. [51] and Peters et al. [52]).

EXTERNAL AUDITING: COMMERCIAL-BASED SYSTEMS

The systems discussed in this section are likely to only scratch the surface of possible auditing applications in use. Many systems are likely to be in development or use, but because they are proprietary, there is no knowledge about them.

Arthur Andersen

Arthur Andersen (AA) has developed expert systems for the consulting group's clients. For example, Arthur Andersen ([56, 57] and Mui and McCarthy [58]) discuss two systems designed to interface with the electronic data-gathering analysis and retrieval system. FSA (Financial Statement Analyzer) takes as input an ASCII file of annual-report-like information and develops a set of ratios. ELOISE (English Language Oriented Indexing System for EDGAR) provides a means to examine a text data base in order to find relevant information for an inquiry. (These projects are discussed in more detail in this book and in O'Leary [59].) However, there have been no discussions in the literature relating to internal projects to aid the AA auditing process.

Arthur Young

Arthur Young (AY) has taken a single-product, multiple-component, middle-out strategy in the development of their decision support system, AY/ASQ, a software designed to automate the audit process for manufacturing environments. AY/ASQ was developed in an Apple McIntosh environment. The operation for each of the applications is similar to the other applications. The system consists of several modules including Decision Support, Office, Trial Balance, Time Control, and Data-bridge.

The Decision Support module is the module of most interest for this chapter. That module features the ability to reference the computer file stored documentation for the AY audit process. In addition, the system guides the audit planning process through a "smart questionnaire" approach. This smart questionnaire approach ensures that the auditor performs certain procedures. Then when it is indicated to the computer that those procedures have been followed, the rest of the checklist is updated.

Future enhancements likely will include the development of similar modules for different industries and the development of a module to analyze internal controls.

Peat, Marwick, Main

Peat, Marwick, Main (PMM) apparently has taken a multiple-project approach to the development of expert systems in auditing. Their best known system is Loanprobe, also known as CFILE. The development of that system is chronicled in a sequence of papers, including Kelly, Ribar, and Willingham [23], Ribar [60–62], and Willingham and Ribar [63]. CFILE is a rule-based system developed using INSIGHT 2 (now Level 5). A rule-based approach is used because of the classification nature of the problem. (Similar classification problems have been solved using a rule-based approach.) It is estimated that CFILE has three person-years of development time (Ribar [60]).

CFILE derives its name from credit file analysis and is designed for use in bank audit loan loss evaluation. In particular, it aids the process of estimating the dollar amount of the reserve for the bank's portfolio of loans.

AUDPREX (Kelly [64]) is a proposal to develop an expert system to aid in the design of audit programs in the area of inventory systems. Such a system would be used as an aid to determine the type, timing, nature, and amount of substantive procedures.

In contrast to CFILE, another system designed to aid in the interpretation of Statement on Auditing Standards (SAS) #80 on accounting futures was done by a single researcher within a period of several weeks (Ribar [60]). This included the time required by the researcher to learn the expert system shell, INSIGHT 2. For the SFAS-based system, the professional literature provided much of the guidance.

Price Waterhouse

There are no systems reported at Price Waterhouse (PW). However, PW recently has developed a technology center. At the technology center, PW is exploring the use of multiple technologies in auditing, including the use of decision support systems and expert systems.

GOVERNMENTAL AUDITING

Governments face the problem of auditing and reviewing large volumes of tax returns and filings of various types. The large volume often means that humans are unable to process all the documents in a cost-effective manner. Alternatively, even if it were possible to process all the volume, often budgetary constraints limit the number and quality of persons that could be employed. As a result, the need for systems aimed at processing similar documents submitted to the government is likely to be very high. The successful development of the following systems indicates that such systems may be widespread in the near future.

Each of the following systems has been developed as either a consulting project or as an activity of an internal AI staff.

Reviews of SEC Filings

Currently, human financial analysts use analytic review of corporate filings at the Securities and Exchange Commission (SEC) to check the correctness of the filings. Arthur Andersen [56] (see also Mui and McCarthy [58]) developed FSA as a LISP-based prototype to explore the possibility of using a computer program to compute and analyze ratios. FSA includes the ability to "understand" the text in the filings so that it may gather relevant information required to complete an analytic review of the return. Such a system would limit the need for human financial analysts to perform those activities and free their time for other activities. FSA is also described in a separate chapter of this book.

From a research perspective, this system is one of the first functioning systems to employ the approach summarized in DeJong [65] to read and understand natural language. Briefly, that approach reads a part of the sentence. It then predicts what will follow in the remainder of the sentence. Then it checks its prediction against what it actually finds to confirm and guide its search for meaning in the rest of the text. The system continues in this manner, predicting and substantiating while generating its understanding of the text.

Pennsylvania State Audit for Taxes

Hall et al. [66] address the problem of determining which organizations to audit to achieve the maximum collection of monies due the state of Pennsylvania. Accordingly, the overall audit goal is to improve audit productivity.

Unfortunately, this problem is difficult to solve since there is little understanding about which organizations should be audited. Thus, there is little available expertise to build into the system. As a result, Hall et al. [66] developed a system that would learn and develop the necessary expertise.

The general research goal of the paper is to determine how a computer program can be programmed to learn. In order to accomplish that goal, they chose a genetic learning approach. Genetic algorithms learn by employing different combining rules on responses, such as inversion and mutation. For example, the system may combine the two sets of characteristics abc and cde to form abe in its search for a better set of characteristics.

IRS Auditing of Tax Returns

Little has been released on the Internal Revenue Service (IRS) efforts to date. A summary of many of the IRS projects in process or planned is provided in a separate chapter in this book and in Brown and Streit [67]. However, it faces a problem that is similar to other government activities in that it has a number of documents to process in a short time and is subject to budgetary constraints.

Danish Customs Auditing of Value-added Tax Accounts

Recently, Danish customs authorities employed a consulting firm to develop an expert system to help them audit value-added tax (VAT) accounts (Lethan and Jacobsen [68]). The system was designed to develop more effective VAT auditing and to improve the VAT examiner's productivity. As in other government applications, there is a great deal of work to be done, and the expert system is designed to do some of the work in order to improve the productivity of the examiners.

In order to acquire the knowledge necessary for the system, the knowledge engineers found that they almost had to become ''experts'' in the VAT auditing process. Further, in order for the system to be used by Danish customs officers at the sites of the companies that were being investigated, the system would have to be developed for use on an IBM-PC and the knowledge base would have to be in Danish.

The system is a prototype that was designed for release in 1988. The system was developed using the expert system shell KEE.

Contributions and Extensions of Government Audit Systems

Each of these systems is important because they capture the knowledge of experts in their knowledge bases and allow for productivity improvements. Each of these systems is designed to allow computer processing of some human information-processing activities while allowing humans to focus on other more important issues.

However, there are some additional contributions. The FSA was one of the first actual implementations of DeJong's [65] approach to understanding text. The Pennsylvania state tax system is the first audit system to be able to learn. The VAT system demonstrates an easy-to-forget capability of expert systems that the knowledge does not have to be recorded in English; the system does not care in what language is the knowledge.

Systems of this type are not just limited to these applications. Instead, those situations where there are a large number of documents to process and those situations where there is interest in determining filing violations are all conceptually congruent with these applications. In addition, although each of these applications is associated with a government, such applications are not limited to government but could be extended to almost any business that processes large amounts of the same kind of documents.

INTERNAL AUDITING

The functional area of auditing that probably has received the least attention is internal auditing. Although internal auditors likely are going to be able to make use of many of the developments in each of the other categories of auditing discussed in the preceding some applications have been aimed at the unique requirements of internal auditing.

Decision Support for Internal Audit Planning

Boritz [69] presented an initial report on the development of a desktop decision support system for internal auditing planning. That system (Boritz [70]) has recently become available to the commercial market through the Institute of Internal Auditors (IIA) as a product known as Audit MASTERPLAN (AMP).

AMP includes two approaches to measuring risk (based on Boritz [71]) and includes the IIA's Standards for Professional Practice of Internal Auditing. AMP is designed for most industries (financial, industrial, service, and manufacturing). AMP has five components: systems management, risk factors management, audit portfolio management, personnel skills management, and a long-term planning and budgeting module.

In the original report (Boritz [69]), the research focus was on the user interface and the inclusion of knowledge into the procedures of the system rather than the storage of a separate knowledge base. Boritz and Kielstra [72] described a methodology for the assessment of risk using audit and inherent risk.

Price Analysis

A problem that continues to make headlines throughout the country is the spending activities of the federal government, for example, the $200 ashtray. In a sequence of at least three papers Dillard et al. [73, 74] and Ramakrishna et al. [75] proposed the development of an expert system to aid in the examination of the reasonableness of an expenditure.

Their discussion is primarily aimed at federal government acquisitions. However, as they note, price analysis is also a problem in private enterprise.

PAYPER: An Expert System to Examine Payroll and Personnel Files

PAYPER (Payroll-Personnel) is a prototype expert system (O'Leary and Tan [76]) developed using the expert system shell EXSYS, designed to aid in the audit of payroll and personnel files. It does this by investigating patterns of conditions that are met. As a simple example, not only should hours worked and pay rate meet certain constraints, but also hours worked times pay rate plus vacation pay must meet certain constraints.

The primary theoretical contribution of PAYPER is that it uses expert systems, multiple-condition symbolic rules to extend traditional EDP single-field numeric audit tests. By taking into account relations between the fields, this approach allows tighter and more comprehensive analysis of the data.

The Internal Audit Risk Assessor (TIARA): The Equitable

There is only limited information available on TIARA as developed by Inference Corporation for The Equitable. A brief summary of the system is available (Inference, no date) and further inquiries to Inference Corporation did not yield any additional information except that the system was not used by The Equitable.

As originally discussed, TIARA presents a methodology for assessing risk. Some of the variables used in that decision include strength/experience of the unit's management team, the unit's internal control consciousness, changes in the unit's basic industry/market, and the length of time since their last audit. The system was designed to provide a means to enable rapid identification of high-priority audits and consistent assessment of audit risk.

Coopers & Lybrand: Internal Audit Systems

Recently, Coopers & Lybrand have begun promoting a general internal audit system that:

- Employs audit planning and tracking.
- Allows automatic sample selection from mainframe data.
- Automatically identifies patterns in sample data.
- Has intelligent on-line questionnaires for policy testing and specific regulation.
- Provides explanations for questions.
- Records internal auditor comments during the audit.
- Displays policy documents on-line.
- Generates work papers.
- Prints branch exception reports.

Continuous Audit of On-line Systems

Vasarhelyi et al. [77] argue that recent advances in hardware and software technology are engendering increasingly complex information systems environments, thus requiring increasingly complex audit approaches. Further, as firms increase in size because of mergers and economies of scale, the quantity of auditing demands on the auditor is increasing.

However, the same technologies that increase the complexity of the information systems environment can be used to the advantage of auditing those systems. Not only can decision support systems be used to assist auditors, but also the computer can be used to perform additional auditing. In particular, because of the large amount of data, human auditors may not be able to provide an effective or efficient audit. As a result, it is desirable to build systems that continuously audit portions of the data base as transactions occur.

The quality of these audit systems is dependent on the ability of the modeler to capture the expertise of auditors in the metrics and analytics used to model that expertise. Research in systems of this type needs to explore those approaches that capture that expertise best.

Fraud Detection

There have been at least two studies (Tenor [78] and Lecot [79, 80]) that have used expert systems to investigate the possibility of fraud as part of the internal audit function. Tenor [78] discusses an off-line fraud detection system for deviant file use. Lecot [80] describes an on-line system designed to determine fraudulent credit card use. In each case the focus of these systems was on determining if a user of a service of the firm is a legitimate user. Conceptually, the intrusion detection systems discussed under EDP systems and the continous audit system discussed immediately preceding are similar to these systems.

The approach of each system is to first establish a profile for each of the legitimate users that defines expected and possible behaviors. Then when that user makes use of the system, that use is compared to the profile to determine if it matches. Those comparisons are based on the notion that ''early warning symptoms'' can be captured in those user profiles.

VALIDATING AND VERIFYING EXPERT SYSTEMS

An important aspect of developing expert systems is the validation and verification of those expert systems. Validation refers to the relationship between the recommendations generated by the system and the recommendations generated by the human counterpart. For example, a typical validation test would involve a comparison of the system to the expert. Verification refers to the correctness of the implementation in the particular technology chosen to develop the system. For example, verification involves ensuring that there are no rules that result in circular reasoning. A recent summary of the research in validation and verification of expert systems is provided in O'Leary [81].

DANGERS IN EXPERT SYSTEMS DEVELOPMENT

One of the dangers of the current approach to most knowledge engineering projects is that there is preoccupation with what is rather than what should be. On one expert system project of which the authors are aware, it was realized that a mathematical programming approach would provide a better solution to a subproblem than using a sequence of rules. The linear program was able to provide a better solution than simply mimicking an auditor's behavior. There is no need to use satisfying procedures when optimal solution generation processes can be used.

Preoccupation with the type of knowledge representation can be dangerous. For example, Biggs et al. [27] found auditors do not think in if–then rules. Turning dialogues with auditors into such rules may lead to a loss of information.

In a related study, Gal and Steinbart [82] examined the development of two expert systems for investigating the nature of audit judgment. The evidence presented in that paper indicates that ''refinements made to those prototype systems resulted in evaluations which reflect more of the decision criteria actually used by the auditor.'' That is, the initial systems developed may not properly represent judgment.

Another danger in the development of expert systems is that the more computers do, the less auditors need to do. This has at least two implications. First, we must remember that expert systems are a move to automate the audit process. As with the introduction of all automation projects, the number of human workers decreases. Thus, we can expect to see a decrease in the number of auditors to accomplish the same amount of work. Second, if the system knows something, then the auditor may not need to know that information. As a result, auditors may forget important information that they have learned or may not learn things that are important. Reportedly, AY has tempered the inclusion of activities in AY/ASQ so as to minimize the negative implications of the system knowing "too much" and the auditor forgetting or, worse yet, not learning.

Another danger is that the auditor would blindly depend on the system's recommendations. This could occur in at least two situations. First, if the auditor does not have the necessary foundation then decisions made by the system cannot be questioned. Second, if the auditor does not "interact" with the system, then the system's suggested course of action will be executed. As a result, it is important to place the responsibility for the actions on the auditor, not the system.

The impact of training and performance effects of a knowledge-based system are discussed in Blocher et al. [83].

SOURCES OF EXPERT SYSTEM CONTRIBUTIONS

The journal *Auditing: A Journal of Theory and Practice* has become a primary source of publication of academic papers on expert systems. *Expert Systems Review*, published by the University of Southern California, School of Accounting, is a new publication aimed at disseminating information about AI and expert systems in accounting and business. It provides more of a focus on expert systems and AI in general rather than just auditing systems.

Three primary meetings have fostered the presentation of results on expert systems in auditing and accounting. The University of Southern California and Deloitte, Haskins & Sells Audit Judgment Symposium have featured the first presentation on many of the systems discussed in this chapter. This is clearly established by reviewing the references. In addition, the Measures in Management College of The Institute of Management Sciences has also featured initial and subsequent discussions on many of the papers listed in the references at the semiannual meetings of the Operations Research Society of America, The Institute of Management Sciences. In the fall of 1988, the University of Southern California and Peat, Marwick, Main Foundation sponsored the First Annual International Symposium on Expert Systems in Business, Finance and Accounting. Many of the papers from that meeting were published in *Expert Systems Review*.

As the major accounting firms started developing their own statistical audit software, they made it available to universities so that they could integrate it into their programs. At least one of the firms, AY, is considering allowing distribution of their software to academic institutions. This tendency is likely to continue with other firms following suit.

CONCLUSIONS

Recently developed audit-based expert systems have moved beyond the initial rule-based systems to include such knowledge representation methods as frames and semantic networks. The systems went beyond just employing heuristics in the context of decision-making processes to include developments such as learning and natural-language understanding. In addition, expert systems have moved out of academe and into commercial applications.

As summarized in this chapter, there are a wide variety of prototype and commercial systems in operation. Expert systems remain an important tool to:

- Simulate the procedures through which an auditor goes.
- Test our understanding of the knowledge in a particular area of auditing.
- Test the use of technological developments in artificial intelligence in audit-based expert systems.

REFERENCES

1. Hayes-Roth, F., Waterman, D. A., and Lenat, D. B., *Building Expert Systems*, Addison-Wesley, Reading, MA, 1983.
2. Turbin, E. and Watkins, P., "Integrating Expert Systems and Decision Support Systems," *Management Information Systems Quarterly*, June 1986, pp. 121–138.
3. Amer, T., Bailey, A., and De, P., "A Review of Computer Information Systems Research Related to Accounting and Auditing," *Journal of Accounting Information Systems*, Vol. 2, No. 1, 1987, pp. 3–28.
4. Bailey, A., Meservy, R., Duke, G., Johnson, P., and Thompson, W., "Auditing, Artificial Intelligence and Expert Systems," in *Decision Support Systems: Theory and Applications*, C. Holsapple and A. Whinston (eds.), Springer-Verlag, Berlin, 1987.
5. Bedard, J., Gray, G., and Mock, T. J., "Decision Support Systems and Auditing," in *Advances in Accounting*, B. Schwartz (ed.), JAI, Greenwich, CT, 1984.
6. Borthick, F., "Artificial Intelligence in Auditing: Assumptions and Preliminary Development," *Advances in Accounting*, B. Schwartz (ed.), JAI, Greenwich, CT, 1987, pp. 179–204.
7. Chandler, J., "Expert Systems in Auditing: The State of the Art," *Auditor's Report*, Vol. 8, No. 3, 1985, pp. 1–4.
8. Dillard, J. F. and Mutchler, J. F., "Knowledge Based Expert Systems in Auditing," *Working Paper*, Ohio State University, July 1984.
9. Messier, W. F. and Hansen, J. V., "Expert Systems in Auditing: A Framework and Review," in *Decision Making and Accounting: Current Research*, S. Moriarty and E. Joyce (eds.), University of Oklahoma Press, Oklahoma City, OK 1984, pp. 182–202.
10. O'Leary, D., "The Use of Artificial Intelligence in Accounting," in *Expert Systems for Business*, Silverman, B. (ed.), Addison-Wesley, Reading, MA, 1987.
11. Bailey, A. D., Meservy, R., and Turner, J., "Decision Support Systems, Expert Systems,

and Artificial Intelligence: Realities and Possibilities in Public Accounting," *Ohio CPA Journal*, Spring, 1986, pp. 11–15.

12. Borthick, F. and West, O., "Expert Systems—A New Tool for The Professional," *Accounting Horizons*, Vol. 1, No. 1, 1987, pp. 9–16.

13. Elliot, R. K. and Kielich, J. A., "Expert Systems for Accountants," *Journal of Accountancy*, September 1985.

14. Flesher, D. and Martin, C., "Artificial Intelligence," *Internal Auditor*, February 1987, pp. 32–36.

15. McKee, T., "Expert Systems: The Final Frontier?" *CPA Journal*, July 1986, pp. 42–46.

16. Hansen, J. V. and Messier, W. F., "Expert Systems for Decision Support in EDP Auditing," *International Journal of Computer and Information Sciences*, Vol. 11, 1982, pp. 357–379.

17. Holstrom, G., "Sources of Error and Inconsistency in Audit Judgment," Working Paper No. 70, School of Accounting, University of Southern California, 1984.

18. Hogarth, R., *Judgment and Choice*, Wiley, Chichester, 1985.

19. Dillard, J. and Mutchler, J., "Expertise in Assessing Solvency Problems," *Expert Systems*, August 1987, pp. 170–178.

20. O'Leary, D., "Expert Systems in a Personal Computer Environment," *Georgia Journal of Accounting*, Vol. 7, 1986, pp. 107–118.

21. Holstrom, G., Mock, T., and West, R., "The Impact of Technological Events and Trends on Audit Evidence in the Year 2000: Phase I," in *Proceedings of the 1986 Touche Ross/University of Kansas Symposium on Auditing Problems*, R. Srivastava and N. Ford (eds.) School of Business, University of Kansas, Lawrence, KS, 1987, pp. 125–146.

22. Ashby, R., *Introduction to Cybernetics*, Wiley, 1965.

23. Kelly, K. P., Ribar, G., and Willingham, J., "Interim Report on the Development of an Expert System for the Auditors Loan Loss Evaluation," in *Proceedings of the Touche Ross/University of Kansas Audit Symposium*, 1987, pp. 167–188.

24. Hansen, J. V. and Messier, W. F., "A Knowledge-based Expert System for Auditing Advanced Computer Systems," *European Journal of Operational Research*, September 1986, pp. 371–379.

25. Hansen, J. V. and Messier, W. F., "A Preliminary Investigation of EDP-XPERT," *Auditing: A Journal of Practice and Theory*, Vol. 6, No. 1, 1986, pp. 109–123.

26. Messier, W. F. and Hansen, J. V., "A Case Study and Field Evaluation: EDP-XPERT," Paper presented at the Audit Judgment Symposium, University of Southern California, February 1988.

27. Biggs, S., Messier, W., and Hansen, J., "A Descriptive Analysis of Computer Audit Specialists' Decision-making Behavior in Advanced Computer Environments," *Auditing: A Journal of Theory and Practice*, Vol. 6, No. 2, 1987, pp. 1–21.

28. Denning, D., "An Intrusion Detection Model," *IEEE Transactions on Software Engineering*, Vol. SE13, No. 2, 1987, pp. 222–232.

29. Chandler, J., Braun, H., and Dungan, C., "Expert Systems: Operational Support for Audit Decision Making," Paper presented at the University of Southern California Symposium on Audit Judgment, February 1983.

30. Dungan, C. "A Model of an Audit Judgment in the Form of an Expert System," University of Illinois, Ph.D. Dissertation, 1983.

31. Dungan, C. and Chandler, J., "Analysis of Audit Judgment through an Expert System," Faculty Working Paper No. 982, University of Illinois, November 1983.

32. Dungan, C. and Chandler, J., "Auditor: A Microcomputer-based Expert System to Support Auditors in the Field," *Expert Systems*, October 1985, pp. 210–221.

33. Braun, H. M., "Integrating an Expert System and Analytical Review Techniques for Making an Audit Decision," Paper presented at the ORSA/TIMS meeting in Miami, October, 1986.

34. Kelly, K. P., Expert Problem Solving for the Audit Planning Process, Ph.D. Dissertation, University of Pittsburgh, Pittsburgh, PA, 1984.

35. Kelly, K. P., "Modeling the Audit Planning Process," *Expert Systems Review*, Vol. 1, No. 1, 1987, pp. 3–7.

36. Biggs, S. and Selfridge, M. "GCX: An Expert System for the Auditor's Going Concern Judgment," Paper presented at the National Meeting of the American Accounting Association in New York, 1986.

37. Selfridge, M., "Mental Models and Memory: Expert Systems and Auditing in the Year 2000," Paper presented at the USC Audit Judgment Conference, February 1988.

38. Selfridge, M. and Biggs, S., "GCX, A Computational Model of the Auditor's Going Concern Judgment," Paper presented at the Audit Judgment Symposium, University of Southern California, February 1988.

39. Selfridge, M. and Biggs, S., "GCX: Knowledge Structures for Going Concern Structures for Going Concern Evaluations," Paper presented at the First International Symposium on Expert Systems in Business, Finance and Accounting, University of Southern California, September 1988.

40. Dillard, J. F. and Mutchler, J. F., "Knowledge Based Expert Computer Systems for Audit Opinion Decisions," Paper presented at the University of Southern California Symposium on Audit Judgment, 1986.

41. Dillard, J. F. and Mutchler, J. F., "A Knowledge-based Support System for the Auditor's Going Concern Opinion Decision," Working Paper, Ohio State University, 1987.

42. Meservy, R. D., "Auditing Internal Controls: A Computational Model of the Review Process," Ph.D. Dissertation proposal, University of Minnesota, October 1984.

43. Gal, G., "Using Auditor Knowledge to Formulate Data Constraints: An Expert System for Internal Control Evaluation," Ph.D. Dissertation, Michigan State University, 1985.

44. Meservy, R. D., Bailey, A., and Johnson, P., "Internal Control Evaluation: A Computational Model of the Review Process," *Auditing: A Journal of Theory and Practice*, Vol. 6, No. 1, 1986, pp. 44–74.

45. Bailey, A. D., Duke, G. L., Gerlach, J., Ko, C., Meservy, R. D., and Whinston, A. B., "TICOM and the Analysis of Internal Controls," *Accounting Review*, Vol. 60, 1985, pp. 186–201.

46. Grudnitski, G., "A Prototype of an Internal Control System for the Sales/Accounts Receivable Application," University of Texas Working Paper, presented at the University of Southern California Symposium on Audit Judgment, 1986.

47. Steinbart, P., "The Construction of an Expert System to Make Materiality Judgments," Ph.D. Dissertation, Michigan State University, 1984.

48. Steinbart, P., "The Construction of a Rule-based Expert System as a Method for Studying Materiality Judgments," *Accounting Review*, January 1987.

49. Mock, T. and Vertinsky, I., "DSS-RAA: Design Highlights," Paper presented at the University of Southern California Audit Judgment Conference, February 1984.

50. Mock, T. and Vertinsky, I., *Risk Assessment in Accounting and Auditing*, Research Monograph No. 10, The Canadian Certified General Accountants Research Foundation, Vancouver, British Columbia, Canada, 1985.

51. Dhar, V., Lewis, B., and Peters, J., "A Knowledge-based Model of Audit Risk," *AI Magazine*, Vol. 9, No. 3, 1988.

52. Peters, J., Lewis, B., and Dhar, V., "Assessing Inherent Risk During Audit Planning: A Computational Model," University of Oregon, March 1988.

53. American Institute of Certified Public Accountants (AICPA), "The Auditor's Consideration of an Entity's Ability to Continue as a Going Concern," *Statements on Auditing Standards, No. 59*, New York, 1988.

54. Schank, N. R., "Reminding and Memory Organization," Research Report No. 170, Department of Computer Science, Yale University, 1979.

55. Bailey, A., Han, K., Stansifer, R., and Whinston, A., "A Formal Algorithmic Model Compatible with Conceptual Modeling in Accounting Information Systems," University of Texas Working Paper, December 1988.

56. Arthur Andersen & Co., "Financial Statement Analyzer," December 1985.

57. Arthur Andersen & Co., "ELOISE," December 1985.

58. Mui, C. and McCarthy, W., "FSA: Applying AI Techniques to the Familarization Phase of Financial Decision Making," *IEEE Expert*, Vol. 2, No. 3, 1987, pp. 33–41.

59. O'Leary, D., "Accounting Regulation-based Expert Systems," *Research in Accounting Regulation*, Vol. 1, 1987, pp. 123–137.

60. Ribar, G., "Uses of Expert Systems Technology at Peat Marwick Main," *Expert Systems Review*, Vol. 1, No. 1, 1987, pp 1 and 5.

61. Ribar, G., "Development of an Expert System," *Expert Systems Review*, Vol. 1, No. 3, 1988.

62. Ribar, G., "Expert Systems Validation: A Case Study," *Expert Systems Review*, Vol. 1, No. 3, 1988.

63. Willingham, J. and Ribar, G., "Development of an Expert Audit System for Loan Loss Evaluation," in *Auditor Productivity in the Year 2000*, A. Bailey (ed.), Arthur Young, Reston VA, pp. 171–186.

64. Kelly, K. P., "Audit Programming Expert System Project," 1986.

65. DeJong, G., *Skimming Stories in Real Time*, Ph.D. Dissertation, Yale University, 1979.

66. Hall, M., Meservy, R., and Nagin, D., "Audit Knowledge Acquisition by Computer Learning," Paper presented at the ORSA/TIMS Meeting, New Orleans, May 1987.

67. Brown, C. and Streit, I., "A Survey of Tax Expert Systems," *Expert Systems Review*, Vol. I, No. 2, 1988, pp. 6–12.

68. Lethan, H. and Jacobsen, H., "ESKORT—An Expert System for Auditing VAT Accounts," in *Proceedings of Expert Systems and Their Applications—Avignon 87*," EC2, Avignon, France, 1987.

69. Boritz, J., "CAPS: The Comprehensive Audit Planning System," Paper presented at the University of Southern California Symposium on Audit Judgment, 1983.

70. Boritz, J., "Audit MASTERPLAN," *Audit Planning Software*, Institute of Internal Auditors, 1986.

71. Boritz, J., "Scheduling Internal Audit Activities," *Auditing: A Journal of Theory and Practice*, Vol. 6, No. 1, 1986 pp. 1–19.

72. Boritz, J. and Kielstra, R., "A Prototype Expert System for the Assessment of Inherent Risk and Prior Probability of Error," 1987.

73. Dillard, J. F., Ramakrishna, K., and Chandrasekaran, B., "Expert Systems for Price Analysis: A Feasibility Study," in *Federal Acquisition Research Symposium*, U.S. Air Force, Williamsburg, VA, 1983.

74. Dillard, J. F., Ramakrishna, K., and Chandrasekaran, B., "Knowledge-based Decision Support Systems for Military Procurement," in *Expert Systems for Business*, B. Silverman (ed.), Addison-Wesley, Reading, MA, 1987, pp. 120–139.

75. Ramakrishna, K., Dillard, J. F., Harrison, T. G., and Chandrasekaran, B., "An Intelligent Manual for Price Analysis," in *Federal Acquisition Research Symposium*, U.S. Air Force, Williamsburg, VA, 1983.

76. O'Leary, D. and Tan, M., "A Knowledge-based System for Auditing Payroll–Personnel Files," University of Southern California, February, 1987.

77. Vasarhelyi, M., Halper, F., and Fritz, R., "The Continuous Audit of Online Systems," Paper presented at the University of Southern California Audit Judgment Conference and the National Meeting of the American Accounting Association, 1988.

78. Tenor, W., "Expert Systems for Computer Security," *Expert Systems Review*, Vol. 1, No. 2, 1988, pp. 3–5.

79. Lecot, K., "An Expert System Approach to Fraud Prevention and Detection," *AI-88 Artificial Intelligence Conference*, Long Beach, CA.

80. Lecot, K., "An Expert System Approach to Fraud Prevention and Detection," *Expert Systems Review*, Vol. 1, No. 3, 1988, pp. 17–20.

81. O'Leary, D., "Verifying and Validating Expert Systems," Paper presented at the First International Symposium on Expert Systems in Business, Finance and Accounting, University of Southern California, September 1988, to appear in P. Watkins and L. Eliot (eds.), *Expert Systems in Business and Finance*, Wiley, New York, forthcoming.

82. Gal, G. and Steinbart, P., "Knowledge Base Refinements as an Indication of Auditor Experience," Paper presented at the University of Southern California Symposium on Audit Judgment, 1986.

83. Blocher, E., Krull, G., Scalf, K., and Yates, S., "Training and Performance Effects of a Knowledge-based System for Analytical Review," Paper presented at the First International Symposium on Expert Systems in Business, Finance and Accounting, University of Southern California, September 1988.

5

ANSWERS: An Expert System for Financial Analysis

Edward Blocher

INTRODUCTION

This chapter describes an expert systems approach for analysis of financial statements. The expert system featured in the chapter is ANSWERS, a product of Financial Audit Systems. This system is designed for a very specific type of financial analysis, that done by auditors as part of planning an audit and in performing certain evidence-gathering procedures. However, the financial analysis concepts that are integrated into the system are quite general in applicability, and as a result there are a number of nonauditor users of the system.

The first section of the chapter describes briefly the various uses of financial analysis, with a focus on audit uses. Following, there is a discussion of the different approaches to building expertise into financial analysis software, with some specific illustrations. Then, there is a demonstration of the ANSWERS system, which includes a brief users' guide to the two modules of the system: trend analysis and projection analysis. The trend analysis module develops relevant financial ratios, trends, and reasonableness tests as a basis for the financial analysis of an entity under study. These ratios, trends, and tests are then used in the system to trigger relevant comments and suggestions from a knowledge base of financial analysis expertise. The comments and suggestions include (a) definitions of key terms and ratios; (b) explanations of observed relationships in the data, the possible causes, implications for other accounts or relationships, and so on; (c) suggestions for appropriate approaches for further investigating the condition, if desired; and (d) suggestions for management action.

The projection module consists of selected forecasting models, including exponential smoothing and regression analysis, which provide a toolkit for a number of financial analysis applications.

Following the description of the system, there is a section that describes how an expert system of this type can be used in training. The results of a study of the use of the ANSWERS system in training auditors are then presented and discussed. Last, the chapter presents a description of how the ANSWERS system was developed, including the development of design specifications, knowledge acquisition, programming, development, testing, and maintenance. The chapter then concludes with a look forward to the next decade of development of systems with applications in financial analysis.

FINANCIAL ANALYSIS APPLICATIONS

This section considers the various applications of financial statement analysis. For this chapter, the term *financial analysis* is used to describe those analytical and other techniques, which are used to interpret financial statements to answer the following questions:

1. Are the statements fairly stated and free of material errors and frauds?
2. How is the company performing, in terms of the growth and profitability of operations, relative to prior years or to industry averages?
3. How is the company performing in terms of financial position, liquidity, leverage, and solvency?
4. What operating and financial issues are in need of current management attention?
5. What are the possible effects on the financial statements of a certain operating or financial plan?

Financial Analysis by the Auditor

The auditor uses financial analysis when performing analytical procedures that are now required by the American Institute of Certified Public Accountants (AICPA) auditing standards. Analytical procedures involve the use of ratio analysis, trend analysis, and reasonableness testing to uncover unexpected relationships within the financial data and inconsistencies between reported financial and operating data. These procedures are used to plan the audit by identifying accounts or transaction classes that have the highest risk of significant error or misstatement. Analytical procedures are particularly effective for detecting errors or frauds that arise because the account of concern is not reported completely; for example, there are some unreported sales or unreported liabilities. Other, nonanalytical forms of evidence are relatively strong at substantiating the existence and proper evaluation of the reported assets but relatively less effective for establishing the completeness of the reported amount.

Analytical procedures are also very effective for detecting overstatement of receivables, inventories, and payroll since they provide an analytical base to predict what these balances should be as a basis for comparison to the reported (but unaudited) amount. For example, fraudulent overreporting of receivables and inventories and "ghost" employees in payroll are often readily detected by analytical tests that integrate the relevant financial and operating data to determine if the reported amount is reasonable. One recent study reported that almost one-third of financial statement errors were initially signaled by analytical procedures (Hylas and Ashton, 1982). To illustrate, one fraud (Crown Aluminum) could have been caught in this manner by using a simple analytical means to determine that the inventory reported by the client exceeded the physical capacity at certain locations. Further investigation showed that the inventory was fraudulently overstated by approximately 100%. For reasons such as this, the recent report of the Treadway Commission on Fraudulent Financial Reporting recommended strongly that analytical procedures are a primary tool for auditors to identify fraudulent financial statements.

Financial Analysis by the Controller or Financial Executive

The financial executive has a number of roles, three of which are (a) to prepare accurate and timely financial reports, (b) to provide expert interpretation of the reports in terms of financial condition and in terms of the company's progress toward its financial and operating objectives, and (c) to prepare special financial reports and analyses to facilitate management decision making.

The financial executive achieves these objectives through the use of financial analysis:

1. To identify and explain financial and operational problems before they become critical.
2. To examine reports for accounting errors by comparison to budgets, by use of ratio analysis, and by testing the reasonableness of selected financial data vis-à-vis related operational data.
3. To review financial data with an eye to discovering the potential for management or employee fraud or theft.
4. To prepare forecasts of sales, expenses, and other account categories that are necessary for effective budgeting and for management decision making.

Financial Analysis for the Consultant

Here we are interested in the consultant, accountant, or financial advisor who either prepares financial reports for small companies and individuals and/or is asked from time to time to provide expert advice regarding these financial statements. The clients are generally looking for expert advice regarding their strengths and weaknesses, how they compare to similar businesses or entities, advice regarding certain business plans or financial decisions, and information regarding current and potential financial problem areas. Additionally, these clients will often request the consultant to prepare projected financial statements for the purpose of requesting a loan, for business planning, or for some related purpose. These services require a significant amount of knowledge of financial statement relationships and of financial data projection techniques, elements provided in the ANSWERS system.

Financial Analysis for the Business Owner

The owner of a business or commercial entity often needs expert financial advice regarding business expansion, extending or obtaining credit, and the tax effects of certain transactions, analysis of the profitability and financial condition of the entity or business, among other questions. "Automated" financial analysis of basic financial statement data is an important way that the ANSWERS system can service these needs.

TYPES OF EXPERT SYSTEMS FOR FINANCIAL ANALYSIS

There are three types of expert systems commonly used for financial analysis applications. This section describes the three types of systems and gives some examples of each. The three types of systems are (a) insight-facilitating systems, (b) decision-facilitating systems, and (c) decision-making systems.

Each of the three types of systems can be described in terms of how it supports the various elements of the decision process, as outlined in Figure 1. This simple model shows that the first step in financial analysis is to acquire relevant data. This is followed by an analysis of the data using ratios, trends, graphs, forecasting models, and related techniques. These analyses produce "insights," which means an observation of a significant financial condition or relationship that is unexpected or requires management's attention. Finally, these insights are the basis for a decision, which might be an investment decision or an audit decision, for example.

Insight-facilitating Systems

The systems that are "insight facilitating" have the objective of producing relevant trends and ratios, facilitating the user's analysis and developments of insights about the financial data under review. The input to these systems is raw data, and the output of the system is simply the trend, ratio, and graphical analyses (see Table 1). The user then reviews these analyses to obtain specific insights about the entity under review. Different users will likely have different insights about the financial condition of the entity, and the quality of these insights depends directly upon the expertise of the user.

Insight-facilitating systems have really no expertise at all, except that which is involved in determining which ratios will be calculated, how they will be calculated, how the graphs will be presented, and so on. In effect, these systems place most of the work on the user. However, they can be quite useful in assisting the user by

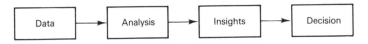

Figure 1 Financial analysis decision process.

TABLE 1. Types of Expert Systems for Financial Analysis

Type of System	Input to System	Output of System	User's Role
Insight facilitating	Data	Ratios Graphs	Develop insights
Decision facilitating	Data	Ratios Graphs Insights	Make decisions
Decision making	Data; query by the system	Recommended decision	Decision implementation

eliminating the "pencil-pushing" aspects of the decision task. Two examples of the many systems of this type are the NEWVIEWS system by Q. W. Page Associates and INSIGHT by Layered. Both of these systems are integrated accounting systems that provide financial reports, specific analysis of the financial data including ratio analyses, and graphs. An example of how a system of this type might work is shown in Tables 2 and 3. Table 2 is the financial statement data for an example firm, and Table 3 shows a report of selected financial ratios from this data. The user of the system would use these reports to develop specific insights about the firm's financial condition—profitability, liquidity, capital structure, and so on. Take a minute to review these reports and develop some of your own insights. How would you rate the firm's liquidity, profitability, and potential as an equity investment?

Decision-facilitating Systems

A second type of system is designed to achieve somewhat more than data analysis and presentation. This second type of system, the decision-facilitating system, produces insights as well as trends, ratios, and graphs. These insights are installed in a knowledge base of relevant comments and suggestions that are triggered, as appropriate, by specific conditions in the data. For example, a significant decrease in the current ratio would produce a set of comments and suggestions regarding the proper interpretation of this observation. These comments would include a definition of the current ratio and how it is typically interpreted (i.e., as a measure of liquidity), an explanation of the significance of this change in this ratio for this entity (e.g., a decline in liquidity reflects a reduced ability to meet short-term debt obligations), suggestions for further investigation (e.g., has some portion of current asset and/or current liabilities been misclassified or reported inconsistently), and suggestions for management action (e.g., consider more systematic means for cash control and develop new sources of long-term debt).

In contrast to the insight-facilitating type of system, this system embodies financial analysis expertise in these comments and suggestions. Like the insight-facilitating systems, they produce the reports of trends, ratios, and graphs, but in addition, the user receives a report of the insights an expert analyst would obtain under the specific condition for the data under review. These insights can then be used to supplement those derived independently by the user or, as a second opinion,

TABLE 2. Example Company: Selected Financial Data

Account Description	1982	1983	1984	1985	1986	1987
Cash	25,141	25,639	32,977	34,009	49,851	30,943
Accounts receivable	272,450	312,776	368,267	419,731	477,324	542,751
Prepaids	3,982	4,402	5,037	5,246	5,378	6,648
Inventories	183,722	208,623	222,128	260,492	298,696	399,533
Property and equipment (net)	47,578	49,931	55,311	61,832	77,173	91,420
Other assets	18,734	20,738	23,075	26,318	36,248	39,403
Total assets	551,607	622,109	706,795	807,628	944,670	1,110,698
Accounts payable	49,831	64,321	70,853	80,861	94,677	78,789
Accrued expenses	86,087	102,650	113,732	131,899	143,159	164,243
Notes payable	99,539	118,305	182,132	246,420	237,741	390,034
Long-term debt	62,622	43,251	35,407	32,310	128,432	126,672
Deferred taxes payable	7,551	7,941	8,286	8,518	9,664	11,926
Other liabilities	5,279	5,521	5,697	5,593	5,252	4,695
Total liabilities	310,909	341,989	416,107	505,592	618,925	776,359
Capital stock	73,253	87,581	79,009	71,601	81,238	73,186
Retained earnings	167,445	192,539	211,679	230,435	244,507	261,153
Total stockholders' equity	240,698	280,120	290,688	302,036	325,745	334,339
Total liabilities and equity	551,607	622,109	706,795	807,628	944,670	1,110,698
Net sales	982,244	1,095,083	1,214,666	1,259,116	1,378,251	1,648,500
Cost of goods sold	669,560	739,459	817,671	843,192	931,237	1,125,261
Depreciation expense	8,303	8,380	8,972	9,619	10,577	12,004
Interest expense	11,248	13,146	14,919	18,874	16,562	21,128
Income tax expense	26,650	34,000	38,000	32,800	26,500	25,750
Dividends paid	13,805	17,160	19,280	20,426	20,794	20,807
Net income	32,563	37,895	41,809	39,577	35,212	37,787
Number of common shares outstanding at year end	12,817	13,714	13,728	13,684	14,023	13,993
Market price per share	38	43	55	65	43	31

to in effect challenge the thinking of the unaided user. The utility of this type of system is that it allows the user the flexibility to use the system's insights as provided or to discard one or more of the insights because they presumably are not relevant due to other conditions known to the user which are not reflected in the financial data input to the system. This is similar to having an unobtrusive and sensitive expert leaning over your shoulder, one who will quietly defer to your own better judgment.

The only widely available system of this kind now available is the ANSWERS system. This system will be described more fully later in the chapter. To see how it contrasts to the insight-facilitating type of system, review Table 4, which is the insights report of the ANSWERS system for the data shown in Table 2. Compare

TABLE 3. Listing of Selected Financial Ratios for Example Company (and annual % change)

	1983	1984	1985	1986	1987
Accounts receivable turnover	3.74	3.57	3.20	3.07	3.23
	—	−4.54%	−10.36%	−4.06%	5.21%
Current ratio	1.93	1.71	1.57	1.75	1.55
	−6.31%	−11.39%	−8.18%	11.46%	−11.42%
Dividends per share	1.25	1.40	1.49	1.48	1.49
	15.74%	12.00%	6.42%	−0.67%	0.67%
Percentage of days payables outstanding	26.89	29.27	30.98	32.58	25.46
	—	8.85%	5.84%	5.16%	−21.85%
Gross margin, %	32.47	32.68	33.03	32.43	31.74
	2.01%	0.64%	1.07%	−1.81%	−2.12%
Gross profit	355,624.00	396,995.00	415,924.00	447,014.00	523,239.00
	13.73%	11.63%	4.76%	7.47%	17.05%
Inventory turnover	3.77	3.80	3.49	3.33	3.22
	—	0.79%	−8.15%	−4.58%	−3.30%
Long-term debt to equity, %	15.44	12.18	10.69	39.43	37.89
	−40.66%	−21.11%	−12.23%	268.84%	−3.90%
Accounts payable turnover	13.39	12.30	11.62	11.05	14.14
	—	−8.14%	−5.52%	−4.90%	27.96%
Quick ratio (acid test)	1.19	1.09	0.99	1.11	0.91
	−5.55%	−8.40%	−9.17%	12.12%	−18.01%
Return on total assets	0.14	0.14	0.12	0.09	0.08
		0.00%	−14.28%	−25.00%	−11.11%
Return on equity	0.15	0.15	0.13	0.11	0.11
	—	0.00%	−13.33%	−15.38%	0.00%

your insights developed from Table 3 to those outlined in Table 3. Note that, for brevity, the two comments shown in Table 4 are only 2 of the 21 comments that were produced by the ANSWERS insights report for the example company. The number of comments for a given entity depends directly upon the number of significant changes in ratios or trends for the underlying data.

The data in Table 2 is actually taken from the last several years of existence for the W. T. Grant Company, which filed for bankruptcy in 1975. The data shown is actually for the years 1968–1973. A keen analysis of this bankruptcy is presented by Largay and Stickney (1980), who show that most of the financial ratios for W. T. Grant did not change dramatically for the five years in question. A review of Table 3 shows this to be generally accurate, except for the change in long-term debt. The critical information, which is not present in Table 3, is the change in cash flows from operations for W. T. Grant over this period. Largay and Stickney estimate these cash flows to have been negative in all but one of the years shown and decreasing steeply for the last three years. This is a strong signal of the pending bankruptcy. The thorough analysis prepared by a system of this type can be helpful for detecting the more difficult to find problems such as that illustrated here. These systems provide the "second guess" the analyst sometimes needs.

TABLE 4. ANSWERS Report for the Example Company*

Observations	Comments
1. Cash flow to total debt decreased	A significant decline generally indicates a weakening of the company's liquidity. This can be a signal of increasing financial risk.
	Is this change consistent with changes throughout the industry?
	What steps are being taken by management to address the increased financial distress?
	Does the company have the ability to respond effectively to increased financial distress?
	Has the company recently entered into significant debt-financed plant or equipment expansion?
	Could debt be restructured to help reduce current maturities?
2. Cash flow from operations decreased	Often, one way to improve cash flow is to arrange more favorable credit terms. Restructuring the arrangements with both suppliers and customers can be equally advantageous.
	If the company has income but little or no positive cash flow, perhaps there are overvalued assets that can be written down to provide income tax benefits.
	Perhaps a review of investments and other assets would reveal resources that could be converted to cash without significantly effecting the company's financial position.
	Is there some way the company could reduce or restructure its debt to help relieve the related interest cost?

* This is a part of a computer-generated report from the ANSWERS software system.

Decision-making Systems

The final type of system is that which is often called the "true" expert system because it includes all phases of the financial analysis task—from data collection to final judgment. At this time there are few widely available systems of this type that run on a microcomputer. These expert systems are developed by artificial intelligence (AI) companies such as Syntelligence and CPA firms such as Arthur Andersen and Coopers & Lybrand. A useful review of some of these systems is presented in a recent paper by Holsapple et al. (1988).

AN ILLUSTRATION: THE ANSWERS SYSTEM

This section presents a brief description of the two modules of the ANSWERS system: ratio analysis and projection analysis. Following, there is a discussion of the use of the system in a training application (Blocher, 1988; Blocher, Krull, Scalf, and Yates, 1988; Blocher and Willingham, 1988; Porter and Blocher, 1988).

The Trend Analysis Module

The trend analysis module is designed to focus on the three most critical audit areas—accounts receivable/sales, inventory/cost of sales, and payroll—and a general overview of the financial condition for the entity, which we call simply financial analysis. These are the four so-called report groups of the system. Data entry, calculations, and the related knowledge base of comments and suggestions are separate for each of the four groups. This partition of the knowledge base is intended to simplify the user's access to the system and to facilitate the focus of each user session on a specific analysis objective.

To further simplify the system and to facilitate ease of use, each of the four report groups is further subdivided into four or more "categories," which reflect specific subobjectives for each of the report groups. For example, the categories under the financial analysis report group are liquidity, capital structure, profitability, and the analysis of the going concern issue for the entity. These report groups and the related categories are outlined in Figure 2. Note that each category is associated with one or more financial ratios. It is these ratios that are the heart of the system.

Data entry. The data ANSWERS uses to compute these ratios are taken from the account balance detail provided by most microcomputer-based accounting or auditing systems (spreadsheet systems, general ledger systems, etc.) plus some special data items (mostly operating data) that must be entered directly by the user. Using a data transfer utility, the financial data in these microcomputer systems is pulled into the ANSWERS system in a way that allows ANSWERS to use it directly.

Ratio entry. A special feature of the ANSWERS system is that it allows the user to modify, delete, and/or create new ratios or categories. This degree of flexibility allows the more experienced user to customize the system to his or her own specific needs.

Observations, Comments, and Suggestions. The principal benefit of the system is the delivery of the expertise contained in the comments and suggestions. An example of these comments and suggestions was shown in Table 4. The comments and suggestions are "triggered" by significant changes in the ratios shown in Table 3 or by relationships among these ratios. For this purpose, a significant change is determined by the user, who selects an amount and/or percentage of threshold for triggering these ratios and relationships. A triggered ratio or relationship is called an "observation," and specific, tailored comments and suggestions are tagged to each of these observations. These comments and suggestions are thorough and complete, having been developed from the efforts of a team of CPAs, accounting and finance faculty, and consultants.

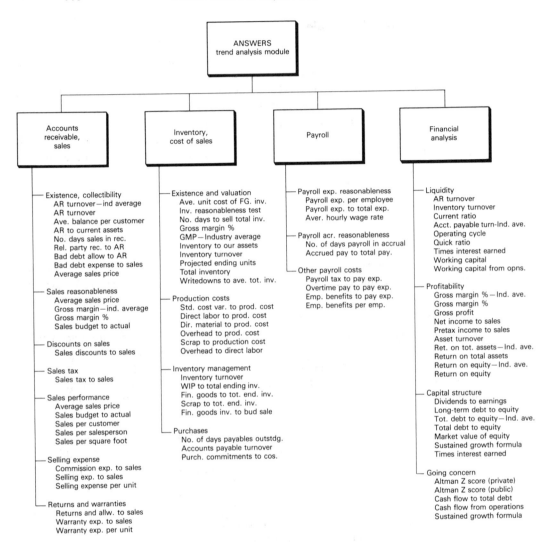

Figure 2   The ratio analysis module.

Entering comments and suggestions.   As for the direct entry or modification of ratios, the user has the ability in the system to modify, delete, or add new comments and suggestions. Again, the intent here is that the system can grow with the experienced user through cumulative updating and modification directly by the user.

Graphical support.   In addition to tabular and textual reports, the system provides a convenient way to document the analysis done and to present the results

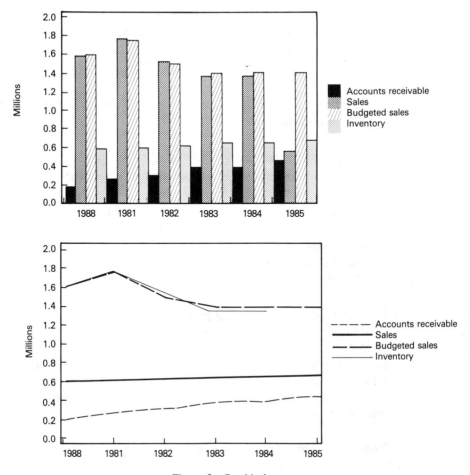

Figure 3 Graphical reports.

in an easy-to-interpret graphical form. The graphs can be obtained either through a menu based on category and ratio or a menu based on observations. Of course, the graphs can be obtained in a variety of forms (line, bar, pie, and values), a variety of colors, and a variety of scales. See Figure 3 for an illustration of selected graphical formats.

Projection Analysis Module

The projection analysis module is a somewhat different element of the system. It is built around a regression analysis tool that has been enhanced to provide expert comments and warnings regarding the use of the system. In contrast to the ratio module that analyzes annual or quarterly account balance data, this module develops regression models from a relatively small amount of financial and operating data.

The role of the projection module is to provide the ability to perform statistically accurate forecasting applications. The forecasting applications can be used in a number of ways, including both in a prospective and a retrospective manner.

Prospective uses.   In this case the user's intent is to forecast some future event, such as sales levels. These uses include:

- Preparing budgets, forecasts, and financial projections.
- Reviewing the financial projections of a client, subsidiary, important vendor, a potential acquisition, and so on.
- Cash management by forecasting weekly, monthly, or quarterly cash needs.

Retrospective uses.   In this case the user's intent is to forecast some current or past event, and the forecast will be used to evaluate the reasonableness of the reported amount:

- In the audit application, current period's sales are forecasted by a model developed from prior years' data as a basis for testing analytically the reasonableness of reported monthly or quarterly sales amounts.
- In a management control use would be to forecast sales at various locations, regions, or units as a basis for evaluating the reasonableness of the reported amounts. The same approach could be used to analyze reported expenses from these locations or units.

Regression reports.   The results of a regression application are reported in tabular and graphical form, as for the ratio analysis module. Illustrations of these reports are shown in Tables 5–7 and Figures 4 and 5. Tables 5–7 present the tabular reports—the raw data, the regression equation, and the forecasted amounts— while Figures 4 and 5 present the related graphs.

Additionally, the user is automatically provided a comment or warning, only when appropriate, if a statistical assumption or other indicator of model validity is violated. For example, a set of warning messages is included to deal with the possibility of data shift in a time series model. This is indicated by a significant Chow test, and the implications of a failure of the test are presented both on the screen and on any printed report so that the user will be appropriately warned about the limited reliability of the model and of its forecasts under these conditions.

In addition to the warning messages, a number of automatic heuristics are built into the system to deal with data and modeling problems such as autocorrelation and nonconstant variance of residuals. Because of these triggered warnings and automatic heuristics, the regression module can be characterized as an ''intelligent'' forecasting tool.

TABLE 5. Regression Example Data

Report date: 11/30/85 Prepared by: Reviewed by:	Original data values for PLANT Example Client, Inc. June 30,1985		Page 1
Date	Sales	Advertising	Index
June 1982	2,745.00	354.00	2,009.00
July 1982	3,200.00	456.00	2,190.00
August 1982	3,232.00	525.00	1,878.00
September 1982	2,199.00	145.00	1,856.00
October 1982	2,321.00	199.00	2,168.00
November 1982	3,432.00	543.00	1,899.00
December 1982	4,278.00	1,189.00	2,463.00
January 1983	2,310.00	212.00	1,999.00
February 1983	2,573.00	284.00	2,190.00
March 1983	2,487.00	246.00	1,894.00
April 1983	2,484.00	278.00	2,134.00
May 1983	3,384.00	498.00	2,100.00
June 1983	2,945.00	224.00	1,874.00
July 1983	2,758.00	312.00	2,265.00
August 1983	3,394.00	485.00	2,435.00
September 1983	2,254.00	188.00	1,893.00
October 1983	2,763.00	276.00	2,232.00
November 1983	3,245.00	489.00	2,004.00
December 1983	4,576.00	1,045.00	2,109.00
January 1984	2,103.00	104.00	2,195.00
February 1984	2,056.00	167.00	2,045.00
March 1984	4,874.00	1,298.00	2,301.00
April 1984	2,784.00	398.00	1,893.00
May 1984	2,345.00	187.00	2,345.00
June 1984	2,912.00	334.00	2,094.00
July 1984	2,093.00	264.00	1,934.00
August 1984	2,873.00	333.00	1,783.00
September 1984	2,563.00	143.00	1,977.00
October 1984	2,384.00	245.00	1,857.00
November 1984	2,476.00	232.00	2,189.00
December 1984	2,364.00	322.00	2,093.00
January 1985	3,458.00	435.00	1,567.00
February 1985	2,786.00	234.00	1,923.00
March 1985	2,390.00	123.00	1,894.00
April 1985	2,376.00	446.00	1,276.00
May 1985	2,894.00	1,200.00	1,576.00
June 1985	4,673.00	1,789.00	2,593.00
July 1985	2,783.00	475.00	2,453.00
August 1985	3,874.00	584.00	2,736.00
September 1985	3,053.00	1,103.00	1,598.00
October 1985	3,040.00	220.00	1,576.00
November 1985	2,494.00	876.00	2,398.00
December 1985	2,784.00	834.00	1,783.00

TABLE 6. Regression Projection Report

Report Date: 11/30/85   Projections report for plant   Page 1
Prepared by: Example Client, Inc.
Reviewed by: June 30, 1985

Projected account: sales
Based on relationships with: advertising

Period		Projected	Actual	Actual over/ (under) projected	Percentage over (under)	Rank
January	1985	2,963.70	3,458.00	494.30	16.68	9
February	1985	2,500.91	2,786.00	285.09	11.40	10
March	1985	2,245.34	2,390.00	144.66	6.44	12
April	1985	2,989.03	2,376.00	(613.03)	(20.51)	6
May	1985	4,725.05	2,894.00	(1,831.05)	(38.75)	1
June	1985	6,081.18	4,673.00	(1,408.18)	(23.16)	4
July	1985	3,055.80	2,783.00	(272.80)	(8.93)	11
August	1985	3,306.76	3,874.00	567.24	17.15	8
September	1985	4,501.72	3,053.00	(1,448.72)	(32.18)	3
October	1985	2,468.68	3,040.00	572.32	23.14	7
November	1985	3,979.07	2,494.00	(1,485.07)	(37.32)	2
December	1985	3,882.37	2,784.00	(1,098.37)	(28.29)	5
		42,699.61	36,605.00	(6,094.61)	(14.27)	

Report Date: 11/30/85   Projections report for plant   Page 2
Prepared by: Example Client, Inc.
Reviewed by: June 30, 1985

Ranges for various confidence intervals:

The projected balance is the best estimate of the value for each period. Using the following values, SALES can be projected with 95% confidence to be the projected balance ± 436.45. Ranges for other confidence intervals may be found in the following:

Confidence Level (%)	Allowable Range
50	± 151.42
70	± 231.59
80	± 289.48
85	± 325.11
90	± 365.20
95	± 436.45
99	± 601.24

TABLE 7. Regression Report: Statistical Measures

Report Date: 11/30/85	Results of statistical checks	Page 1
Prepared by:	Example Client, Inc.	
Reviewed by:	June 30, 1985	

Model is OK

The ANSWERS PROJECTION Module was able to complete a projection model for your data and relationships. No significant statistical problems were detected in the computation of the projections.

Report Date: 11/30/85	Regression equation for plant	Page 1
Prepared by:	Example Client, Inc.	
Reviewed by:	June 30, 1985	

Calculation note: stepwise search for best model.
Regression equation:

$$Sales = 1962.145947 + (2.302422 \times Advertising)$$

Standard error of Estimate = 222.680434
F value ("statistical validity") = 271.122997
Coefficient of determination (R squared) = 0.903373
Ratio of standard error to mean of projected variable = 0.078091

Predictor	t Value
Advertising	16.465813

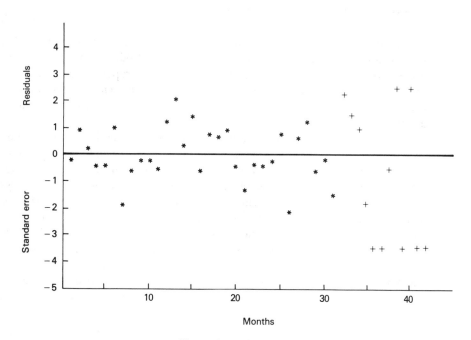

Figure 4 Residual plot.

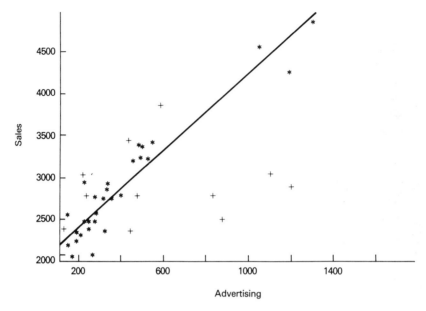

Figure 5   Regression plot.

Use of the ANSWERS System in Training

A potentially important application for financial expert systems such as ANSWERS is to facilitate the training of analysts, auditors, and others. In mind here is not the training of the auditor or analyst to use the system properly, but rather, the use of the system to enhance conventional training methods. That is, the system can be used to facilitate the teaching of basic concepts and techniques of financial statement analysis.

There are a number of ways the system could be used in training. For example, the system could simply be used as a solution key, a benchmark for student performance in selected exercises involving financial statement analysis. However, more productive use is likely to be obtained from direct student use of the system in learning. For example, the system could be used in the following way. The comments and suggestions knowledge base could be partially or completely removed, and the students, working in teams, would be given the exercise to develop partial or complete knowledge bases (comments and suggestions) within the system. The students' systems could then be contrasted in a class meeting as a basis for class discussion about what the knowledge base *should* look like. To facilitate this discussion, the students' knowledge bases could be applied to some case data they had already analyzed in a pencil-and-paper fashion as a basis for a comparison to their earlier analysis of that case. Alternatively, the knowledge bases might be applied to some new data, and the resulting analyses could be used as a basis for class discussion.

Generally, the system would be used as an addition to the conventional lecture and class discussion techniques currently used for the financial analysis course. The use of the system could enhance the effectiveness of the traditional methods since it provides immediate feedback and since the use of computer-interactive systems is often more motivating for the students than simple pencil-and-paper exercises.

Experimental Results

The ANSWERS system was recently used in an experiment to examine the relative effectiveness of the system as a decision aid and/or as an aid in teaching. The task context was what a senior auditor faces when planning the audit, that is, the review of the client's unaudited financial statements to determine those accounts and transaction cycles having the greatest risk of misstatement. The techniques that are used to complete this analysis typically include the ratio analyses commonly associated with financial statement analysis. Auditors call these techniques *analytical procedures*.

The participants in the study were senior-level auditors of an international CPA firm who were participating in a training course for computer audit coordinators. Thirty-three auditors participated, 16 being trained in the conventional manner and the other 17 receiving lecture and discussion plus an exercise using the ANSWERS system.

The data were analyzed using analysis of covariance, where the covariates were selected measures of the auditors' perceptions of financial analysis usefulness and the number of months of audit experience. There was no statistically significant mean effect, interaction effect, or covariate effect for the training treatment. This finding suggests that the training effect might be very small or very context specific, that is, dependent on the specific type of student and task situation. Additionally, the study was exploratory in the sense that there was a relatively small pool of subjects and because they were all from the same CPA firm. Moreover, the subjects in this experiment simply used the system in analyzing some example data. Thus, they in effect had a relatively passive use of the system. A more thorough, active involvement with the system might be required to obtain the expected training effect, say, one wherein the experimental task was to develop a portion of the knowledge base from scratch and then to use that knowledge base on the case data. The results of the student's knowledge base could then be compared to that of the ANSWERS system as a basis for class discussion and learning. A follow-up study is now being designed with a richer experimental task and a larger subject pool to further investigate the potential effect of a system of this type on the effectiveness of training.

DEVELOPMENT OF THE ANSWERS SYSTEM

The development of the ANSWERS system took place over a series of stages beginning in January 1984.

Stage 1. *Design*: January through December 1984, including formulation of the objectives, market, and basic specifications of the system and the development and review of a prototype.

Stage 2. *Development*: January through April 1985, including development of the detailed specifications, initial development of the knowledge base, and high-level review of the system by potential users.

Stage 3. *Coding and redevelopment*: May through September 1985, including completion of the knowledge base, completion of the initial code, and redesign of the system to incorporate new system features.

Stage 4. *Testing and documentation*: October through December 1985, including development of the manual for the system and a tutorial and the testing of the system.

Stage 5. *Introduction of the system*: January 1986.

Stage 6. *System refinement*: January through May 1986, including development of a user's guide, training materials, and developing system enhancements.

Stage 7. *Version 2*: a new version of the system is now being prepared. The new version will have a completely redesigned knowledge base, an enhanced regression module, and other new features.

Design and Specifications

The idea for the ANSWERS system came about in late 1983. The motivation was the recent growth at that time in the use of the microcomputer and particularly of microcomputer audit systems. For example, a number of auditors were looking into the use of LOTUS 1-2-3 for preparing audit schedules and working papers. Financial Audit Systems (FAS) had recently released the FAST! system, a relational data base type of audit system. ANSWERS was conceived as a companion system, one that would enhance the use of the FAST! system by facilitating the detailed financial analysis of the auditee's unaudited financial statements as part of the process of audit planning. Recent auditing standards of the AICPA were putting increasing focus on greater care in audit planning generally and on the use of analytical procedures in particular. *Analytical procedures* is the term used in auditing for the detailed financial analysis of unaudited financial data. So, the utility of such a system seemed clear, and the growth in use of microcomputers by auditors seemed to show that the timing was just right for such a system.

The first step in the design was to define the nature of the planned system and to identify carefully its market niche. It was decided that initially the system would be marketed only to CPA firms and that it would be in effect an automated analytical procedures system. Though a number of auditors had begun to use the spreadsheet systems to perform some types of analytical procedures, a comprehensive system with its own knowledge base was not then available in the market.

The design plan was to develop two modules of the system: *trend analysis*, which would focus on the traditional financial analysis of the financial statement data, and *regression analysis*, which would provide the auditor an opportunity to do some high-level forecasting and reasonableness testing. Because the two modules required somewhat different expertise from both a development and use standpoint, the development of the two modules followed different patterns, as noted in the following.

The next step was to develop broad system flowcharts of the two modules as a basis for ease of review of system requirements, specifications, and functionality. The overall scope of the system was determined at this time. For example, the decision was made to focus on the three most critical audit areas and the areas wherein fraud and misstatement are most common: accounts receivable, inventory, and payroll. These were the three initial *report groups* of the system.

Then there was a determination of the proper system specifications. Here, it was planned that the system would be able to run on the IBM-DOS or compatible type of computer, which was then the predominant type of system being purchased by CPA firms. Also, it was decided that the system would be coded in FOXBASE for screen handling and TURBO-PASCAL for calculations, an approach that was then being used for all FAS software products. Additionally, the system would have graphics capability and be "menu driven" in a manner similar to the other FAS products.

Following the development of these specifications, there was a focus on the development of a prototype system that consisted of screen descriptions and "mock-up" screen displays. The intent was to start from a concrete idea of what we wanted the system to look like to the user. This "bottom-up" approach to design was taken in order to assure that we achieved a system that had the user first in mind. An example mock-up, the flowchart, and screen descriptions done in this phase are shown in Figures 6 and 7 and Table 8. Note, however, that these example screens are descriptive of the nature of the system at that early point in the design process and do not describe the system as it is today.

At this time the prototype was reviewed with a number of significant FAS customers. As a result of this process, an additional report group focused on an overall financial analysis of the entity was added to the system to provide an evaluation of the entity's liquidity, profitability, capital structure, and going concern problems, if any. Also, a number of changes to the knowledge base were made as a result of these reviews.

Development

The development phase began in early 1985 with the hiring of a project manager. During these few months there was a concentration on the completion of the knowledge base. Experts within academia and in the accounting profession participated in the review of the knowledge base and in the development of the new financial analysis report group. Also, at this time we dealt with certain development issues related to the proper definitions of the ratios in the system, how to handle missing data, the

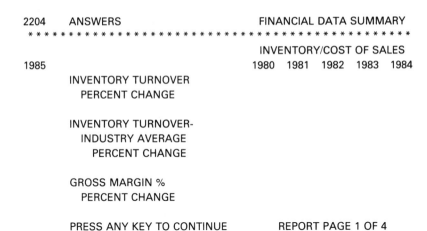

Figure 6 Illustrative screen mock-up.

proper forecasting techniques to use, and related issues. Always, the objective was to remain within the context of a working trial balance data base (limited, if any, operational data or general economic data), which dictated certain limitations on what analyses could be included in the system.

Coding and Redevelopment

At this phase we began to produce the program code and to develop the regression module. This was an important phase of the project in that working with the programmers for the first time we became aware of problems and opportunities that we had not anticipated.

It was a straightforward and easy decision to use the FOXBASE and TURBO-PASCAL languages in the coding rather than one of the AI languages such as LISP or Prolog. First, our objective for the system was to provide a summary of comments and suggestions and not a yes–no type of decision. The system was to be advisory rather than diagnostic. And perhaps most important, the use of FOXBASE and TURBO-PASCAL allowed us to run on a basic microcomputer with modest (384K) memory and without special compiler enhancements. At the time it was not possible to do this with the available AI languages.

The regression analysis module was also being developed at this stage. Proceeding from technical specifications, a small design team of academics worked with a programmer to develop the desired system. A critical aspect of the development of this module was the inclusion of statistical checks and warnings to in effect include some diagnostic statistical expertise in the system. Rather than to provide output of statistical measures and forecasts, the system was being designed to automatically

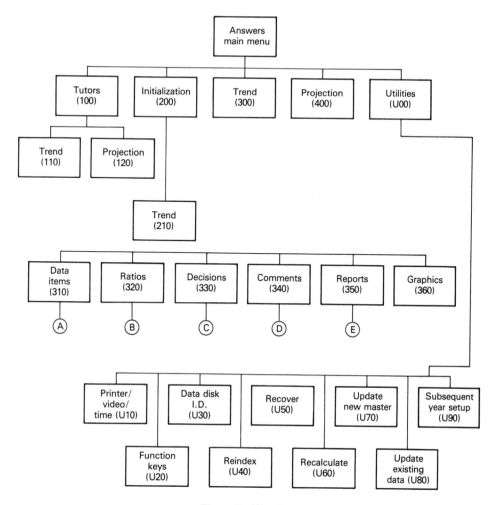

Figure 7   Flowchart.

perform a number of statistical checks and to report appropriate warning messages *only if* it were appropriate to do so. For example, one of the warning messages dealt with the possible incidence of autocorrelation of residuals. This was detected by using the Durbin–Watson statistic, and if signaled, certain transformations of the data were undertaken automatically to attempt to produce a statistically reliable model from the available data. These transformations included deseasonalization, detrending, the use of the log transform, and the use of the square root transform. Other statistical checks included the Chow test for a shift in the data underlying a time series model, the F test for model statistical validity, and the rank order correlation approach to detect nonconstant error variance.

TABLE 8. Screen Functions and Descriptions

Screen	Function	Description
3000	SELECT	If the user selected regression on the super analytical review main menu, he or she would go to this screen and then choose the account function or the multiple-location analysis function.
3100	SELECT	This is the menu for the account function. The user selects which account is to be analyzed and indicates what type of data is available (annual, monthly, quarterly).
3105	MESSAGE . . . IF	If the user indicates that only annual data is available, then this warning message is presented.
3110	ENTER	The user is asked to input the number of periods of data available, base period, and audit period.
3115	MESSAGE . . . IF	If too small a number of periods is given, this warning message appears.
3120	MESSAGE/ENTER	A warning about data accuracy is given; the user chooses between monthly and quarterly data, if necessary.
3130	MESSAGE	Identify and define the dependent variable for the regression analysis.
3135	MESSAGE	If the user indicated a prior year's model in 3100, then 3135 shows this model.
3145	SELECT	User selects whether to continue to use prior year's model, to modify it, or to delete it.
3150	ENTER	Allows modification of model, if selected in 3145.
3200–3210	ENTER	These screens prompt for the independent variables the user will include in the model.
3220	MESSAGE	The screen gives a warning about the accuracy of the data.

Testing and Documentation

In this phase, the system beta test version was sent out to several major customers. Feedback consisted primarily of suggestions for improving the knowledge base and report formats. Also at this time a manual was prepared by a special documentation team, including in part some of the programmers and designers from earlier phases of the project. The written text of the manual was then given to an editor for final preparation.

In a simultaneous effort, the regression analysis module was being tested by the development team and some statistical experts from academia.

System Refinement

The next stage, following the formal introduction of the system in January 1986, was a period of a few months in which there were a number of small refinements to the system. These included a short user's guide and a tutorial data disk. Also, there were changes made to speed the operation of the system and to simplify the operation of the system with windows.

Version 2

The current phase is a comprehensive effort to revise the system with an emphasis on renewal of the knowledge base. The comments and suggestions are being rewritten for clarity, to reduce duplication, and to include additional categories. Also, additional transforms are being added to the regression module, and the number of regression warning messages is being increased to cover additional possible combinations of statistical problems.

In response to user interest, the new version of the system will have shorter menus, more extensive use of windows, and enhanced graphics capability. Additionally, there will be more extensive use of industry data and industry ratios.

A LOOK TO THE FUTURE

To conclude, a few specific observations seem important and relevant regarding trends in financial analysis system development in the coming years. The trends are in part reflective of more significant trends affecting the development of expert systems generally. The trends are (a) greater simplification and focus on ease of use, (b) increased focus on more common problem domains (horizontal rather than vertical market applications), and (c) increasing high cost of knowledge acquisition. Much of the analysis of these trends is developed from two recent surveys (Coopers and Lybrand, 1988; University of Minnesota, 1987) and from market analyses presented in Harmon et al. (1988), Harmon and King (1985), and the *Expert Systems Strategies* newsletter.

Greater Simplification

A number of observations in the previously cited surveys point to the need for increased attention to simplification in expert system development. The complexity of these systems is viewed as a potential obstacle to many users, especially those in the horizontal markets. The complexity of the system is related to the number of rules in the system, the type of user interface, and the nature of the hardware and software environment needed to support these systems.

In terms of complexity, Bobrow et al. (1986, pp. 886–887), and Harmon and King (1985, pp. 197–198) have noted that applications of expert systems have been most successful in simpler decision domains, those for which the human expert would ordinarily be able to complete the decision analysis in 1 hour or less.

In looking to the user interface, increased attention here is a natural outgrowth of the increased user demands for quality, flexibility, and ease of use. Moreover, the emphasis on the user interface is simply one additional aspect of the maturing of the design, development, and marketing of expert systems generally and a growing understanding of their proper role in the firm.

More Common Problem Domains

A second important trend is the move toward what is called "intelligent generic software," "smart workstations," or "enhanced application software" (Harmon and King, 1985, pp. 9–12, 231–233; Bowerman and Glover, 1988, p. 352). The thinking behind these concepts is the importance of placing the expertise in the most accessible point, within the software most commonly used for day-to-day problems. This means intelligent enhancements to existing systems, such as general ledger systems, planning and scheduling systems, and so on. Though they may not be designed directly to solve a specific problem, these systems can provide helpful advice and suggestions that can greatly improve user performance in these common application domains.

Together with the move to more common application areas, the system will become more "transparent" to the user in that the logic and advice can be more readily explained, and the user will have the ability to easily modify the knowledge base. The systems will in effect become more flexible, and more useful to the experienced user. The system can grow with the increase in expertise of a given user through direct user modification. In effect, the system designer and the user have a "creative partnership" wherein the system continuously changes to meet the changing needs of the individual user.

High Cost of Knowledge Acquisition

A third important trend is the increasing high cost of acquiring knowledge for these systems (Bender, 1987; Bobrow, et al., 1986, pp. 191–192; Harmon and King, 1985, p. 199). Though known for their decision-making success, it is not always the case that the expert can explain the decision process. Also, though they may reach the same judgment, different experts may follow quite different judgment processes, which can make it appear that the experts are in disagreement and can add considerably to the difficulty in knowledge acquisition.

Perhaps more generally, it is becoming increasingly clear that decision scientists and experts alike are struggling with a limited knowledge of the expert decision process. Little is known, for example, of what cognitive skills or personality traits might be significantly related to decision performance.

SUMMARY

This chapter has described how the task of financial analysis can and has been applied using expert systems. The ANSWERS system was illustrated as one example of systems of this type. Additional discussion included possible applications of these systems to training accountants and managers and a brief look at the possible future directions for the development of these types of systems.

REFERENCES

FAS, "ANSWERS Users' Manual," Financial Audit Systems, Prentice Hall Professional Software, 2400 Lake Park Drive, Smyrna, GA 30080.

BENDER, E. "The Knowledge Engineers," *PC World*, September 1987, pp. 172–179.

BLOCHER, E. AND K. A. SCALF, "Developing an Expert System for Financial Analysis," *International Journal of Policy and Information*, June 1988, pp. 101–115.

BLOCHER, E., G. KRULL, JR, K. A. SCALF, AND S. V. N. YATES, "Training and Practice Aid Effects of a Knowledge-Based System for Analytical Procedures," Presented at the First International Symposium on Expert Systems in Business, Finance and Accounting, University of Southern California, September 30, 1988.

BLOCHER, E. AND J. J. WILLINGHAM, *Analytical Review: A Guide to Analytical Procedures*, Shepard's McGraw-Hill, New York, 1988.

BOBROW, D. G., S. MITTAL, AND M. J. STEFIK, "Expert Systems: Perils and Promise," *Communications of the ACM*, September 1988, pp. 880–894.

BOWERMAN, ROBERT G., AND DAVID GLOVER, *Putting Expert Systems into Practice,* Van Nostrand Reinhold Co., New York, 1988.

COOPERS & LYBRAND, "Expert Systems in the Financial Services Industry: A Survey Report," Coopers & Lybrand, New York, 1988.

HARMON, P. AND D. KING. *Expert Systems*, Wiley, New York, 1985.

HARMON, P., R. MANS, AND W. MORRISSEY, *Expert Systems Tools and Applications*, Wiley, New York, 1988.

HOLSAPPLE, C. W., K. Y. TAM, AND A. B. WHINSTON, "Adapting Expert System Technology to Financial Management," *Financial Management*, Autumn 1988, pp. 12–22.

HYLAS, R. E. AND R. H. ASHTON, "Audit Detection of Financial Statement Errors," *Accounting Review*, October 1982, pp. 751–765.

LARGAY, J. A. AND C. P. STICKNEY, "Cash Flows, Ratio Analysis, and the W. T. Grant Bankruptcy," *Financial Analysts Journal*, July–August, 1980, pp. 51–84.

PORTER, G. AND E. BLOCHER, "Entering the Age of Expert Systems," *Financial Executive*, May–June 1988, pp. 44–49.

University of Minnesota, "Survey of Fortune 500 Firms' Use of Expert Systems," The Management Information Systems Research Center, 1987.

6

The Financial Statement Analyzer

Chun Ka Mui
Carolyn F. Hassel
Lisa C. Curtis

INTRODUCTION

Many corporations and government agencies seeking to reduce their paper-processing overhead are investigating new technologies to help automate the transmission, receipt, analysis, and output of strategic business documents. This chapter focuses on a pilot system developed for the U.S. Securities and Exchange Commission (SEC) to help in analyzing financial documents.

The EDGAR (Electronic Data Gathering, Analysis and Retrieval) pilot system enabled volunteer corporations to submit required filings electronically (as opposed to paper submissions). While developing this pilot, the SEC wanted to assess the ultimate feasibility of an automated system that would include interpretive and extractive processing. This type of processing was required to extract data from relatively free-form financial filings. Because its legislatively mandated goal is to make all filed information on registered corporations available to the trading public, the SEC was exploring the potential for a processing system that would monitor filings for compliance with security laws and also convert that nonuniform data into easily accessible information.

During development of the EDGAR pilot, the SEC commissioned Arthur Andersen to build two knowledge-based systems: ELOISE (English Language-Oriented Indexing System for EDGAR) and FSA (Financial Statement Analyzer).

ELOISE

ELOISE is a prototype system that analyzes electronically stored text to detect concepts of interest to the SEC. The prototype can detect concepts found in proxy statements, a common type of SEC filing. ELOISE searches each document retrieved from the EDGAR system for specific concepts of interest. For example, ELOISE might be instructed to look for an antitakeover proposal, such as a company proposing to change its bylaws to add a new class of stock.

FSA

FSA[1] is a prototype that analyzes financial information contained in EDGAR's filings. Specifically, 10K and 10Q filings contain financial statements that the SEC needs to assess to perform financial analysis. Two primary problems exist with using the electronically received filing information in automated financial analysis. First, because the electronically received information is in a textual format, it is reviewed manually rather than by an automated numerical process. The second problem relates to the electronic filings: certain types of information are required in the financial statements, but individual filers adapt the format, wording, and organization to fit their unique needs. This lack of structure makes analysis difficult.

Financial analysts spend a significant portion of their time manually retrieving information needed to perform analytical reviews of SEC filings. Much of this information is embedded in:

- Financial statements.
- Parenthetical remarks.
- Footnotes.
- Management discussion and analysis.

The manual process of retrieving this information is inefficient because it is extremely time consuming, and as a result, less time is available for substantive analysis.

FINANCIAL DECISION MAKING

Human information-processing theorists hypothesize that decision making can be divided into a number of phases [2]. The first phase embraces those cognitive activities concerned with explicitly recognizing relevant information in the decision maker's environment and is referred to by terms such as *information acquisition* or *intelligence*. This first step can include some preliminary interpretive data processing; however, its primary purpose is to set the stage for later problem-solving activities that process first interpretations into final decisions.

This initial exploratory activity was recently studied in a series of process-tracing experiments [3–6]. Each of these experiments asked experienced subjects to talk aloud while solving a significant financial problem. Protocols transcribed from these recorded sessions showed extensive important use of financial statement data. Figure 1 illustrates Bouwman's explanation of this process [4].

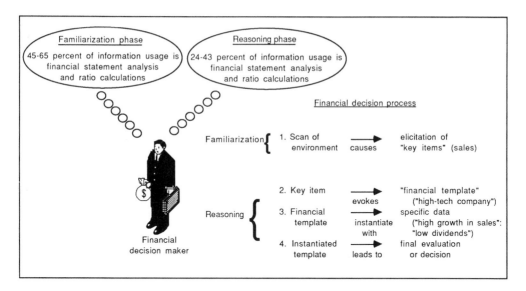

Figure 1 The financial decision process.

Bouwman divided financial decision making into two phases, familiarization and reasoning. His subjects included two groups of experts making two types of decisions. Financial analysts evaluating a stock for possible investment formed the first group, and loan officers evaluating a multimillion-dollar participation loan formed the second. As Figure 1 illustrates, analyzing financial statements and calculating financial ratios comprised significant information usage in both phases—but in the first phase especially.

According to Bouwman, as Figure 1 shows, financial decision making consists of the following steps:

1. Scan the environment and background values to identify key items such as "sales" or "net income."

2. Evoke financial templates for companies or industries from long-term memory (e.g., "high-tech company" or "late recessionary industry").

3. Search for instantiations of these templates with specific information (i.e., a more directed reading of initial data).

4. Evaluate, or decide overall.

In rough terms, the first step corresponds to familiarizing, while the second, third, and fourth accrue to reasoning. The instantiations called for explain the continued use of financial statement and ratio data throughout the entire decision process.

Bouwman developed this description of the decision process after several experimental studies of financial decision making. Bouwman's two-phase description should not be generalized to cover most actual users; however, it does constitute a widely applicable framework for analyzing issues involved in providing automated support for financial problem solving. The next section uses that framework in discussing artificial intelligence (AI) approaches to front-end processing of corporate financial data.

STANDARDIZED PROCESSING FOR FAMILIARIZATION PURPOSES

Surveys of financial decision makers and detailed laboratory studies of those decision makers in action establish the primary use of financial statements in investment, loan, and restructuring decisions. However, because financial statements are first in importance, an interesting data availability paradox occurs.

On one hand, the amount of presently available corporate financial data is clearly overwhelming. For instance, the required corporate filings with the SEC exceed 4 million pages annually. This viewpoint is best expressed in the following analysis of a previously cited process-tracing study [7]:

> Individuals who, as a result of their professional position, act as proxies for other investors, all felt inundated with corporate financial information they felt was of questionable value.

On the other hand, present financial data sources are inadequate in many respects. Research suggests that this judgment applies even to the vast array of computerized financial data services available [8, 9]. Present sources do not adequately account for a wide range of company sizes and types, and they do not make it possible to aspire to high levels of uniform classification and retrieval for heterogeneous corporations.

The solution to these seemingly contrasting problems lies in some knowledge-based processing of disaggregated and uninterpreted financial data. While present data services work well in many cases, they would work better if their input were made more uniform and interpretive.

Such front-end processing would require considerable accounting knowledge concerning the composition of financial statement numbers, and it would also require the ability to extract those accounting numbers (and related conceptual ideas) from unformatted textlike footnotes and proxy statements. Such interpretive and extractive processing is a formidable task and is difficult to build into a computerized system. This difficulty is probably the reason that most present-day financial expert systems aim at decision support for the problem solving's reasoning phase rather than its familiarization phase. Such reasoning support systems are not uniform because they attempt to emulate a disparate group of expert decision makers. Support for familiarization can be uniform, however. In fact, the SEC's EDGAR project sought such support.

THE FINANCIAL STATEMENT ANALYZER

FSA represents a first step at applying AI techniques to the familiarization phase of financial analysis. It performs ratio analysis using corporate annual reports (10K) as the information source. Building the system required approximately 18 man-months of effort, from approximately July 1985 to February 1986, with a project team consisting of SEC and Arthur Andersen personnel. Results of this work are on file with the SEC [10].

An object-oriented system, FSA's structure is modeled after the accounting domain's knowledge structure. Explicit knowledge representation and natural-language processing techniques were molded to technical requirements imposed by the problem domain. In order to extract key financial data from corporate annual reports, the system had to systematically interpret tabular financial statements and textual footnotes. FSA explicitly represents accounting knowledge needed to perform ratio analysis. It incorporates natural-language processing techniques to parse textual footnotes.

Analysis is organized using a message-passing control structure. Each financial statement item is a computational object having a local state (composed of slots) and operators (represented as methods) and communicating via messages. One type of operator, the FIND-YOURSELF method, is a procedure that can search a particular financial document for its value. Invoking this procedure occurs when the value is needed. For example, a ratio (such as QUICK-RATIO) receiving a FIND-YOURSELF message sends a FIND-YOURSELF message to each item in its formula, waits for replies, and then applies these values to the formula. A statement item (such as RENTAL-EXPENSE) receiving a FIND-YOURSELF message would search the company's financial documents for its value. In the case of RENTAL-EXPENSE, the object would search the income statement and, if that failed, the textual footnotes. The nature and complexity of this search is completely hidden from the FIND-YOURSELF message sender.

This message-passing control structure makes analysis a demand-driven process. Data search must be explicitly invoked via a message to an object. This control structure follows the Actor model [11]. The result is a modular system that allows for easy expansion and maintenance, with FSA's search behavior closely modeling the heuristics of human accounting problem solvers.

FSA currently understands balance sheets, income statements, and their accompanying footnotes. It can extract necessary data and perform ratio analysis. For example, it uses (1) the *quick ratio* to measure a firm's ability to pay off short-term obligations without relying on inventory sale, (2) the *current debt-to-equity ratio* to measure how much a firm has been financed by short-term debt, and (3) the *times fixed charges earned ratio* to measure a firm's ability to pay fixed charges.

KNOWLEDGE REPRESENTATION

Figure 2 depicts FSA as it currently exists. The main system input is a company's financial documents, including statements and footnotes. Two knowledge bases support the system: one contains accounting and financial knowledge and the other contains semantic structures that drive footnote processing. Users are financial analysts interacting with the system to initiate queries and resolve ambiguities. For an overall grasp of FSA's functions, one must understand how the two knowledge bases are used in interpretive and extractive processing. Each is described in what follows.

Account Hierarchy

FSA uses a structured representation of accounting knowledge covering the composition of financial statements and the relationships between statement items. This knowledge is needed to interpret loosely structured financial statements and to extract accurate account values from them. FSA models its financial knowledge after chart of account hierarchies used in the accounting profession [12]. Such structures constitute a standard method for organizing financial information, and it was found that accounting problem solvers intuitively attempt to organize financial data into such hierarchies before trying to reason with it.

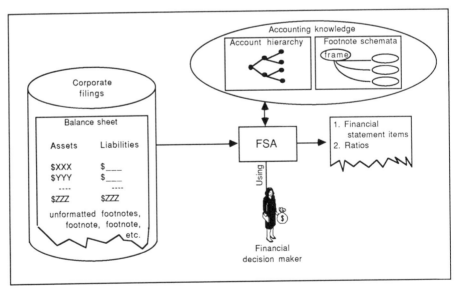

Figure 2   An overview of FSA operation.

Charts of accounts lead naturally to taxonomic classification using a semantic network formalism. Figure 3 illustrates a small portion of FSA's accounting semantic network (the actual network is much larger). Each node represents an object corresponding to some financial item. The taxonomic relationships within the network are SUB-ACCOUNT-OF and ISA, corresponding to the canonical SUBCLASS and INSTANCE relationships. Charts of accounts contain many levels of general accounts and subaccounts, as the SUB-ACCOUNT-OF relationship represents. The ISA relationship represents that each account may be designated in different ways. Figure 3 indicates the SUB-ACCOUNT-OF relationship with a solid arrow and the ISA relationship with a dashed arrow. For example, UNBILLED-RECEIVABLES is a subaccount of ACCOUNTS-RECEIVABLE, and RESERVE is an ALLOWANCE-FOR-DOUBTFUL-ACCOUNTS.

Reasoning is performed within the semantic network through heuristic and algorithmic methods attached to each object. Methods (like FIND-YOURSELF) use the network directly to reason about aggregations and alternative interpretations. The inheritance hierarchy formed by the network enables descriptive and procedural information to move from accounts to subaccounts and instances.

The semantic network's efficacy in representing accounting knowledge was essential for eliciting knowledge from domain experts. The network could be presented in much the same way that a chart of accounts is normally depicted, which in turn maps well to an expert's intuitive image of the domain. Experts could then take direct roles in structuring the knowledge base, thereby lessening problems that arise when knowledge engineers must translate from the expert's domain language to an AI representational language. Experts could also describe their analytical methods directly in chart of account terms.

By design, this application of semantic networks exhibited the desirable qualities of representational systems proposed by Rich [13], representational adequacy and inferential inadequacy. These properties correspond to (1) adequately representing knowledge needed in the domain and (2) successfully manipulating representational structures to derive new structures, structures replicating human inference of new knowledge from old. This representation also displayed acquisitional efficiency, the ability to acquire new information easily.

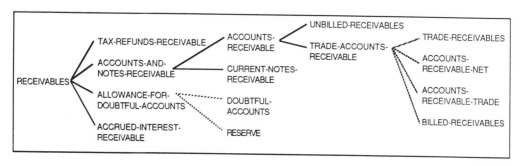

Figure 3 A subset of account hierarchy.

The system's search strategy and representation structure enabled us to easily identify knowledge base deficiencies. Most omissions were new instances for the network. One example of an omission arose when processing a particular hospital's financial statement. The statement referred to RECEIVABLES as PATIENT-RECEIVABLES. For version control reasons, FSA required that this new information, PATIENT-RECEIVABLES is the same as RECEIVABLES, be inserted manually. However, system-controlled acquisition could also have been implemented.

Footnote Schemata

FSA faced financial statement footnotes that significantly challenged automated analysis. Footnotes tend to be unstructured collections of text and tables, with information spread over multiple sentence fragments and interwoven with numerical tables. This anomalous syntactic structure foiled attempts to build a full syntactic parser, one using grammar based on systematic formalisms such as augmented transition networks or charts [14].

Consequently, in conjunction with semantic analysis, footnote syntax was partially parsed. Special objects in the semantic network were defined, and they represented financial items to be found within the textual footnotes. These special objects, *schemata*, were used to represent accounting knowledge contained within footnotes. Figure 4 shows a sample schema for RENTAL-EXPENSE. We designed these schemata directly from our experiences in designing and implementing the earlier SEC prototype ELOISE. ELOISE read corporate proxy statements, looking for certain corporate antitakeover provisions, and was patterned on the semantically driven top-down approach developed by DeJong in FRUMP [15].

FSA uses DeJong's prediction and substantiation model to interpret footnotes,

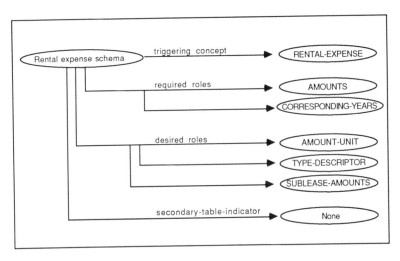

Figure 4   A rental expense schema.

which integrates with financial statement processing's demand-driven nature. The system activates schemata via FIND-YOURSELF messages and then invokes methods that *predict* and then try to *substantiate* each schema role. A text analyzer developed specifically to deal with a footnote's loose syntactic structure performs substantiation. FSA's text analyzer relies on weaker methods than its ELOISE and FRUMP counterparts because footnotes have neither the strong grammatical structure found in ELOISE's legal proxy statements nor the simple grammatical clarity found in FRUMP's UPI news stories. Our text analyzer proved sufficient for FSA's domain.

TECHNICAL ARCHITECTURE

FSA has several functional components, as indicated by Figure 5. As a workbench-type of system, it has several facilities for the user: selecting the company to be analyzed, displaying the appropriate statement, choosing the ratio to be calculated, setting system parameters, and displaying system traces. The user chooses these functions by pointing a mouse at the appropriate area of the FSA panel. A front-end subsystem allows new financial statements to be added to the system. This subsystem is not accessible to the user and therefore must be loaded separately for the FSA programmer. This method of loading statements is not intended to be part

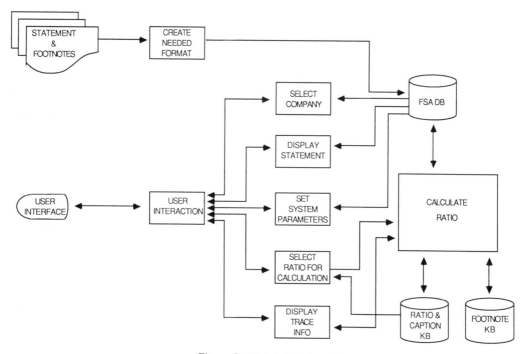

Figure 5   FSA technical architecture.

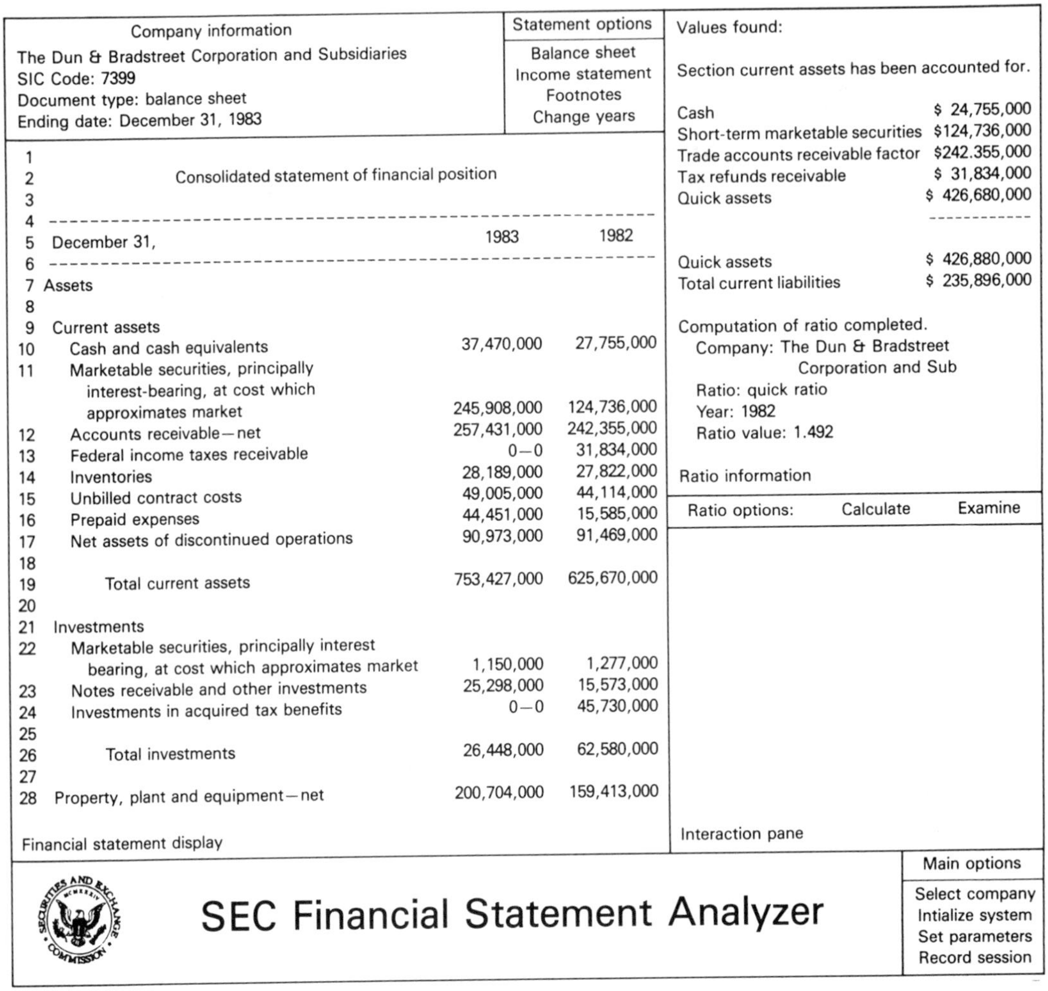

Company information	Statement options	Values found:
The Dun & Bradstreet Corporation and Subsidiaries SIC Code: 7399 Document type: balance sheet Ending date: December 31, 1983	Balance sheet Income statement Footnotes Change years	Section current assets has been accounted for. Cash $ 24,755,000 Short-term marketable securities $124,736,000 Trade accounts receivable factor $242.355,000 Tax refunds receivable $ 31,834,000 Quick assets $ 426,680,000

```
 1
 2                    Consolidated statement of financial position
 3
 4  ------------------------------------------------------------
 5   December 31,                              1983        1982
 6  ------------------------------------------------------------
 7  Assets
 8
 9  Current assets
10    Cash and cash equivalents              37,470,000   27,755,000
11    Marketable securities, principally
         interest-bearing, at cost which
         approximates market               245,908,000  124,736,000
12    Accounts receivable—net              257,431,000  242,355,000
13    Federal income taxes receivable             0—0    31,834,000
14    Inventories                           28,189,000   27,822,000
15    Unbilled contract costs               49,005,000   44,114,000
16    Prepaid expenses                      44,451,000   15,585,000
17    Net assets of discontinued operations 90,973,000   91,469,000
18
19         Total current assets            753,427,000  625,670,000
20
21  Investments
22    Marketable securities, principally interest
         bearing, at cost which approximates market  1,150,000  1,277,000
23    Notes receivable and other investments 25,298,000  15,573,000
24    Investments in acquired tax benefits        0—0   45,730,000
25
26         Total investments                26,448,000   62,580,000
27
28  Property, plant and equipment—net      200,704,000  159,413,000
```

Financial statement display

Quick assets $ 426,880,000
Total current liabilities $ 235,896,000

Computation of ratio completed.
   Company: The Dun & Bradstreet
                Corporation and Sub
   Ratio: quick ratio
   Year: 1982
   Ratio value: 1.492

Ratio information

Ratio options:	Calculate	Examine

Interaction pane

SEC Financial Statement Analyzer

Main options

Select company
Intialize system
Set parameters
Record session

Figure 6   FSA user interface.

of the operational FSA system; the integrated FSA–EDGAR system would pass statements to the FSA application directly from EDGAR.

User Interface

The overriding factor guiding the design of the interface was the desire to provide an interface that is both powerful and user friendly. In the case of FSA, power and user friendliness can be translated to functionality and flexibility. The capabilities required by the SEC analysts and that FSA provides are:

- The ability to analyze any company in the data base.
- The ability to view data stored in the system's data base. This data includes financial statements and the footnotes to those statements.
- The ability to calculate any ratio for a company as long as the necessary data is in the data base.
- The ability to monitor and review calculations made by the system.
- The ability for the user to provide input when the system encounters an ambiguous situation.

In order to provide these capabilities, the user interface is designed to be a financial analyst's workbench. The conversation between the analyst and the system is very flexible, with the analyst having a great deal of control over what the system should do.

To implement this flexibility, the user interface uses a large, high-resolution bit-mapped screen on the workstation. The screen layout is organized so that the analyst can see a large amount of information at once. With this format, the analyst can more quickly assimilate larger amounts of financial information. Figure 6 shows a sample screen after a ratio has been calculated.

SYSTEM RESULTS

Several criteria were used to evaluate the success of the FSA prototype. These criteria included the system's ability to locate and properly calculate the ratios, the ease with which new captions and ratios could be added to the system, and the system's capability of formatting the information so that it could be easily understood.

Financial statements for 30 companies were entered into the system. Ratio calculations were tested on each statement and footnote case. A total of 95 ratio calculations were tested, representing an even mix of balance sheet, income statement, and footnote interpretation. The results of those tests were:

Thirty balance sheet ratios: 29 correctly processed, 97% success rate.

Thirty income statement ratios: 29 correctly processed, 97% success rate.

Thirty-five footnote ratios: 31 correctly processed, 85% success rate.

Ninety-five total ratios: 89 correctly processed, 94% success rate.

Of the six cases that the system processed incorrectly, two were deemed ambiguous or very peculiar by the analysts in a manual review. The other four errors were instances where additional programming logic could be developed to correctly process them; one was a case of an imputed footnote with no dollar values that impacted the value of the original caption, and the other three were instances of footnotes with complex sentence structures.

Overall, the FSA system's ability to successfully process 94% of the ratios tested is favorable. The project's original goal was to achieve a success rate shaped by the "best efforts" possible within the time frame. These results clearly surpass what was envisioned by that objective.

INTEGRATION WITH EDGAR

The FSA prototype was developed to demonstrate the feasibility of using advanced automated techniques to analyze financial statements and footnotes. The current system is not intended to be an operational system. The type of work necessary to turn the system into an operational component of the EDGAR system falls into two categories: enhancement and integration.

Enhancements are those functional elements that are not part of the prototype but are either necessary components of an operational system or extensions of its functional capabilities. The prototype effort concentrated on the core of the financial analysis problem and intentionally did not address these enhancements.

Integration refers to the technical efforts necessary to turn FSA into an operational component of EDGAR. Integration issues address the technical architecture of the EDGAR–FSA application, namely, the hardware and software considerations necessary to enable the two systems to share data and the ability to invoke FSA through EDGAR.

ENHANCEMENTS

This section outlines various enhancements, some necessary and some desirable, to make FSA an operational system.

Translation of EDGAR Filings

One major enhancement necessary to make the prototype system operational is the development of a translation module. Such a module would allow FSA to use the financial statements and accompanying footnotes stored within EDGAR. FSA deals with financial tables that are in a spreadsheetlike representation and text that is in a simple ASCII string format. This representation allows for easy access of data (e.g., captions and amounts) from the tables and text from the footnotes. To analyze a company's filings without placing restrictions on the filer, FSA must be able to understand the format of the data stored by EDGAR and translate it into its required format.

The need for a translation module was recognized at the beginning of the FSA project. Because the problem was considered potentially difficult but definitely solvable, the prototype project concentrated its efforts on the more crucial parts of the analysis problem. For the purpose of the prototype, the financial tables and accompanying footnotes are manually entered and then translated by FSA. The person entering the data directs the translation process. In an operational system, FSA needs to be able to read the filings in the format stored by EDGAR and, without any manual assistance, translate them into its required format.

Additional Knowledge

The prototype system was developed using data from companies in the service industry. For the operational system, it would be necessary to study the characteristics of other industries to ensure the completeness of the current knowledge bases. Each industry is likely to have some unique characteristics, and it may be necessary to recognize knowledge about the specific industry when analyzing a company's financial statements. For example, manufacturing companies are likely to express their inventory much differently than banks. The effect of these differences creates either a single, more complete knowledge base or additional knowledge base pieces for each industry. In either case, the extensible, modular, object-oriented design of FSA allows additional knowledge such as this to be easily added to the system.

Other logical extensions of the FSA knowledge bases include additional ratios, expanded knowledge regarding particular captions and synonyms (especially those found in the income statement, which was not important to the prototype ratios), and additional schemas for captions that can be found in the footnotes.

Automatic Self-Enhancement

FSA is designed to know when it has insufficient knowledge. At these points, it has a facility to query the analyst for additional information. The capability to capture these responses and incorporate them into the system's knowledge bases would allow the system to independently handle more and more cases over time. This capability would be a logical and valuable enhancement to the present system. The development of this module could reduce the effort of expanding the knowledge, as previously described.

Increased Analysis Capabilities

The current FSA system computes standard ratios from a company's financial statements. An additional enhancement that would greatly add to the functionality of this process would be to use the results of the current system as the input to a more sophisticated analysis system. Such a system could contain qualitative "decision rules" or statistical analysis functions. It could use industry trend statistics, previous years' filings, and comparative corporations' data to help the user further analyze the significance of ratios calculated by the system.

Integration. FSA is currently a stand-alone system. It is implemented in the LISP programming language; uses KEE (Knowledge Engineering Environment), a development tool that supports object-oriented, knowledge-based architectures;

and runs on the Symbolics 3600 series LISP machine, a powerful single-user workstation. The sample test cases were entered manually and reside on storage local to the Symbolics computer. No communication interface currently exists between FSA and EDGAR.

In order to make FSA operational, it would be necessary to integrate it with EDGAR. Integration would enable communication interfaces to be established between the two systems. These interfaces would allow EDGAR users to invoke FSA and would allow the two systems to share necessary data.

Various alternatives exist for this level of integration, and the advantages and disadvantages of each must be examined in light of the overall architecture of the EDGAR–FSA system. Three alternative architectures are envisioned:

- Few users running the system on individual, specialized workstations.
- Primarily batch operation, with low-volume interactive use through EDGAR terminals.
- Primarily interactive, on-line use.

The first architecture suggests that the FSA application could continue to operate on the current Symbolics hardware or be ported to another sophisticated workstation with similar capabilities. The workstation would be linked to the SEC's IBM mainframe for the purpose of downloading financial data and uploading results. The analysts would call up specific statements on their individual workbenches for review.

In the second scenario, FSA would be a back-end batch-processing module for EDGAR. This module could operate on a workstation or be ported to a mainframe language or tool. The calculation of ratios for a set of financial statements would be triggered either by the receipt of new filings or explicit invocation by an EDGAR user. The calculation results would then be sorted in a financial data base to be accessed by EDGAR. In addition, an occasional on-line user could request analysis be done interactively.

The third alternative architecture would be to have FSA as an on-line, interactive system. In this case, a functionally distributed workstation architecture might not be financially feasible for high-volume use. A high-volume on-line architecture would necessitate that FSA reside on the mainframe.

FUTURE USES OF FSA TECHNIQUES

Many opportunities exist for minimizing the processing time and manual effort required for analyzing structured documents such as financial statements. In its pilot form, FSA used object-oriented techniques to successfully process (with 94% accuracy) information it interpreted from balance sheets and income statements. If brought to production, the capabilities of such a system would not only provide the benefits associated with turn-around time reduction and an increase in the financial analysts' productivity, but also would provide a means of efficiently and consistently applying certain government policies and regulations.

In January 1989, the SEC awarded the contract to build the long-awaited full-scale EDGAR system [16] that will within four years allow all firms to file electronically. When this foundation is completed, the infrastructure will be in place for FSA, ELOISE, as well as other advanced applications that capitalize on the newly captured repository of information.

FSA required two types of knowledge: (1) document format and English language knowledge and (2) extensive domain knowledge about the financial concepts, ratios, and terminology. Highly structured, consistently formatted documents that contain factual, nonstylistic language offer a high probability for successful automated interpretation. In turn, it may be easier to build a system to automate the interpretation process for this type of document. Similarly, a narrow domain restricts the opportunity for error in interpretation.

The natural-language processing techniques used in FSA can be applied to many business applications. DELICE, a system developed by Arthur Andersen for the French Ministry of Foreign Affairs (MFA), demonstrates the applicability of these techniques to another domain. DELICE assisted the MFA in interpreting birth, marriage and death acts for all French citizens abroad. The office of the MFA receives hundreds of requests for copies of individual acts daily. For legal reasons, they cannot send a photocopy; they must write a summary, or extract, providing the pertinent elements of the act. To reduce costs and improve their efficiency, DELICE was developed.

Recent advances in technology help to solve many of the integration issues initially faced in 1986 at the completion of FSA. Advances in interfaces to mainframe data bases, very large scale integrated design and hardware platforms, knowledge base development tools and object-oriented languages, and distributed architectures make the production implementation of FSA a much more viable task.

REFERENCES

1. C. Mui and W. E. McCarthy, "FSA:Applying AI Techniques to the Familiarization Phase of Financial Decision Making," *IEEE Expert*, February 1989, pp. 38–48.
2. H. A. Simon, *The New Science of Management Decision*, Harper Brothers, New York, 1960.
3. K. Ericsson and H. Simon, "Verbal Reports as Data," *Psychological Review*, Vol. 87, No. 3, 1980, pp. 215–251.
4. M. J. Bouwman, "Towards Expert Systems: The Analysis of Expert Financial Behavior," Technical Report, Department of Accounting, University of Oregon, Eugene, OR, 1985.
5. S. F. Biggs, "Financial Analysts' Information Search in the Assessment of Corporate Earning Power," *Accounting, Organizations and Society*, Vol. 9, No. 3/4, 1984, pp. 313–323.
6. M. J. Anderson, "Some Evidence on the Effect of Verbalization on Process," *Journal of Accounting Research*, Vol. 23, No. 2, 1985, pp. 843–852.

7. M. J. Anderson, "The Investment Decision—An Analysis Using Verbal Protocols," Ph.D. Dissertation, Michigan State University, East Lansing, MI, 1982, p. 85.

8. R. B. McElreath and C. D. Wiggins, "Using the Compustat Tapes in Financial Research: Problems and Solutions," *Financial Analysts Journal*, January/February 1984, pp. 71–76.

9. G. Foster, *Financial Statement Analysis*, Prentice-Hall, Englewood Cliffs, NJ, 1986.

10. Arthur Andersen & Co., "Final Report on the Financial Statement Analyzer to the Securities and Exchange Commission," Technical Report, Arthur Andersen & Co., Chicago, IL, December 1985.

11. C. E. Hewitt, "Viewing Control Structures as Patterns of Passing Messages," *Artificial Intelligence*, Vol. 8, No. 3, pp. 323–364.

12. B. E. Cushing, *Accounting Information Systems and Business Organizations*, Addison-Wesley, Reading, MA, 1982.

13. E. Rich, *Artificial Intelligence*, McGraw-Hill, New York, 1983, Chapter 7.

14. T. Winograd, *Language as a Cognitive Process: Syntax*, Vol. 1, Addison-Wesley, Reading, MA, 1983.

15. G. F. DeJong II, *Skimming Stories in Real Time: An Experiment in Integrated Understanding*, Ph.D. Dissertation, Yale University, New Haven, CT, 1979.

16. J. Matthew, "EDGAR Project Is Set," *Wall Street Computer Review*, Fall 1987, pp. 33–41.

7

The Development of an Expert System That Estimates Casualty Insurance Loss Reserves

Betty C. Horn

INTRODUCTION

This chapter describes the development of RESERVE, a rule-based expert system that estimates casualty insurance loss reserves. Loss reserves are liabilities incurred by insurers for unpaid claims arising from insured events. *Statement of Financial Accounting Standards No. 60* requires the liability to "be based on the estimated ultimate cost of settling the claims (including the effects of inflation and other societal and economic factors), using past experience adjusted for current trends, and other factors that would modify past experience" [1, para. 18].

The proper valuation of the loss reserve liability is of interest to numerous parties, including management, state insurance regulators, the Internal Revenue Service, the Securities and Exchange Commission, and public accountants who audit property/casualty insurers. Estimated loss reserves represent a significant portion of the balance sheet of a property/casualty insurer. In 1987, aggregate industry loss reserves were 58% of liabilities [2]. In the same year, loss and loss adjustment expenses were 78% of premiums earned [3].

RESERVE is a prototype expert system. Waterman [4] defines a prototype system as one that performs credibly across the entire problem but has been subjected to limited evaluation procedures. Two evaluations were performed on RESERVE and are described later in the chapter. Another limitation of RESERVE is that it estimates loss reserves for one line of casualty insurance, automobile liability insurance. The decision to model one line of insurance is discussed in a later section.

This chapter concentrates on the development process and is organized into three sections. First, the process of estimating loss reserves as described in the domain literature is presented. Second, the knowledge-engineering steps used to develop RESERVE are discussed. These steps include participant and problem identification, knowledge acquisition, knowledge representation, encoding, testing, and evaluation of RESERVE. Last, conclusions are presented and further development of RESERVE is explored.

ESTIMATING LOSS RESERVES

Several methods exist for estimating loss reserves. When historical data exist, loss reserves are most often estimated by projecting historical data. Peterson [5] discusses two projection methods. The first method projects historical loss data, or "development data." The second method uses separate projections of claim frequency and average loss severity. A claim is a unit of demand for payment arising from an insured event, and a loss is the dollar value of a claim.

The estimation process begins with reliable data bases of historical data. Casualty insurers accumulate historical development data for paid losses and for incurred losses to satisfy regulatory reporting requirements. However, paid claim counts and incurred claim counts data may not be accumulated, especially by small insurers.

The validity of using development data for projection purposes is a judgmental decision. Berquist and Sherman [6], Peterson [7], and Salzmann [8] have emphasized the need for judgment in (a) assessing the reliability of data bases, (b) interpreting data patterns and the effects of any changes in certain variables, (c) selecting development factors, (d) selecting the appropriate projection method, and (e) evaluating the reasonableness of the computed ultimate losses. The estimation process represented in RESERVE is for the judgments in items (b)–(e). RESERVE assumes that the data bases are reliable.

Data Bases

Historical data are grouped into data bases using two criteria: homogeneity and credibility. Homogeneity requires the grouping of losses and claims by similar attributes, such as reporting and payment patterns. A data base possesses credibility when the volume of data is sufficient to provide a reliable basis for statistical projection. Homogeneity is achieved by segregating data into smaller, homogeneous groups of losses and claims, but the data base must not be so small that credibility is sacrificed.

Casualty insurance companies maintain separate data bases for different lines of insurance: workers' compensation, general liability, professional malpractice, automobile liability, and so forth. Additionally, data bases are separated by liability and physical damage. These separations help achieve homogeneity because the reporting and payment periods differ significantly among the various types of coverages. For example, physical damage claims are generally settled more quickly than liability claims, and the losses are more easily determined. Liability claims have longer settlement periods because they may require the determination of fault and may involve litigation. Additionally, liability losses may include noneconomic damages, which are more difficult to estimate.

An Example of Estimation

Tables 1–3 present an example of the computational portions of estimating loss reserves by projecting historical paid losses. Table 1 is a data triangle of cumulative paid loss data with accident years on one axis and development periods on the other axis. The example is for data that will be fully paid in seven years, or 84 months. These data are used to estimate ultimate paid losses, which are projections of the total paid losses that will occur for each of the seven accident years displayed in the data triangle.

An estimation of loss reserves by projection of paid loss development data is presented in Tables 2 and 3. The development data in Table 1 are used to compute development factors, which are displayed in Table 2. Development factors are the multiplicative increases in the development data from period to period. In Table 2, a cell entry is computed from the development data in Table 1 by dividing the cumulative paid loss in a development period by the cumulative paid loss in the prior development period. For example, in Table 1, the 1986 accident year cumulative paid loss at 12 months is $53,995 and at 24 months is $121,470. The development factor of 2.250 shown in Table 2 for 12–24 months in accident year 1986 is computed by dividing $121,470 by $53,995.

Several methods exist for computing the development factors to be used in the estimation. Computational methods in Table 2 include a simple average, an average excluding high and low, and the average of a judgmentally selected number of recent years. The selection of an appropriate computational method is a judgmental decision. One factor that influences the selection of the computational method is the trend observed in the development factors within a development period (down a column). When paid loss development factors are being selected, the trend in the claim closure rate may also be considered. For example, if the claim closure rate is increasing, the paid loss data in recent years are more fully developed than the data in earlier years. When incurred loss development factors are being selected, the trend in case reserve adequacy is considered. For example, if case reserve adequacy is stable and the incurred loss development factors are increasing, then a computational

TABLE 1. Cumulative Paid Loss Data by Months of Development (U.S. dollars)

Accident Year	12 months	24 months	36 months	48 months	60 months	72 months	84 months
1981	26,383	53,666	62,500	65,355	66,916	67,038	67,135
1982	31,034	59,324	68,678	71,978	73,467	74,002	
1983	36,425	71,482	80,546	85,910	87,168		
1984	39,238	79,327	91,515	95,935			
1985	42,861	95,673	111,338				
1986	53,995	121,470					
1987	66,560						

TABLE 2. Paid Loss Factors by Months of Development

Accident year	12–24 months	24–36 months	36–48 months	48–60 months	60–72 months	72–84 months	84–96 months
1981	2.034	1.165	1.046	1.024	1.002	1.001	
1982	1.912	1.158	1.048	1.021	1.007		
1983	1.962	1.127	1.067	1.015			
1984	2.022	1.154	1.048				
1985	2.232	1.164					
1986	2.250						
Average	2.069	1.153	1.052	1.020	1.005	1.001	
Average excluding high/low	2.063	1.158	1.048	1.021			
Three-year average	2.168	1.148	1.054	1.020	1.005	1.001	
Selected	2.168	1.148	1.054	1.020	1.005	1.001	1.000
Cumulative	2.692	1.242	1.082	1.026	1.006	1.001	1.000

method that gives more weight to the data of recent years would be used. In Table 2, the three-year average was selected for demonstrating the computations.

Changes in numerous variables can affect the validity of using historical data to project ultimate losses. These changes cause the conditions in the current period to differ from the conditions that existed when the data were accumulated. These variables are classified into three groups: (a) exposure, (b) internal, and (c) external. Exposure variables affect the amount of risk an insurer underwrites. Exposure variables include the quality of insured risks, volume fluctuations, net retention limits, policy limits, and business mix. An example of business mix in automobile liability insurance is the relative proportion of personal and commercial coverages. The net retention limit is the amount of risk that the insurer does not reinsure. Internal variables arise from changes in claim processing and payment procedures within a company. Internal variables include changes in data processing, accounting, claim philosophy, and case-reserving practices. The external variables are legislation, judicial decisions, economic inflation, and social inflation. Social inflation arises from changing societal views of the obligation to injured parties. The effects of changes in all of these variables are difficult to quantify, but loss data may be adjusted or development factors may be adjusted. Judgment is required to determine when an adjustment is needed and to determine the magnitude of any adjustment.

The example in Table 2 does not include any adjustments for changes in variables. The cumulative factors shown on the bottom row of Table 2 are computed by cumulative multiplication of the selected development factors. Multiplication begins with the oldest development period. In this example, $1.000 \times 1.001 = 1.001$, $1.001 \times 1.005 = 1.006$, and so forth. The cumulative development factors are used to project ultimate paid losses (Table 3) by multiplying the cumulative factors by the cumulative paid losses (Table 1) for each accident year. Total paid

TABLE 3. Projected Ultimate Losses and Estimated Loss Reserves (U.S. dollars)

Accident Year	Cumulative Paid Loss* (a)	Cumulative Development Factor† (b)	Projected Ultimate Paid Loss [(c) = (a) × (b)]	Estimated Loss Reserves [(c) − (a)]
1981	67,135	1.000	67,135	0
1982	74,002	1.001	74,077	75
1983	87,168	1.006	87,691	523
1984	95,935	1.026	98,430	2,495
1985	111,338	1.082	120,468	9,130
1986	121,470	1.242	150,866	29,396
1987	66,560	2.692	179,179	112,619
Total estimated loss reserves				154,238

* From Table 1.
† From Table 2.

losses are subtracted from the projected ultimate paid losses to compute the loss reserve liability.

The example presented in Tables 1–3 is for paid loss data. The same process is performed for incurred loss data and, if claim counts data are available, for projected claims. After the various projections are computed, a projection method is selected. Selection of the projection method requires judging how well the assumptions of the various methods are satisfied.

Reasonability tests are performed on the selected ultimate losses. These tests consist of comparisons of implied loss ratios and implied average severities with industry averages and with the insurer's historical data. The loss ratio is the ratio of ultimate losses to earned premiums. The loss ratio is implied when the estimated ultimate loss is used in the ratio. Implied average loss severity is computed by dividing the estimated ultimate losses by the projected number of total claims. Judgment is required to assess the reasonableness of the implied losses and to determine the extent of any adjustment when the selected losses are assessed as unreasonable.

KNOWLEDGE ENGINEERING

Knowledge engineering is the process of developing an expert system. The knowledge engineering steps include participant and problem identification, knowledge acquisition, knowledge representation, encoding, testing, and evaluation. Buchanan et al. [9] have described the iterative nature of developing an expert system. In developing RESERVE, the steps of knowledge acquisition, knowledge representation, encoding, and testing were iterative as the system evolved. The knowledge-engineering steps in the development of RESERVE are described next.

Participant and Problem Identification

The actuarial consulting group of an international accounting firm participated in the development of RESERVE. The participants consisted of the domain expert, whose estimation process is represented in RESERVE, and additional actuaries, who assisted in evaluating the system. The firm also supplied cases to be used in developing and evaluating RESERVE. The domain expert is a Fellow in the Casualty Actuarial Society, is a member of the American Academy of Actuaries, and had 9 years experience as a property/casualty actuary. This level of experience is consistent with research results that approximately 10 years of study and experience are required to be recognized as an expert [10].

The researcher performed the knowledge engineering functions. The researcher's first activities were to read extensively in the loss reserve literature and to discuss the estimation of loss reserves with several casualty actuaries, professors of insurance, and public accountants who audit property/casualty insurers. From these activities the researcher gained a general understanding of the loss reserve estimation process, including the computational and judgmental aspects that were discussed in the previous example of loss reserve estimation.

The literature revealed that insurers maintain separate data bases for different lines of insurance. The researcher tentatively decided that a single line of insurance would be appropriate for an initial attempt to model the estimation of loss reserves. The researcher narrowed the choice to workers' compensation or automobile liability using two criteria. First, the line should be large relative to other lines of insurance. Smaller lines of business, such as fidelity, inland marine, ocean marine, and others were rejected based upon the size of the line of business. Second, a liability line should be modeled because the physical damage lines are more easily estimated using appraisals, engineering reports, and other independent data. The liability lines that are the most difficult to estimate due to delays in discovery and evolving exposures are professional malpractice, product liability, and general liability. These lines were eliminated because of their complexity.

The first meeting between the domain expert and the researcher resulted in several accomplishments. First, the concept of an expert system was explained to the domain expert. Second, the single line of automobile liability insurance was selected to be modeled. This decision was based upon the researcher's tentative conclusion and the domain expert's preference. Third, after reviewing the list of literature that the researcher had read, the domain expert recommended some additional literature. By reading the literature preferred by the domain expert, the researcher became familiar with the terminology used by the domain expert prior to beginning the knowledge acquisition phase of development.

Knowledge Acquisition

Numerous interviews with the domain expert were conducted over a period of several months. The interviews were taped, which served as a source of reference for rule development. The structure of each interview was planned, and the researcher followed

Waldron's [11] guidelines on planning appropriate types of questions. Three phases were planned for each interview. First, the expert reviewed RESERVE at its then current stage of development by reading printouts of RESERVE's knowledge base and of RESERVE's reports. Second, the domain expert introduced new knowledge. Third, when the researcher believed that enough knowledge had been acquired to represent the new knowledge in the knowledge base, the interview was terminated, the next interview was scheduled, and the topic of the next interview was established.

The initial approach for knowledge acquisition was the domain expert's explanation of the estimation process using a hypothetical case. This approach allowed the researcher to clarify concepts and processes as the expert proceeded through the case. After the researcher had grasped the general structure of the domain expert's estimation process, the researcher diagrammed the process. Although this diagram was refined at subsequent meetings with the domain expert, it served as a basis for identifying variables and their respective values and for segmenting the estimation process into four judgmental subproblems as follows:

1. Interpreting data patterns and the effects of any changes in variables.
2. Selecting development factor computational methods.
3. Selecting the projection method.
4. Evaluating the reasonableness of the computed ultimate losses.

These four judgmental subproblems were identified in the estimation example presented previously. Separate systems were developed for each of the subproblems, and subsequent interviews focused on acquiring the knowledge to solve a subproblem. The four separate systems were combined into RESERVE after the last subproblem was modeled. A diagram of RESERVE is presented later. Three advantages of developing separate expert systems for each subproblem were identified by the researcher: (a) concepts that affected an individual subproblem were more easily identified, (b) the expert could concentrate on all possible situations within the subproblem, and (c) each of the four systems was easier to debug.

A matrix technique proved to be efficient for some areas of knowledge acquisition. This technique evolved when the domain expert was explaining the selection of development factor computational methods. The domain expert sketched a matrix to show how different combinations of values for multiple variables caused different conclusions. For example, the trend in paid loss development factors (down the column in Table 2) may be increasing and the rate of claim closure is unknown. This combination results in using the three-year average for the paid loss development factors at 12, 24, and 36 months. In RESERVE the permissible values for the trend in paid loss development factors are stable, erratic, increasing, and decreasing. The permissible values for the rate of claim closure are stable, accelerating, decelerating, and unknown. The rate of claim closure is unknown when claim counts data are not available. The domain expert used a matrix of all possible combinations to ensure that all situations were included in the knowledge base. The matrix technique was used extensively to determine that all variable values and their interactions with other variables had been considered in developing the knowledge base.

Knowledge Representation and Encoding

The knowledge in RESERVE is represented as if–then rules. RESERVE is modeled on EXSYS, an expert system development tool that contains all of the elements of an expert system except the knowledge base. EXSYS was selected because of its abilities to activate an external program from any rule and to print a report from any rule. These two abilities are used in RESERVE to activate LOTUS 1-2-3 for computations and to print reports of intermediate decisions that supply input data for the LOTUS worksheet.

RESERVE uses a forward-chaining inference structure. Forward chaining in EXSYS causes each rule to be evaluated in the order of occurrence. This structure was used for two reasons. First, the subproblems must be sequentially solved. Second, one of the planned evaluations of RESERVE was for another actuary to review RESERVE's reasoning process. Forward chaining facilitated the reasoning evaluation by requiring the researcher to sequence the rules in a logical order. The following description of RESERVE reveals the sequential nature of the estimation process.

Three software packages are used in the estimation process. Multiple software is used because both judgment and computation are required. RESERVE projects ultimate paid losses and ultimate incurred losses. The projection of ultimate losses using claim frequency and average severity is not modeled in RESERVE because claim counts data are not always available. When claim counts are available, RESERVE uses the information in selecting a projection method and in the reasonability tests. The flow of the estimation process through the three software packages consists of the following:

1. The data triangles are entered into a loss reserve computational software package. This software computes development factors using multiple methods and also computes various ratios and averages from the data triangles. The computational software is not used again in the estimation process.

2. When RESERVE begins an estimation, RESERVE queries the user about the particular case being estimated. The user inputs values for data base attributes, for data patterns, and for exposure, internal, and external variables. When RESERVE has sufficient information to select a development factor computational method that is appropriate for the case being evaluated, a development factor report is printed and LOTUS 1-2-3 is activated. A sample development factor report is presented in Appendix A.

3. The actual numerical development factors were computed in step 1 (see Table 2 for an example). The selected numerical development factors are entered on the LOTUS worksheet, and projected ultimate claims, ultimate paid losses, and ultimate incurred losses are calculated. The user notes which projection method for ultimate losses results in the higher loss. When the user exits LOTUS 1-2-3, RESERVE is reentered at the rule that generated the development factor report.

4. The next query by RESERVE asks which loss projection method, paid or incurred, is the higher. The user inputs the answer based upon the user's observation in step 3. RESERVE now has sufficient information to select the loss projection method and to specify any needed adjustments to the selected ultimate losses. These adjustments are for data that do not reflect the effects of certain reinsurance contracts and for legislation and judicial decisions. The source of adjustments for legislation and judicial decisions is discussed later. RESERVE prepares a selected ultimate report, and LOTUS 1-2-3 is again activated. Appendix A contains a sample of the selected ultimate report.

5. Selected ultimate losses are calculated on the LOTUS 1-2-3 worksheet. The reasonability tests data are also calculated at this step, and the reasonability tests data are passed through a file to RESERVE for use in the next step.

6. RESERVE begins a sequence of 12 reasonability tests that examines the consistency between the knowledge about changing variables and the reasonability tests data. Reasonability tests are discussed in more detail later. When a rule that evaluates a reasonability test is true, RESERVE prints a reasonability test report that identifies the test and that specifies an adjustment to selected ultimate losses. A sample of this report is also contained in Appendix A.

7. LOTUS is activated when RESERVE determines that an adjustment to the selected ultimate losses is needed. The specified adjustment is made, and the reasonability tests data are recalculated. The values for the reasonability tests are again passed by a file to RESERVE, and the rule for the next reasonability test is evaluated.

Steps 6 and 7 are repeated until all 12 tests are evaluated. The last test always activates LOTUS regardless of the need for an adjustment to allow the user to print a copy of the LOTUS worksheet. The worksheet documents the selected development factors, the selected ultimate losses, and the adjustments made because of the reasonability tests.

8. RESERVE then queries the user for total selected ultimate losses, total cumulative paid losses, and carried loss reserves to make its final conclusion as to loss reserve overstatement or understatement. The final output report of RESERVE is also included in Appendix A.

Figure 1 presents a diagram of the estimation process, and Table 4 presents a list of the individual variables classified as exposure, internal, and external. Each type of variable has the potential to materially affect the estimation of loss reserves. Changes in the different types of variables, however, affect the estimation process in different ways.

Exposure variables are variables that affect the amount of risk that a company underwrites. When exposures are increasing or decreasing, projections of historical data will not reflect the increase or decrease. RESERVE considers changes in exposure

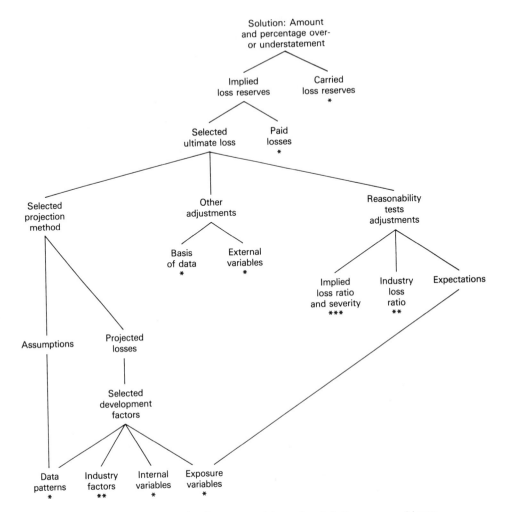

Figure 1 RESERVE's estimation process: (*) user input; (**) programmed input; (***) computed input.

variables that occurred in both the current year, which is the date at which loss reserves are being estimated, and the prior year. Changes in exposure variables affect the estimation process in two ways. First, for significant changes in earned premium growth, in net retention limits, and in the proportions of personal and commercial business, the development factors are adjusted.

Second, changes in exposure variables affect the reasonability tests by creating expectations for changes in implied loss severities and implied loss ratios. Implied loss severities are average severities for each accident year and are computed by dividing selected ultimate losses by projected ultimate claims. Thus, the severities are implied from the projected losses and the projected claims. The loss ratio is

TABLE 4. Individual Variables Within Each Variable Type

Exposure variables
    Rate levels
    Growth
    Net retention limits
    Policy limits
    Business mix
        Personal/commercial coverage
        Geographic territories
        Pools and associations
Internal variables
    Data processing or accounting
    Claim philosophy
    Case-reserving practices
        Claim department personnel
        Definition of a claim
External variables
    Legislative
    Judicial

the ratio of losses to earned premiums and is computed for each accident year. When selected ultimate losses are used in the numerator, the ratio is an implied loss ratio. These expectations, which arise from significant changes in exposure variables, are the bases of the reasonability tests that examine the consistency between the changes in exposure variables and the implied data. When the implied severities and implied loss ratios fall outside an expected range or changes in exposure variables are not consistent with the implied data, the current year or the prior year selected ultimate loss is adjusted.

Two effects may occur from changes in internal variables: (1) the amounts of case reserves may change and (2) the timing of case reserves may change. These two effects bias the data for projection purposes because the development in the period of the change is not comparable to the development in prior periods. When RESERVE concludes that the amounts of case reserves or the timing of case reserves or both have changed, an adjustment is made to the 12- or 24-month development factors selected by RESERVE.

Changes in external variables include legislation or regulatory changes, judicial decisions, economic inflation, and social inflation. Social inflation and economic inflation are handled implicitly in RESERVE by constructing rules that incorporate the domain expert's expectation of percentage increases in average outstanding reserves and implied severities. The inclusion of inflation expectations in the rules creates the need to update the knowledge base annually as social and economic conditions change.

Legislative and judicial changes may arise in any of the states or in any relevant legal jurisdiction. It was impractical to obtain this knowledge for a prototype expert system. RESERVE asks the user to provide any needed adjustment to selected ultimate losses to reflect the effect of any legislation or judicial decisions on the specific case being evaluated. The intended user of RESERVE, at its present stage of development, is either an actuary who possesses this knowledge or a user who has obtained this knowledge from an actuary.

Testing

Testing was a continuous part of the development process. More structured evaluations of RESERVE were conducted after the completion of RESERVE. Criteria were established to determine when RESERVE would be considered to be complete and the evaluations would be performed. These criteria were:

1. The factors and procedures discussed by the Committee on Loss Reserves [12] were explicitly considered. These factors and procedures are listed in Appendix B.
2. RESERVE's estimation was acceptable to the domain expert.
3. The test cases included all major variable changes within the domain.

RESERVE was tested in the early stages of development using the hypothetical cases introduced by the domain expert. As each subproblem of the estimation process was modeled, the system was tested for its ability to derive the theoretically correct solution for all specified input values. Actual loss reserve cases were then used to test RESERVE.

The participating accounting firm provided seven actual cases from three different offices. Test case data consisted of data triangles and a completed input checklist. This checklist, which was developed by the researcher and the domain expert, gathers knowledge about (a) changes in exposure, internal, and external variables for the specific case; (b) the data bases; and (c) the original actuary's estimate and the entity's estimate of loss reserves. The input checklist is presented in Appendix C.

The test cases contained a variety of variable changes. Exposure variable changes in the test cases included significant changes in growth, rate levels, net retention limits, policy limits, and business mix. Two cases had external variable changes arising from legislation. None of the test cases had external variable changes arising from judicial decisions. The domain expert stated that precedent-setting judicial changes are not common in automobile liability. Although the researcher specifically requested cases with a variety of internal variable changes, none of the test cases had significant internal variable changes. Again, the domain expert stated that these changes do not occur frequently.

Data base attributes also varied among the test cases. Three test cases had claim counts data. Two test cases had separate data bases by subline. The sublines of automobile liability are bodily injury, property damage liability, personal injury protection, medical payments, and uninsured motorists' coverage. The sublines were combined to test RESERVE, which estimates loss reserves for the aggregate of the automobile liability sublines. All of the test cases used net retained data, which are loss data net of reinsurance recoverable. Some of the data were combined for personal and commercial coverages, and some represented only personal or commercial coverage. RESERVE can estimate loss reserves for either combined or separated data bases for personal and commercial coverage. The number of months of data in the test cases ranged from 72 to 132 months. The domain expert used 72 months as the minimum development period for automobile liability insurance.

RESERVE was used to estimate loss reserves for each test case. The domain expert reviewed both RESERVE's estimation process and RESERVE's estimate of loss reserves. When RESERVE's estimate was not acceptable to the domain expert, the rules were refined to handle the specific test case situation. Comparisons of RESERVE's estimates with the original actuary's estimates revealed that RESERVE's estimates were not consistently over or under the actual estimates made in practice.

Evaluations

Two evaluations of RESERVE were conducted. The first evaluation was a reasoning evaluation, which consisted of a second actuary reviewing RESERVE's reasoning. This actuary had 14 years experience and is a Fellow in the Casualty Actuarial Society. The researcher met with the reasoning evaluator and provided a written explanation of the structure of RESERVE, a printout of RESERVE's knowledge base, listings of the variables and the variables' values, and some test cases. The researcher requested the reasoning evaluator to comment on any aspect of RESERVE, including (a) the logic of RESERVE's estimation process, (b) the omission or inclusion of variables, (c) the variables' values, and (d) the terminology used.

The reasoning evaluator provided several suggestions concerning business mix variables, data base attributes, dollar-weighted development factors, and the effect of timing of payments. When the test cases possessed the attributes needed to evaluate the suggestions, the effects of the suggestions on RESERVE's estimates were determined. These effects either were insignificant or, in one case, changed the estimate in the wrong direction. Each suggestion was then discussed with the domain expert. The domain expert and the researcher agreed that RESERVE should not be modified at this time for the reasoning evaluator's suggestions. However, further development and testing of RESERVE may reveal that these suggestions improve RESERVE's estimates.

The second evaluation of RESERVE was a performance evaluation, which compared RESERVE's estimates with human experts' estimates. Three additional actuaries, referred to as "performance evaluators," participated in the performance evaluation. Six new cases from three different offices of the accounting firm were randomly assigned to the performance evaluators. Each evaluator interpreted the data pattern trends for input into RESERVE. After the researcher used RESERVE to estimate loss reserves, the case data, output reports, and LOTUS worksheets were returned to the evaluators. The researcher met with the performance evaluators to discuss their evaluations of RESERVE's estimates and to obtain their estimate of loss reserves for their assigned cases.

Table 5 presents comparisons of RESERVE's ultimate loss estimate with the

TABLE 5. RESERVE's Estimates Compared with the Performance Evaluators' Estimates

	Percentage over (under) Original Actuary		RESERVE over (under) Performance Evaluator
Case	RESERVE Using Performance Evaluators' Values	Performance Evaluators' Estimate	
A	2.2	(0.2)	2.4
B	5.4	(1.2)	6.6
C	0.6	0.1	0.5
D	1.8	1.0	0.8
E	1.9	11.1	(9.2)
F	(4.4)	(4.4)	0.0

performance evaluator's estimate. The estimate is stated as a percentage difference from the original actuary's estimate. Use of the original actuary's estimate, which was made in actual practice, does not imply that this estimate is more accurate than either RESERVE's estimate or the performance evaluator's estimate.

Ultimate loss was used as the basis of comparison because the proportion of ultimate loss that has been paid distorts comparison of the loss reserve liability. The higher the proportion of ultimate loss that has been paid, the greater the percentage difference in the loss reserve liability. For example, if RESERVE estimated ultimate losses of $52,000 and an actuary estimated $50,000, RESERVE's estimate would be 4% larger. If cumulative paid losses were $40,000, then RESERVE's estimated loss reserve liability would be $12,000 and the actuary's estimated loss reserve liability would be $10,000, and RESERVE's estimate would be 20% larger. If the cumulative paid losses were $30,000, then RESERVE's estimated loss reserve liability would be 10% larger than the actuary's estimate. The performance evaluators concurred that ultimate loss is a better basis for comparison than the loss reserve liability.

The performance evaluators considered the differences for cases C, D, and F to be insignificant. The performance evaluator for cases A and B stated that RESERVE used incorrect development factors in older development periods. RESERVE used average industry factors for these cases in older development periods because of a data pattern value assigned by the performance evaluator. The data for cases A and B revealed that this was incorrect because the data were fully developed after 36 months, and a development factor of 1.00 should have been used. RESERVE was subsequently modified to correct this error. New estimates were made for cases A and B, with differences of (1.3) and 5.7, respectively.

RESERVE's estimate for case E was significantly lower than the performance evaluator's estimate, although both were larger than the original actuary's estimate. The difference was attributed to a growth rate greater than 400%. RESERVE contains rules that adjust for growth rates, but the largest increment is for growth of 75% or greater. This result indicates the need to either refine the rules to handle more extreme changes or restrict the use of RESERVE when extreme changes have occurred.

TABLE 6.   RESERVE's First Estimate Compared with RESERVE's Second Estimate

| | Percentage over (under) Original Actuary | | |
Case	With Domain Expert's Values	With Performance Evaluators' Values	Differences Caused by Data Pattern Values
A	(1.5)	(1.5)*	0.0
B	1.4	4.5*	3.1
C	(0.6)	0.6	1.2
D	(1.1)	1.8	2.9
E	1.9	1.9	0.0
F	(4.4)	(4.4)	0.0

* After rule modification discussed in text.

RESERVE's estimates were larger than the original actuary's estimate for five of the six evaluation cases. Because the test cases had not revealed a conservative bias in RESERVE, the researcher obtained the domain expert's data pattern values for the evaluation cases. These data pattern values were used to estimate loss reserves a second time with RESERVE. A comparison of RESERVE's second estimates with RESERVE's first estimates are presented in Table 6. Differences occurred in three cases and ranged from 1.2 to 3.1%. These differences indicate a need to either train the user of RESERVE or to develop additional rules to interpret data patterns or both.

CONCLUSIONS

This chapter has presented the development and evaluation of RESERVE, a prototype expert system for estimating automobile liability insurance loss reserves. The development of RESERVE required numerous interviews with one domain expert and continuous testing of the system throughout the development process. Two evaluations of RESERVE were conducted. The first evaluation consisted of a second domain expert's review of RESERVE's reasoning process. This evaluation resulted in several suggested improvements to RESERVE. The second evaluation was conducted to assess RESERVE's performance in estimating new cases. RESERVE showed credible performance in this evaluation. Both evaluations identified areas for further development that should improve RESERVE's estimates.

A limitation of RESERVE at its current stage of development is that it represents the estimation process of one domain expert and is inherently limited to that domain expert's experience and knowledge. The estimation process of RESERVE may not be generalizable to other human experts.

Further development of RESERVE will improve its performance. First, the improvements noted from the evaluations could be incorporated. Second, the involvement of additional actuaries will expand the experiences that are represented in RESERVE's knowledge base. Third, additional methods of estimating loss reserves, such as projecting average claim frequency and average loss severity, might improve RESERVE's estimations. Testing RESERVE's ability to estimate loss reserves for a broader range of case situations should be a part of additional development.

Continued development of RESERVE will require additional evaluations that are appropriate for the development stage. A future evaluation that might be appropriate is a "blind" evaluation [13]. A blind evaluation would use judges who would not know the source of the estimates. This type of evaluation appears appropriate because the correct estimation of loss reserves is not known.

The scope of RESERVE could also be expanded. Possible expansions include evaluating the reasonableness of the data bases, estimating automobile liability loss reserves by subline, and estimating loss reserves for other lines of insurance. Any expansions of RESERVE should be based upon a cost–benefit analysis of developing a highly refined expert system that estimates loss reserves. A cost–benefit analysis should consider implementation and maintenance issues and their costs. Implementation and maintenance issues are beyond the scope of this initial development of RESERVE.

APPENDIX A: RESERVE'S OUTPUT REPORTS

Development Factor Report

Case is SAMPLE

PAID LOSS DEVELOPMENT FACTORS

For paid loss development factors at 12, 24, and 36 months use an average of three methods.

For a paid loss development factor at 48 months use an average of three methods.

For a paid loss development factor at 60 months use an average of three methods.

For a paid loss development factor at 72 months use an average of three methods.

For a paid loss development factor at 84 months use an average of three methods.

For a paid loss development factor at 96 months use an industry factor of 1.01.

For a paid loss development factor at 108 months and over use an industry factor of 1.00.

INCURRED LOSS DEVELOPMENT FACTORS

For incurred loss development factors at 12, 24, and 36 months use an average of three methods.

For incurred loss development factors at 48 and 60 months use an average of three methods.

For an incurred loss development factor at 72 months use an average of three methods.

For an incurred loss development factor at 84 months use an average of three methods.

For an incurred loss development factor at 96 months and over use 1.00.

ADJUSTMENT TO SELECTED DEVELOPMENT FACTORS

The adjustment to the development factors at 12 months is 1.05.

The adjustment to the development factors at 24 months is 1.00.

REPORTED CLAIM DEVELOPMENT FACTORS

Use simple average for all periods.

Selected Ultimate Report

Case is SAMPLE

SELECTION OF PROJECTION METHODS

For selected ultimate use 25% paid and 75% incurred.

ADJUSTMENTS TO SELECTED ULTIMATE LOSS

An increased limits adjustment factor is not needed.
A legislation adjustment factor is not needed.
A judicial adjustment factor is not needed.
Any needed adjustments are user provided.

Reasonability Test Report

Case is SAMPLE

REASONABLENESS TEST ADJUSTMENT

Adjustment is needed for reasonability test NONE; tests are done, print the LOTUS worksheet.

Report of RESERVE's Estimate of Loss Reserves

Case is SAMPLE

RESULTS

Loss reserves are understated; probability is 100/100.

Selected ultimate = 777,846
Paid losses = 623,608
Implied loss reserves = 154,238
Carried loss reserves = 140,000
Carried loss reserve understatement = 14,238
Percentage loss reserve understatement = 0.0923

EXAMINATION OF VARIABLES

Current year change in exposure variables is significant.
Prior year change in exposure variables is none or insignificant.
Changes in internal variables are none or insignificant.
Changes in external variables are none or insignificant.

APPENDIX B: FACTORS AND PROCEDURES OF THE COMMITTEE ON LOSS RESERVES

FACTORS

1. Homogeneity
2. Credibility
3. Data availability
4. Emergence patterns
5. Settlement patterns
6. Development patterns
7. Frequency and severity
8. Reopened claims potential
9. Aggregate limits
10. Collateral sources
11. Reinsurance
12. Pools and associations
13. Operational changes
14. Changes in loss distribution
15. External influences
16. Reasonableness

PROCEDURES

1. Data organization
2. Loss-reserving techniques

APPENDIX C: INPUT CHECKLISTS FOR RESERVE

Current Year

Case Name (or Number) _____
Year _____

The purpose of this checklist is to obtain data input to test an expert system that evaluates automobile liability loss reserves.

CHANGES IN VARIABLES IN CURRENT YEAR

I. Exposure variables
   A. Rate levels have
     _____ increased 20% or less or decreased 10% or less
     _____ increased >20%
     _____ decreased >10%
   B. Net retention limits have
     _____ not changed
     _____ increased
     _____ decreased
   C. Policy limits sold have
     _____ not changed
     _____ increased
     _____ decreased
   D. Policy limits are predominantly
     _____ in excess of net retention limits
     _____ below net retention limits
   E. Business Mix
     Geographic territories have
     _____ not changed
     _____ been added
     _____ been deleted
     The rate level of *added* geographic territories when compared to the rate level of the prior territories is
     _____ comparable
     _____ higher
     _____ lower
     The rate level of *deleted* geographic territories when compared to the rate level of the prior territories is
     _____ comparable
     _____ higher
     _____ lower

The proportion of personal to commercial coverage has

_____ not changed

_____ changed with increasing commercial

_____ changed with increasing personal

The participation in voluntary or involuntary pools or associations is

_____ none

_____ participates and handles claims

_____ participates with claim assessment by the pool or association

The amount of participation in any pool or association for which the company handles the claims has

_____ not significantly changed

_____ changed with comparable rated business

_____ increased with higher rated business

_____ increased with lower rated business

_____ decreased with higher rated business

_____ decreased with lower rated business

II. Internal variables

   A. Case-reserving practices

   Claim adjustors have

   _____ not changed significantly

   _____ changed internally

   _____ changed from outside to inside adjustors

   _____ changed from inside to outside adjustors

   Definition of a claim unit has

   _____ not changed

   _____ changed

   B. Claim philosophy has

   _____ not changed

   _____ changed

   C. Data-processing or accounting changes during the period are

   _____ none or insignificant

   _____ significant

   The backlog of cases has

   _____ not changed significantly

   _____ increased

   _____ decreased

III. External variables

   A. Any legislation during all periods is

   _____ none or insignificant

   _____ significant

   If significant, please specify the adjustment factor(s) that should be used to adjust ultimate losses. The accident years to which the adjustment factor applies should also be specified:

B. Any judicial decisions during all periods are

_____ none or insignificant

_____ significant

If significant, please specify the adjustment factor(s) that should be used to adjust ultimate losses. The accident years to which the adjustment factor applies should also be specified:

DATA BASE ATTRIBUTES

I. Basis for data is

_____ basic limits

_____ net retention limits

_____ gross limits

If basis for data is gross limits, please specify the adjustment factor(s) that should be used to adjust ultimate losses for quota share treaties or other reinsurance contracts:

II. Homogeneity

A. The data bases are (check all applicable situations)

_____ separate by coverage (PIP, BI, PD, etc.)

_____ combined for all automobile liability coverage per the statutory annual statements

_____ combined for personal and commercial and for all geographic territories

_____ separate for personal and commercial

_____ separate by geographic territories

_____ separate for personal and commercial and by geographic territories

Note: It is assumed that the data bases were homogeneous in the prior periods. RESERVE will query for changes that decrease homogeneity because of a changing business mix.

III. Credibility

(*Note*: It is assumed that sufficient volume exists for the data bases to be credible.)

OTHER INPUT DATA

I. Actuary's incurred but not reported (IBNR), or Selected Ultimate, or Implied Reserve (on same bases as data):

II. Carried IBNR, or Book Ultimate, or Carried Reserve (on same bases as data):

III. Please describe any other factors considered when this case was evaluated.

Prior Year

Case Name (or Number) _____

Year _____

CHANGES IN VARIABLES IN PRIOR YEAR

A. Rate levels have
_____ increased 20% or less or decreased 10% or less
_____ increased >20%
_____ decreased >10%

B. Net retention limits have
_____ not changed
_____ increased
_____ decreased

C. Policy limits sold have
_____ not changed
_____ increased
_____ decreased

D. Policy limits are predominantly
_____ in excess of net retention limits
_____ below net retention limits

E. Business mix
Geographic territories have
_____ not changed
_____ been added
_____ been deleted
The rate level of *added* geographic territories when compared to the rate level of the prior territories is
_____ comparable
_____ higher
_____ lower
The rate level of *deleted* geographic territories when compared to the rate level of the prior territories is
_____ comparable
_____ higher
_____ lower
The proportion of personal to commercial coverage has
_____ not changed
_____ changed with increasing commercial
_____ changed with increasing personal
The participation in voluntary or involuntary pools or associations is
_____ none
_____ participates and handles claims
_____ participates with claim assessment by the pool or association

The amount of participation in any pool or association for which the company handles claims has

_____ not significantly changed

_____ changed with comparably rated business

_____ increased with higher rated business

_____ increased with lower rated business

_____ decreased with higher rated business

_____ decreased with lower rated business

ACKNOWLEDGMENT

This chapter is based on my doctoral dissertation at Georgia State University. I appreciate the advice and support of my dissertation committee members. I also thank the American Institute of Certified Public Accountants for the doctoral dissertation grant that supported this research.

REFERENCES

1. Financial Accounting Standards Board, *Statement of Financial Accounting Standards No. 60: Accounting and Reporting by Insurance Enterprises*, Stamford, CT, FASB, 1982.

2. *Best's Aggregates & Averages: Property-Casualty*, 49th Annual ed., A. M. Best Co., Oldwick, NJ, 1988.

3. Ibid.

4. Waterman, D. A., *A Guide to Expert Systems*, Addison-Wesley, Reading, MA, 1986.

5. Peterson, T. M., *Loss Reserving: Property/Casualty Insurance*, Cleveland, OH, Ernst & Whinney, 1981.

6. Berquist, J. R. and Sherman, R. E., "Loss Reserve Adequacy Testing: A Comprehensive, Systematic Approach," *Proceedings of the Casualty Actuarial Society,* Vol. 64, 1977, pp. 123–184.

7. Peterson, op. cit.

8. Salzmann, R. E., *Estimated Liabilities for Losses & Loss Adjustment Expenses*, Prentice-Hall, Englewood Cliffs, NJ, 1984.

9. Buchanan, B. G., Barstow, D., Bechtel, R., Bennett, J., Clancey, W., Kulikowski, C., Mitchell, T., and Waterman, D. A., "Constructing an Expert System," in *Building Expert Systems*, F. Hayes-Roth, D. A. Waterman and D. B. Lenat (eds.), Addison-Wesley, Reading, MA, 1983, pp. 127–167.

10. Simon, H. A., "On How to Decide What To Do," *Bell Journal of Economics*, Vol. 9, 1978, pp. 494–507.

11. Waldron, V. R., "Interviewing for Knowledge," *IEEE Transactions on Professional Communications*, Vol. PC29, 1986, pp. 31–34.

12. Committee on Loss Reserves, "Statement of Principles Regarding Property and Casualty Loss and Loss Adjustment Expense Liabilities," *Proceedings of the Casualty Actuarial Society*, Vol. 65, 1978, pp. 74–89.

13. Turing, A. M., "Computing Machinery and Intelligence," *Mind*, Vol. 59, 1950, pp. 433–460.

8

Expert Systems in Health Insurance: Case Studies at Blue Cross of Western Pennsylvania

David J. Gorney

INTRODUCTION

Health insurance, a seemingly simple commodity to most Americans, has truly evolved into a complex and costly administrative product. In fact, the medical industry now accounts for about 12% of the gross national product. To the covered individuals, it represents perhaps a fringe benefit that one (knock on wood) never has to use. But when one does, it is almost as easy as showing one's coverage card to the physician or provider, and then somehow the services get paid for and that's it. That may be oversimplifying the process in this age of deductibles, exclusions, and multiple coverages, but the point is that an amazing number of computer systems and people labor transparently to input, process, and resolve medical claims. Throughout this entire process, numerous decisions are made, many by computers and many by people, and that is where expert systems have a role to play, a very important role.

At Blue Cross of Western Pennsylvania (BCWP), in Pittsburgh, Pennsylvania, two expert systems were developed and implemented successfully. The first, Plan-Tracker, is an expert system that analyzes the performance of about 77 other Blue Cross and Blue Shield plans nationwide and produces an evaluation, or the report card, on those entities. The intelligent analysis work of PlanTracker has produced excellent results; what took a domain expert four full days to do is now *done in less than 1 hour*.

The second project, culminating in NERSys (Nurse Expert Review System), has likewise produced outstanding results. Claims that suspend from the normal computer-processing cycle for reasons of questionable medical policies or unusual characteristics are resolved by the NERSys knowledge base rather than by manual nurse review. The expert system is handling *over 90% of these claims*, a major productivity improvement. This chapter is about how these successes started as interesting ideas and then something even better followed—they became realities!

IN THE BEGINNING

In the early 1600s, Francis Bacon became famous for his work in inductive logic and the study of learning and thinking processes. He may be best known for the saying "Knowledge is power." In the modern corporate world, Bacon's disciples, especially those who labor in the information services profession, are continually beseiged with requests such as "Why do we gather and store all of this information and then we can't get to it?" or "What are we doing with eight hospital data bases, five account (customer) data bases, and ten different claims-processing systems all storing and processing the same data?" Would Bacon say in this age that perhaps too much of a good thing is one huge corporate headache, or more concisely, "Information overload is weakness."

We shall never know, of course, but we do know that businesses today are suffering from the overall ineffective use of their very own data. In several respects, it was this dilemma that inspired me, as a director with Information Services at BCWP, to begin to explore the technology of expert systems in an attempt to help develop information into its most useful form, knowledge.

The Society of Insurance Research (SIR) sponsored an expert systems conference in 1985 in Toronto, Canada. Complete with technical presentations on expert systems, vendor exhibits, and demonstrations, this conference both amazed and confused me. On the one hand, I listened in a sort of reverent manner as the story of the American International Group (AIG) marine insurance expert system was unveiled. Not knowing much of anything about the underwriting of flood insurance, the concept of the system's knowledge base was intriguing. Then a novice about artificial intelligence (AI), I, like many others, looked for the magic in the system. Lending even more credibility to this concept of expert systems was the presence of IBM at the gathering, conducting a briefing and demonstration of an automobile insurance underwriting expert system. The system's recommendation to reject the 20-year-old male driver with a history of accidents with his sports car did not overly impress me, but one could see the reasoning and common sense embedded in the expert system knowledge base. These and other presentations, nearly all of which implored those of us in attendance to get started now in the development of expert systems, led me to wonder if I and BCWP had not already missed the boat. At any rate, the SIR conference confirmed the fact that it was time to begin. The next question was, how?

FINDING SOME HELP

After returning from the SIR conference, it was time to pick up the pace and begin to work on a project. The obvious recourse at this juncture was to contract for outside help due to our lack of experience, internal resource constraints, and the need to move quickly. That is when I first discovered that help was not easy to find, at least the kind of start-up assistance that was required at BCWP. The collage

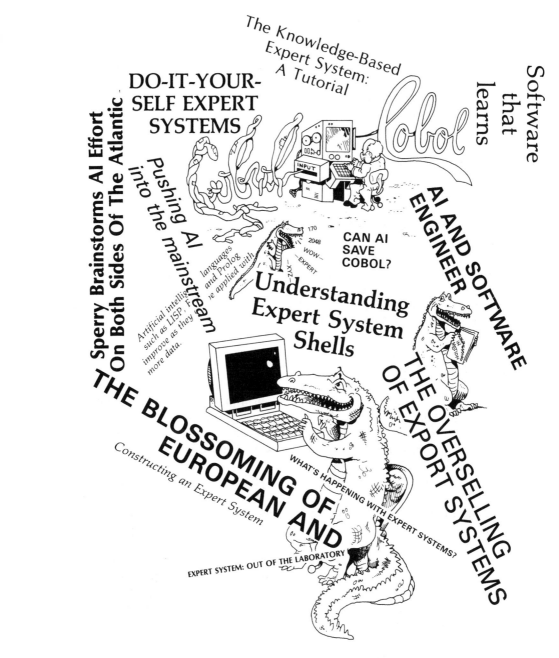

Figure 1

in Figure 1 represents the near avalanche of articles that surfaced continually about AI.

Interestingly enough, from my office window I could see the headquarters of the Carnegie Group Incorporated (CGI), one of the most credible and well-known AI vendors. However, CGI, a vendor specializing in manufacturing- and engineering-type applications, was not interested in serving the insurance industry. Syntelligence of California, conversely, was working with insurers but seemed to be fully booked at that time and had a policy of using their proprietary software to build customer systems. IBM, always worthy of a look, had not yet entered the growing market, at least not for project consulting. The major consulting firms were only beginning to experiment with expert systems. Ironically, although in proximity to Carnegie-Mellon University, BCWP was seemingly without an ally to proceed to develop a project.

Shortly thereafter, at a local computer security meeting, I attended a presentation given by an independent consultant with an avid interest in AI. The consultant's talk was on computer viruses and the potential of using AI to enhance computer security. This was in 1985, long before the now famous virus exposures of 1988. As a result, I invited the consultant to visit BCWP to further discuss some ideas on expert systems. This consultant played a brief but significant role in the start-up of expert systems projects at BCWP.

MANAGEMENT SUPPORT

Corporate management was receptive to a plan to conduct a small research project with the goal of identifying payback. The use of internal staff was out of the question as BCWP was in the process of laying the groundwork for a major new development project using relational data base technology. Thus, outside consulting was the answer. The outside consultant that I had met at the security meeting was brought on board to assist in determining the best business problem to target. During a four-month span of very intensive work, two prototype systems were developed.

The process of getting started was memorable for several reasons. Up to that time, my entire career (originating at Rockwell in 1971 in a typical IBM shop) had consisted of mainframe problems and mainframe-type systems resolutions. I quickly learned that personal computers should not be underestimated as development tools. In a short span of time, I was using DBase III, Kermit, Prolog, and of course, the MS-DOS operating system. I could see that word-processing packages and productivity tools like Side Kick for calendaring, memos, and project management certainly opened new ways of thinking.

In retrospect, what may have changed the most was my perception about the way work is conducted in the conventional large information services setting.

As a manager, constant telephone calls, meetings, and interruptions become the normal diet in the office. The only solution was to allocate evening and weekend time for the prototype development. This project taught me much about reserving time to be productive and, as the results started to appear, to have fun. Companies need to encourage employees to be creative and enjoy their work, sometimes at the expense of rigid and traditional personnel policies. More often than not, BCWP has provided the progressive environment that is needed for innovation. There can be no doubt that one can be much more productive at work if that endeavor is self-motivated. To put it simply, this new expert system development work was fun.

However, those days were not all fun. As can be expected, many in the organization did not know of or understand the project or were openly resentful of it. Curiously enough, the most notable resistance came from the management of the system development group. I had proposed that this area should become involved with the project to share in the learning process. After a period of reluctant participation, system management finally conceded that expert systems were here to stay. Probably a topic for a different book, it is curious how politics, turf issues, and perhaps even jealousy work to hinder new ideas. Most ironic is the situation when these attitudes surface in the change agents of the corporation, the system developers themselves.

Having been through numerous development projects, I long ago learned to cope with these problems and move ahead concentrating on the positive. I also learned that new ideas are often squelched if someone in the senior executive ranks is not a proponent, and that is as it should be. We were fortunate enough to have a proponent in our organization, Mr. Robert Schuler, now the Executive Vice President and Chief Operating Officer of BCWP, then the Senior Vice President of Finance and Information Services. Without his support, the budding expert system projects at BCWP were doomed to oblivion.

One of the initial prototypes was the MAC (Marketing Account Consultant) expert system. The premise behind the MAC expert system was to gather critical information about one specific large corporate client customer into a knowledge base that would then serve to assist the marketing account executive in servicing and selling to that client. Information was to be fed into MAC from corporate subject data bases (Provider or Hospital, Customer, Claims, and Subscriber) in addition to financial and accounting data bases. The on-line public Dow Jones and information retrieval resources were also part of the MAC system.

The bottom line of this project was to provide marketing with a tool to help manage accounts and anticipate problems and requests. Perhaps a bit too abstract for its time, MAC was placed on hold, but it may be reactivated in the future.

At the conclusion of the research contract, it was decided to shift gears in a sense and begin to bring the process of developing expert systems in-house. Budget funds were approved to make expert systems a reality within BCWP.

After a briefing session with senior management, where two project ideas and prototypes were demonstrated, the go ahead was received to begin development of the IPDR (Inter Plan Data Reporting) error analysis expert system, later called

PlanTracker. PlanTracker was chosen as our first project because it offered the possibility of favorably impacting the cash flow process that occurs between all Blue Cross plans, other plans, and ultimately customers.

The PlanTracker system consists of several modules that together represent the report card concept. Figure 2 shows the major components of the system and indicates the flow of information necessary to support it.

Following each processing cycle, COBOL programs are used to extract and summarize the current run's data from files resident on the mainframe. Information is extracted about the total submissions, errors, and valid claims in the aggregate. The data is also broken down by participating plans, error codes, group accounts, and a combination of plans, errors, and groups. This data is compiled for all the

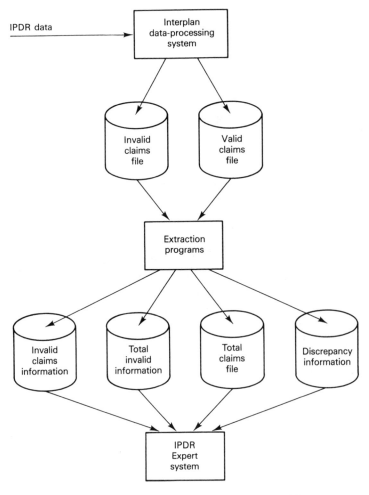

Figure 2   IPDR expert system: high-level system architecture.

```
┌─ Top Level Menu ──────────────────────────────────────────────────┐
│                                                                    │
│     Would you like to:                                             │
│                                                                    │
│              1.        view IPDR run totals                        │
│              2.        analyze IPDR data, organized by error code  │
│              3.        sort plans by some attribute                │
│              4.        analyze a particular plan                   │
│              5.        analyze plans with no claims submitted      │
│              6.        change parameters, settings, defaults, etc. │
│              E         exit from the system                        │
│                                                                    │
│                                                                    │
│     please enter 1, 2, 3, 4, 5, 6, or E ⟹                          │
│                                                                    │
└────────────────────────────────────────────────────────────────────┘

PC Scheme 3.0   Expanded Memory Version   6 July 87
```

Figure 3

accounts, taken together, and for selected accounts identified by the administrator to be closely monitored. Error data is maintained separately for each step of the edit process and is also totaled for overall performance evaluation.

The extracted data is then downloaded to PC-readable media. The PC level system, written in LISP, consists of two modules: a processor and a displayer. The processor module integrates the current run data with a processed historical data file to create an updated history file, performs the statistical analysis necessary to support the report card evaluation, and organizes and sorts the data to allow the user to view the results in various ways with a rapid response time.

The output from the processor module and the knowledge base module provide the input for the display module. The display module provides a menu-driven vehicle for analyzing the processed data in the context of the knowledge base and for investigating the effects of modifying the analysis context by updating the knowledge base. The knowledge base module contains the plan and account profiles, descriptive information about plans and accounts, and other facts that are salient to the interpretation of plan performance data. Figure 3 is a menu screen from PlanTracker.

BLUE CROSS–UNIVERSITY OF PITTSBURGH PARTNERSHIP

In place of using commercial AI vendors, consulting firms, or independent consultants, a relationship began with the University of Pittsburgh AIM (Artificial Intelligence in Management) laboratory, a component of the Katz Graduate School of Business. The AIM laboratory was co-chaired by Dr. Gerrold May and the creator of the Caduceus medical diagnosis system at the university, Dr. Harry Pople.

The university laboratory had developed projects and expert systems with Westinghouse, Alcoa, Mellon Bank, and other well-known corporate entities. The availability of graduate students studying AI and professors with a realistic vision of achieving research goals and practical results made the university a great partner for the development and learning process that BCWP faced. Two of the students became full-time employees after graduation, which reconfirmed the value of the partnership to all participants. Consulting firms and software vendors play a vital role in the computer industry, but the start-up effort at BCWP was made much more rewarding by the strategic cooperation with the AIM laboratory. Dr. May, who eventually became chairman of the AIM laboratory, was particularly valuable for his technical and business advice.

KNOWLEDGE ACQUISITION

The process of acquiring information from a domain expert is part science and part art. The scientific process entails the logistics of extracting information from the expert, recording it, analyzing it, and putting it to eventual use. The art of knowledge acquisition embodies the human behavior skills essential for all systems analysts or knowledge engineers.

In each of our projects, the most positive factor for success was the enthusiastic cooperation of the domain experts of the IPDR (Inter Plan Data Reporting) Administration department and the Medical Review department for the PlanTracker and NERSys projects, respectively.

An interesting reaction was observed at the inception of our knowledge acquisition (K/A) sessions. The domain experts were prone to understating their own knowledge and the scope and breadth of their functions. The director of the IPDR claims department insisted that his functional area and its problems were "not grandiose" enough for us to consider it as a target for a new project.

On the PlanTracker project, a project group was assembled consisting of two Blue Cross analysts (later called, more appropriately, knowledge engineers), two graduate students from the University of Pittsburgh, and the project management. A lesson was learned at the very first interview session with the IPDR domain expert.

The entire project team arrived for the interview, tape recorder ready, when it became apparent that the situation was somewhat intimidating to the IPDR analyst, an extremely nice person with about 25 years experience in error claim problem solving. From that point on, nearly all of the interview sessions were scheduled to be one-on-one if possible.

What is possibly lost in intellect at these meetings by reducing the number of analysts is overcome by ensuring that the domain expert is comfortable and relaxed enough to speak openly about his or her work.

After a session has ended, the real labor begins. Our methodology was to record the interview sessions and then transcribe them for project team review and discussion. It is somewhat incredible to see the typed results of a 1-hour meeting. Fifteen to 20 text pages was not unusual. Initially, we transcribed verbatim, and conceptionally this is the proper mode to use. Seeing the results of a session in this native format can be an awakening experience. The following is a sampling of project transcripts:

> Well, I think another thing we would want to incorporate into the system, which is very hard for us to do manually, is the history of performance . . . manually, we just can't do history with two control plan runs a month with over a hundred plans involved.
>
> This one is a pregnancy diagnostic [claim] but it says it is an Angio Venogram. I have called the hospital for two years, and they have never changed their system. After going for records, I've found that it is all fetal cardiogram. I have to . . . change this revenue code to a fetal cardiogram. They still keep coding it incorrectly. They say that they are doing it this way because of their system, something they cannot or will not change . . . and we definitely do not want to change [our] system to pay Angio Venogram under pregnancy diagnostic because it is wrong.

We learned that humans speak very naturally in a broken, jumpy, and occasionally ungrammatical way. Accustomed to reading carefully scripted speeches or reports, many of us were taken aback by the results of how we communicate verbally. This also applied to the collectors and the collectees of the interview process.

Again we adjusted and decided that project policy would be to alter or clean up the text prior to distribution to the project team and the client.

The labor intensiveness of this process cannot be stressed enough. Transcribing a meeting of several participants is tedious at best. It is no doubt a clerical task. All project members, professionals and students alike, were required to transcribe sessions for the enrichment of the process. One of our best secretaries threatened to leave if given much more of the transcription to do. At one time, our project team consisted of a native Taiwainese, a fellow from India, and a native Israeli, all who possessed some form of accent. There were times when our project meetings resembled subcommittee sessions of the United Nations. It certainly made comprehension of the tapes a challenge at times.

Finally, with regard to keeping the sessions productive, it became apparent that it was critical to get the sessions analyzed quickly. The sooner the client saw the results of the interview, either in the form of prototype demonstrations or written formulated logic, the more enthusiastic he or she became.

As the first project using AI techniques and tools at BCWP, the PlanTracker system design was ultimately a result of considerations of cost, functionality, politics (the ever present!), and the bias of the project designers. In many respects, these factors are commonly considered for any development project.

Costs were actually the simplest consideration. As a project considered to be research oriented, a modest amount of less than $100,000 was set aside to fund the effort. In retrospect, through the participation and involvement of the University of Pittsburgh AI Laboratory, a lot of mileage was extracted from the available funding. Working with graduate students is not without its problems, but all in all, these individuals are highly motivated and come equipped with well-developed intellects. The students were open minded about all design ideas, not having formulated strong opinions concerning one technology or another. Too many members of the information services profession are caught up in the hammer-and-nail syndrome. That is, when the only tool you have ever used is a hammer, every problem looks like a nail.

On the minus side, to some of the students, the project was very temporal in nature and represented one of many high-priority tasks.

NERSys

The second project started at BCWP was the NERSys system. The Medical Review Department at BCWP receives claims that suspend, or "kick out," during the adjudication process on the corporate mainframe processing system. Roughly 2,000 claims each day suspend for reasons of medical policy questions, inconsistencies, or uninterpretable information on the claims. For example, a medical procedure may be noted indicating that a cardiogram was performed. In actuality, a fetal sonogram was done and marked incorrectly. Another policy may be that all pregnancy claims for females under age 12 or over age 50 be reviewed by the medical review nursing staff. When a diagnosis did not match the medical procedure performed, a review was also mandated. As medical technology increased in complexity, the administrative process to handle and pay health insurance claims also became more complex. Nurse reviewers, about seven on staff, received claims daily on computer forms. The result of their review process was to approve the claim as is for payment, reject it partially, or reject the claim in total. Often many activities occurred during this review process. The most costly, in terms of dollars and time, was to request detailed medical records from the hospital.

The objective of the new system was to expedite this review process while hopefully improving the uniformity and quality of the entire endeavor.

A critical objective of the new system was to capture nurse reviewer knowledge. As the project developed from an idea to reality, some experienced and valuable nurse reviewers were lost to retirement or medical problems, which only served to reinforce the need to develop the nurse reviewer knowledge base.

NERSys DESIGN

NERSys could have been structured in many ways. Within the Medical Review Department, the most difficult questions facing the project team were where to begin and, at the opposite end of the spectrum, where to stop, in effect setting the scope of the project. The choices were derived from a setting of roughly 14,000 medical diagnosis codes (chest pains, jaundiced skin, etc.), 4,000 medical procedure codes, and several different categories of claims. These were classified as outpatient, inpatient, dental drug, and so on. After much discussion, it was decided to begin with the outpatient pregnancy diagnostic claims. Pregnancy was selected because its rule or logic set was basically finite in scope. About 200 claims per day fall into this category.

The claims are processed in a batch mode by the inference engine. Nurse reviewers can then selectively review the claims or let them pass into the mainframe payment system. Very routine and repetitive decisions are not reviewed. In any

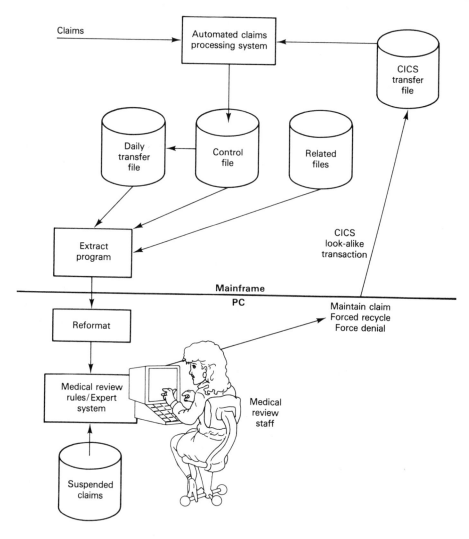

Figure 4   Medical review expert system: high-level system architecture.

case, patient care and medical decisions are not affected by NERSys decisions. A feature of the system allows the nurses to key in a question or concern overruling a NERSys decision. The medical director can then review these "red-flag" situations for potential policy or decision problem areas. This component is especially valuable to ensure that the decisions are verified and to build the much needed confidence and credibility of the ultimate clients of the system, the nurse reviewers. It is also helpful for training new nurses and for the review of new rules in the knowledge bases.

By the end of 1988, NERSys was processing between 10,000 and 12,000 claims per month. Over 90% of the claims are resolved without need of nurse review. Time has been freed up for the nurse reviewers to concentrate on the more complex type of claim problems. The system is also saving dollars with the avoidance of unnecessary requests for medical records to providers and with reduced paper costs.

Because the system groups similar medical cases by medical codes and providers, a possible coding mistake by the provider is now caught before a high volume of records need to be requested. The cost savings from this by-product of the system will save thousands of dollars over time. Finally, the major objective of the system is being fulfilled: making the review process faster while retaining scarce and valuable corporate memory, that is, nurse reviewer knowledge. Figure 4 represents a high-level design architecture of the NERSys system.

TECHNOLOGY SELECTION

Many factors were considered in the evaluation of the appropriate system configuration and software for NERSys and PlanTracker.

Both PlanTracker and NERSys projects posed some interesting design questions: Should the new system be mainframe based or built on a desk-top personal computer? What development language should be used: COBOL, LISP, or an AI shell?

PLANTRACKER HARDWARE–SOFTWARE PLATFORM

As the quantitative analysis of the knowledge developed, the specific development environment had to be selected. The key word is *development* as opposed to *eventual production* or *run environment*. Several factors influenced our decision to design the system on a personal computer. First, the university laboratory owned several of them, but more importantly a variety of software was available for PC development. Also, most of this software was relatively inexpensive. The prototype software selected for the first project was Personal Consultant Plus from Texas Instruments (TI). This product offered an easy-to-learn shell on top of PC Scheme, a TI dialect of LISP. Thus, demo systems can be written in PC Plus, and the fully powerful Scheme LISP could be used to provide ultimate programmer flexibility. The shell also provided built-in features for rule writing, help functions, and why and how explain functions. As it turned out, the PC Plus shell was utilized to construct a throw-away prototype demonstration. The actual development of PlanTracker was done using Scheme on a standard PC using MS-DOS.

WHY NOT A MAINFRAME?

The IBM mainframe system at BCWP was given consideration but ruled out for several reasons. The cost of placing an AI tool on a large IBM system was a constraint. Since our design solution would not be accessed by more than one to five IPDR analysts at one time, the power of the mainframe was not justified on the basis of performance needs. Another consideration was the process of placing a new technology in the IBM large-system environment that was the heart of a 4,000-terminal network. The potential of any degradation to that network caused by a research-type project is politically unacceptable to the technical and management group that oversees the mainframe resources. Even though the central processing unit (CPU) power, memory, and data storage of the mainframe was very appealing, the decision was prudently made to develop on a PC with the eventual probability of porting upward to a more powerful system. No doubt this is why many AI solutions have evolved from the world of the PC. Even after our systems had been implemented successfully, the familiar refrain was heard, ''Why didn't you use COBOL?'' As it turned out, in many ways we could have. Eventually we learned to reverse that question and ask why the problem had not already been solved using COBOL? The PlanTracker system is a hybrid system that uses COBOL to extract mainframe data to be processed on a PC using LISP.

NERSys HARDWARE–SOFTWARE PLATFORM

As with the PlanTracker System, it was decided that NERSys should include an extraction module to bring the suspended claims from the mainframe down to the development machine, a Compaq 32-bit 386 PC.

We decided to look into expert system development shells for the NERSys project. The IBM ESE mainframe product was reviewed. Despite the attractiveness of using the mainframe power, the overall users of the system would be localized in the Medical Review Department. This weakened the case for a mainframe resident system. The Nexpert Object system from Neuron Data was reviewed briefly and offered many attractive and powerful features. However, our knowledge engineers were very proficient in LISP and not in C, the language of the Nexpert software tool.

The GoldWorks software from Gold Hill Computers was eventually chosen due to its wealth of development features including the screen toolkit, the developer's template, and the strong help facility. Sun Microsystems hardware was selected because of its mainframe connectivity, excellent multiple-window facility, and power as a workstation and network server. The risk that was taken was that GoldWorks did not operate outside of the PC platform. A commitment was received from Gold Hill to port the software to Sun, and this was accomplished late in 1988. The Sun system offered the designers the vehicle to build an expert system while planning for the implementation of an interactive text referral system.

During the knowledge acquisition process, it was determined that the nurse reviewers could benefit from loading the various medical references and other documents (bulletins, management memos, etc.) into a text-publishing system. The other advantage of using Sun was its UNIX-based operating system. Eventually UNIX will be transportable to literally all computer vendors, including IBM.

FUTURE PLANS

The expert systems strategy at BCWP has been to only develop projects that offer solid business goals and objectives with limited downside potential, in short, positive business results for business people. This strategy will prevail in the future.

PlanTracker and NERSys will be developed to their fullest extent for eventual use within other Blue Cross and Blue Shield plans and, in some instances, other insurance entities.

In some small way, these systems can help to make each of the Blue Cross and Blue Shield corporations more effective and productive while also introducing the concepts of expert systems to these corporations.

Several other projects are in the process of beginning within BCWP. In general, these projects will enhance claims processing, improve customer service and marketing, and in effect make the organization more competitive and adaptive.

Expert systems have a place in insurance organizations everywhere. The process of insurance is both labor intensive and paper oriented. As the entire industry becomes increasingly more complex, expert systems can be very effective at solving special dilemmas in the functions of membership, claims processing, medical review, actuarial, marketing, and service.

9

Expert Systems in Sales and Marketing

L. L. Odette
L. J. Berkman

INTRODUCTION

Think about the way insurance agents work. They meet you in your home or at your place of business and, in one half hour, gather your basic financial data. They gather information about your family, such as the number of dependents and their ages and sexes. They get a rough idea of your family income, assets, and liabilities. Then within a day or two, the agent (or "financial advisor" as many are now called) returns with an analysis of your situation that in all likelihood emphasizes your exposure to financial ruin. You find your needs analyzed and laid out in all their glory in front of you, with a summary illustration (i.e., sales proposal) about the benefits of life insurance or the advantages of income protection against the event of long-term disability. Perhaps no surprise there, right? Insurance agents sell insurance.

Well, they do not sell all that effectively. The average premium payment that follows from the conventional sales approach is roughly $500 [1]. However, the insurance industry is all too well aware that the average need of the consumer for all the financial products that the company offers may very well be 10 times the average premium this approach produces. After all, deregulation permitted the insurance companies to sell investment products and even banking products through their agency force. To the insurance company of the eighties, in the sales situation described, mentioning only insurance represents a significant lost opportunity. And to the same insurance company, the agency force represents a very expensive ($200,000 five-year training expense per agent) distribution channel that is not quite hitting on all cylinders.

Now think about how bankers work. You go to their place of business to execute some transaction, for example, open an IRA, buy a CD, make a deposit to your account, or apply for a loan. Rarely are your needs analyzed at the bank like they might be when buying insurance (a loan may be the exception to this rule, but only if you equate your needs with what the bankers decide they will give you).

Have you ever heard your banker say "Oh, I see on the form here that you have one of our competitor's CDs that is just about to mature. Would you like to take advantage of our higher rates?" or "I notice that you don't have an IRA or contribute to an employer-sponsored pension plan. You have the money to save—I'd like to show you the advantages of opening an IRA with us." Of course not. Bankers are not salespeople.

But, as in the insurance industry, deregulation has increased the mix of products a bank may sell, with the result that many sell a wide range of investment products and retirement products, even life insurance. The banking industry knows that their bankers do not take the time to understand their customer's needs, so they miss a tremendous opportunity to sell more of their products. They thereby miss the profit that comes from establishing a diverse long-term relationship with the customer. With increasing competition, they may not even keep the customer. With how many different banks do you do business?

These are just two examples of the difficulties that retail financial services firms face in managing their sales activities in a world that is much more complex than it was 10 years ago. Sales productivity is not the only problem area. Competition, increasing consumer sophistication, and economic uncertainty have made it more difficult to do product development and marketing right (i.e., not just on target but quickly and cost effectively). Understanding the needs of the different consumer market segments, developing the products to meet those needs, and managing the sales force to sell to those needs will be critical to the future success of banks, insurance and securities firms.

We have used point-of-sale activities to illustrate the problem these firms face because herein lies the solution. They must find a way to deliver expertise in analyzing a customer's broad financial needs, advice in matching products to needs, and coaching in selling to those needs. Applied Expert Systems (APEX) builds precisely these kinds of systems.

This chapter is a case study on how APEX builds expert systems to help financial services firms more effectively manage their sales and marketing activities. APEX and others have used the APEX development technology and methods to build expert systems for sales and marketing support in the United States, Europe, Japan, and Australia. These systems represent the greatest penetration of expert systems technology into the work force today. The case illustrates just how much the expert systems research of the seventies has been reduced to practice today.

Before discussing the steps in the development of these systems, which include knowledge engineering, coding, and quality assurance (QA), we go into some depth on the APEX approach to the expert system domain choice. Then we elaborate on why so many good expert system opportunities exist in the financial services and why sales and marketing systems are the APEX focus.

Following a discussion of typical output produced by sales and marketing expert systems for financial services, we outline the knowledge engineering steps, coding stages, and QA process used to build them. We conclude the chapter with a discussion of important deployment considerations.

CHOOSING THE DOMAIN

How to Generate Good Candidate Applications

Choosing the domain for an expert system application is, in essence, a search for ways to add value to the activities of an organization. Analyzing and identifying where the value might be is not quite as easy as identifying areas where expertise is scarce or inconsistently applied, areas where productivity is suboptimal, or any of the usual elements appearing in the checklists of the "how to get started in expert systems" talks. That is, to focus solely on the expertise is to miss the point, with the result that choosing the domain takes on the characteristics of a solution in search of a problem. There may very well be significant value in applications targeted at capturing scarce expertise or improving consistency of analysis, but solving a business problem must be the starting point, not a side effect.

One framework for understanding value and therefore choosing an application domain is the value chain analysis popularized by Michael Porter [2]. Value chain analysis starts by analyzing all the activities that a firm performs in designing, producing, marketing, delivering, and supporting its product (Figure 1). These activities are then systematically examined with an eye toward how they interact and can provide sources of competitive advantage within a particular industry. For example, a competitive cost advantage can stem from a low-cost physical distribution system like those operated by the discount stockbrokers in the financial services. Some securities firms have worked this principle to tremendous advantage in providing a wide range of financial services. Alternatively, competitive advantage via differentiation can stem from superior product design, a responsive order entry system, and similarly diverse factors (e.g., some mutual fund companies have 24-hour service and computerized transaction service via computer using a touch-tone phone).

We can not claim that APEX has conceived its sales and marketing applications from the start by a careful analytical process based on some business model such as value chain. Nevertheless, we have always evolved the concept through successive designs with an eye toward how the application delivers value in the context of a particular organization. This has meant emphasizing particular aspects of the generic sales and marketing application over other aspects to better suit a given client situation.

Why So Many Expert Systems Are in the Financial Services

One reason that many of the first expert systems to be commercialized were designed for the financial services industry is that expert systems are particularly well positioned to add value to the activities of these firms. The products of the financial services industry are differentiated from the products of other sectors by their high information

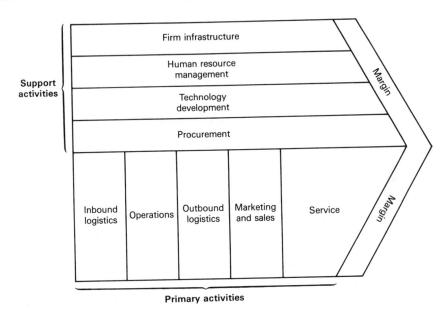

Figure 1   The generic value chain [2]. Candidate expert system applications can be identified by analyzing a firm's value chain for advantageous linkages between production activities. The establishment or improvement of such linkages may be enabled by mechanizing expertise. Production activities of financial services firms, from inbound logistics (news, economic statistics) to service (advice on using products to satisfy needs or meet goals), are information rich. With many linkages adding value through expertise, these activities are good potential candidates for expert systems.

content. The separate production activities of financial services firms, from product development through sales and service, consist primarily of information processing, and most of this is done by people, not computers. The *Wall Street Journal* has reported that workers in the financial services process 24 times more information than workers in other sectors [3].

Though somewhat extreme, a good example of this is the activity of a typical securities trader (Figure 2).

Much of what is done in the production activities of financial services firms adds value to the information via analysis. Of course, analysis is one of the things at which expert systems can be consistently very good (and one of the things that, by all the evidence, at which junior analysts can be woefully inconsistent).

The life insurance and banking examples given earlier are a case in point. These kinds of firms are now able to sell a broad range of products like mutual funds, retirement products, and some banking products. But in the life insurance industry, statistics suggest that current sales forces only realize a fraction of the potential in a particular sales situation (Figure 3). Even with expensive and extensive training, today's life insurance salespeople are not particularly good at analyzing a

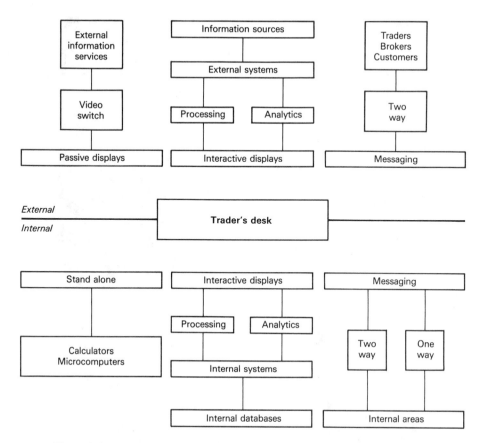

Figure 2   Trading room technology. Securities dealers typically work in a very information-rich environment, where access to and analysis of information can be a source of competitive advantage. External sources of news and quotes from information vendors like Reuters and Quotron, Telerate, and Fundamental Brokers are available through passive video displays. Analytics from vendors like Market-view, Bloomberg and Shark may be interactive, while the trader is in touch by phone with brokers, customers, and other traders. Internal information such as price quotes, in-house research, and trade position data is also available. Data processed by the trader is of two major types: informational (passive, e.g., news, prices, and analytics) and executable (live, e.g., price quotes).

prospect's total financial situation. Nor are they particularly good at matching a product to a need. Sales forces in banks and securities firms are even worse.

In a given sales situation, there are typically several products that may match a particular need. A good deal of value is added to the sales process when the salesperson can easily and consistently match a client's need to a specific product. There is value for the client in obtaining a comprehensive, objective analysis. There is value to the firm in suggesting the right product at the right time.

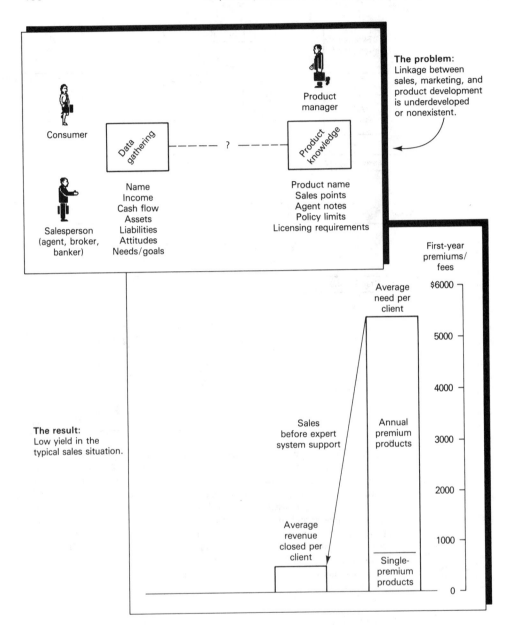

Figure 3. **The problem of financial services firms.** The paper-based link between the sale/service activities and the marketing and product development activities is inadequate to ensure that sales knows about the firm's products and that the firm knows about its clients. The net result of changes in the financial services environment is a greater revenue opportunity in an individual sales situation; conventional sales organizations are only realizing a fraction of that opportunity.

But there is more to the value than just the revenue from the sale. For example, banks skew their sales and marketing budget to marketing, and they are good enough marketers to know that a customer who has bought more than one product from the bank is more likely to stay a customer and therefore more likely to be profitable than a customer with just a single account—value in a product that once sold stays sold. So, there is a good deal of value in a process that facilitates more as well as bigger product sales. And just like insurance and brokerage, as it becomes legal for the banks to offer financial products they could not in the past, it becomes even more important to ensure that those products are sold. Bankers will be asked to gain a greater understanding of their customer's total needs, find the right bank product, and sell it. This can be a tall order in an institutional culture that is not sales oriented today.

It is worth emphasizing that the proliferation of products is a particular problem for all the financial services. The development and life cycle for financial products can be very short these days. Getting a good sense for this is as simple as visiting your stockbroker's office to take in the supermarket ambiance—the overhead paging system blaring "attention shoppers!" pitches for the products of the day.

Bad as the situation is now, the bet is that it will only get worse as changes in the financial services environment around the world continue to realign boundaries and linkages and put pressure on insurance companies, banks, brokerage houses, and other firms to orient to the needs of the consumer (Figure 4). These changes are not the changes in the linkages between global markets that have been so prominent in the press but changes in local regulations and consumer sophistication that affect the personal finances of consumers.

Why Expert Systems for Sales and Marketing

As the rules changed for this information-intensive industry, there have been many opportunities to build strategic information-based applications. Expert system technology has been a large part of many of these applications. The focus of APEX's products has been support for sales and marketing of financial services products. Our approach brings our knowledge of both personal finance and technology to bear on the problem of cost effectively selling financial products to the middle-income market.

The high end of the market is relatively small but profitable and is already served adequately by the financial planning subsidiaries of the life insurance companies or the private banking services of the bank (i.e., if your net worth is at least $500,000, you can have a banker talk to you in person). The needs of this upscale market are different, more geared toward diversification of assets, the minimization of financial risk, and tax consequences. The higher net worth and income of this market segment justifies a more personalized client relationship.

From the experience with this market, it is clear that understanding client needs and building and managing the client relationship is an effective sales approach.

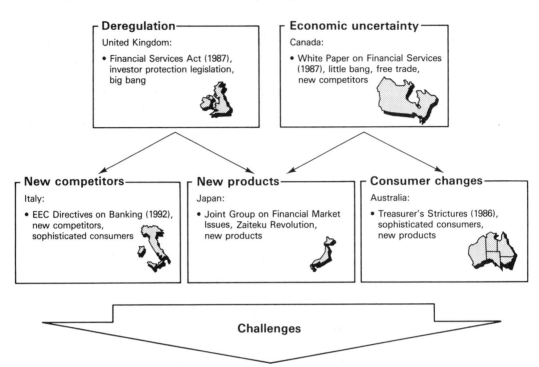

Figure 4   Changes in the world environment for retail financial services. In the 1980s deregulation and economic uncertainty (inflation and recession) have known no national boundaries. The result has been pressure to simultaneously comply with the new regulations and manage the uncertainty while meeting increased competition and developing new products for more sophisticated consumers. The challenge to financial services firms around the world is to better manage their customer relationships while finding ways to control more of their customer's assets. Ultimately this means being customer needs oriented in sales and having more and better information for marketing and product development.

In anything but the upper end of the market, it has just been too expensive to deliver.

As we have outlined in the preceding text, in the new business environment it becomes strategic to try to move this approach downmarket to the retail financial services: the sale of financial products like bank accounts, money market funds, annuities, life insurance, and mutual funds. The target market for these products is often termed the *middle market*, people with modest net worth and income whose financial needs (educating children, purchasing a home, providing for retirement) often outstrip their financial resources and whose financial resources cannot support the current delivery mechanisms for needs analysis and advice. For example, advice from a financial planner may cost $1,000 to deliver; microcomputer-manufactured advice, usually based on spreadsheets and boilerplate text producing a one-size-fits-all report, may cost $250 to deliver.

However, analyzing needs and delivering advice is only one part of the equation if the application is to be strategic. Servicing the middle market demands integration across the corporate functions of marketing, product development, information systems, and sales. The sales and marketing application area is strategic because changes in the attitude, behavior, and life style of the middle market will force a financial services institution to deploy its resources differently in order to capture and maintain a large share of what is a cost-conscious and value-oriented group.

Why have the requirements of serving the middle market changed? In the United States, the ongoing process of deregulation, increasing consumer sophistication following on the heels of events like the introduction of the Individual Retirement Account (IRA), and the disintermediation of the traditional financial institutions due to the high interest rates of the early eighties, have put pressure on the marketing and distribution channels of the retail financial services firms. Increased competition is also a factor; in 1985 there were 500 more life insurers in existence than there had been 10 years earlier [4].

On the one hand, the marketing and product development functions of the firm need to be much better informed about consumer needs and more targeted to their chosen market segments as product development and proliferation is very costly. On the other hand, the distribution channels, like bank branches and life insurance agents, are very costly and provide little value to the consumer. A typical insurance agent costs $200,000 to train over 5 years, with about 85% attrition over that period. In competition with automatic tellers and effective direct mail campaigns like those waged by the mutual fund companies, there is increasing pressure to improve the effectiveness of a branch operation of a bank, securities firm, or insurance company in selling an expanding array of products: to somehow find the right cluster of products for the particular consumer and to establish and maintain an intimate and trusted client relationship while making the sale in as few calls as possible.

Several expert system applications have been designed and built to satisfy this need. The Union Bank of Finland has built a system called Investment Key [5] to give advice on consumer investment strategies, simulate portfolio sell–buy decisions, including their tax implications, and suggest particular investment products to implement the investment strategy.

Sanwa Bank has developed a system in this domain called Best Mix that is in use in its retail banking operations in Japan. Other banks and insurance companies in Japan have similar projects in development [6], and the recent tax reforms [7] will make the Japanese consumer more aware of the need as well as making the process easier to perform.

The APEX sales and marketing systems are the most sophisticated of this class of applications, designed to meet the needs of the middle market and the financial institutions serving it.

The APEX systems are built around a core expert system that performs financial needs analysis given basic financial data provided by the client. Financial needs analysis encompasses the creation of a systematic set of monetary objectives and action plans for an individual or a family. Analysis of goals is tempered by the family's income and net worth. The analysis includes many considerations:

- Tax planning.
- Education planning.
- Estate planning.
- Investment advice.
- Retirement planning.
- Risk (insurance) planning.

For many people, a well-executed financial plan can make a significant difference in whether they achieve their investment goals and increase their long-term net worth by lowering taxes and marshalling expenses and in some cases by allowing them to be better informed of financial alternatives.

The client data and the expert's recommendations are stored together in the second major piece of the application, a marketing information system. In many cases, particularly where the information/transaction systems have been product oriented and not customer oriented, this is the first time that the home office has access to detailed consumer information. Extracts of the base information can be exported into conventional data base systems for query and reporting or may be configured as a platform for a marketing/product development expert system.

The kind of marketing information that can be obtained is unique because for the first time it permits the marketer to understand the market needs in depth based on expert-level financial analysis of thousands of cases and not rely solely on crude life-cycle models that only consider a few demographic variables like age, salary, marital status, and number of dependents.

The final piece of the APEX system is a sales scripting module that is connected to an on-line product catalog and provides capability for matching specific products to customer needs. In addition to the value added to the sales process, the sales script acts as a training mechanism for the sales person. New products added to the product catalog one day will appear in the sales script the next day, supplying appropriate sales points and other information for the agent (like commissions to be made on the sale, where to get additional information about the products, and how many points the sale will contribute toward the "Hawaiian Vacation" sales contest).

The output of the application is a series of reports generated via a natural-language production module that tailors the text to the individual client's situation. The organization, tone, and content of the client report are specific to the individual client. The agent's report suggests particular products and corresponding sales points that are tailored to the client given the attitudinal information supplied by the client on the questionnaire.

Sales and Marketing Is a Worldwide Problem
for Financial Services

The APEX sales and marketing system described in the preceding has proven itself in the U.S. market as a very cost-effective and strategic application satisfying the need stated earlier: to sell an expanding array of products against increasing competition to a more sophisticated consumer. For example, insurance companies have seen their close ratios and commissions per sale more than double, and one-half as many calls are required to close a sale. But the same need is present in many other national markets (Figure 4).

Australia and Canada, for instance, have experienced deregulation of the financial services with results very similar to the results in the United States, namely, increased competition and consumer sophistication and postderegulation restructuring of the financial services industry. The strategic impact of expert systems for sales and marketing support has not been lost on firms in these countries; hence APEX and others have been actively building systems outside the United States.

In the United Kingdom, by contrast with Australia and Canada, deregulation was accompanied by much stiffer regulation regarding the ways financial services were to be delivered to the consumer. The interpretation of the regulations requiring intermediaries to "know your client" and give "best advice" has been the major topic of discussion in financial services firms in the United Kingdom for the last two years. Therefore, compliance with the regulations, more than competition or changing consumer attitudes, has been the chief concern of the industry. Sales and marketing expert systems have been perceived by U.K. firms as the ideal mechanism for ensuring that their intermediaries comply with the regulations. Individualized, high-quality ("best advice"), consistent, and unbiased advice sanctioned by the firm and complete with audit trail is all the agent is allowed to give to the customer.

European financial services firms see something quite different as the major threat to the status quo: competition. In 1992 the barriers to trade in goods and services are due to be removed. Already the industry is feeling the effects as Italian entrepreneurs bid for Belgian banks in anticipation of the new era [8]. In Europe, the APEX approach to sales and marketing becomes a defensive weapon by which national banks and insurance companies can defend their markets.

All these pressures have not been unforeseen, nor are they entirely new. What is different is the speed with which change is happening and the worldwide impact. There have been piecemeal attempts in the past to address the challenges via new sales procedures, computerized illustration systems, and financial planning software or support groups. These attempts have not had much success so far.

Some of the failings of earlier technological solutions can be traced to the scope of the application; computerized illustration systems generate too many numbers to be immediately useful to the customer and provide little selling help to the agent. The failure of other systems can be traced to the critical deployment factors; many financial planning systems have tended to turn the salesperson into a computer jock, requiring many hours spent at the PC preparing a plan instead of selling.

The APEX solution as embodied in the system output described later reflects the lessons learned from the mistakes of the past. We discuss the APEX design approach in a later section but point out here the importance to proper design of paying careful attention to the way people work: culture, infrastructure, and compensation schemes. This is a system design truism; nevertheless, it is quite difficult to accomplish.

APEX SALES AND MARKETING SUPPORT SYSTEMS

Input

In reading the text of the following section on the system output, keep in mind that the format, tone, and content of the reports vary substantially from system to system, reflecting the organizational factors already outlined, as elucidated during the design phase of development. These particular illustrations do, however, capture the salient features of all the sales and marketing systems APEX has developed.

The starting point in the production of the analyses is the data collection process, often accomplished via a questionnaire called a fact finder, although many financial services companies have data bases of client information that already have information sufficient for the expert system.

The job of the fact finder is to determine the basic client information: name, rank and serial number, income, assets, and liabilities. One of the advantages of the expert system technology is the ability to make sense of incomplete and inconsistent information, exactly the kind of financial information most people have about themselves.

More important perhaps than the basic facts and figures is the attitudinal information that can be gathered with the fact finder. This kind of information concerns the individual's attitudes toward various kinds of risk, the goals that are important to them, and the priorities that are attached to the goals. The attitudes, goals, and priorities are the sorts of soft information that an expert system can make very good use of; in the systems APEX builds, both the reasoning of the expert and the structure of the documents are based on the attitudinal information.

For the reports illustrated here we use the fictional case of the Altons, a young couple of moderate means whose goals are to educate their children, provide adequate funds for their retirement, buy a sailboat, and provide financial security for the family over the long term.

Once the basic information has been obtained from the fact finder or client data base, the client data is sent to the expert for processing. The result is a series of reports that, in the case of the U.S. and Australian systems, go to the client and the salesperson. The U. K. version produces a single report summarizing the analysis and recommendations for the salesperson. An extract of the data is also available to populate the marketing data base.

All instances of the system to date have been architected for batch operation. Interactive systems are certainly feasible, but they carry a big negative; they force or encourage the salesperson to spend time with the computer that could be spent with the client. Even if the client is present, the technology can hinder the process of the salesperson establishing credibility and trust and focusing on making a decision. Batch systems have the great advantage of putting the technology out of sight, letting the interactivity between client and agent be of a personal nature.

INSTANCES OF THE SYSTEM OUTPUT

The output of all APEX systems is a series of reports generated via a natural-language output module that tailors the report text to the individual client's situation. The organization, tone, and content of the client report are specific to the individual client; the agent's report suggests particular products and corresponding sales points that are tailored to the client using the attitudinal information supplied by the client on the questionnaire.

The text generation technology is an implementation of a high-level document description language that enables document definition from section through paragraph and sentence to individual words in sentences. Automatic pluralization and gender are just two of the capabilities of the language that enable the text to be flexible enough to be read as if it had been written by a human (e.g., the client and his or her wife or husband and children) and not just a boilerplate.

The need for such a capability is indicated by market research. The value of expert systems that produce analysis for human consumption is greatly reduced if that analysis is perceived to have been written by a machine. The personal touch is important.

The following sections describe the two major reports produced by the APEX sales and marketing systems, the client report and the sales report.

Client report.   The client report is a document designed to provide (where warranted) a take-away summary of specific recommendations for expressed needs. A major design criterion is that the report provide selling support for the salesperson.

The text in both the client and sales reports is generated via a text generation system that is driven from the observations and recommendation that result from the expert processing. The text generation system is the high-level document description language described earlier. About 30% of the total code is devoted to producing the text.

The client report is designed to look and read as if it were prepared by a human; no two are alike. With valuable advice delivered in a manner the client deems valuable, the salesperson is positioned to be more professional and to have recommendations considered more seriously.

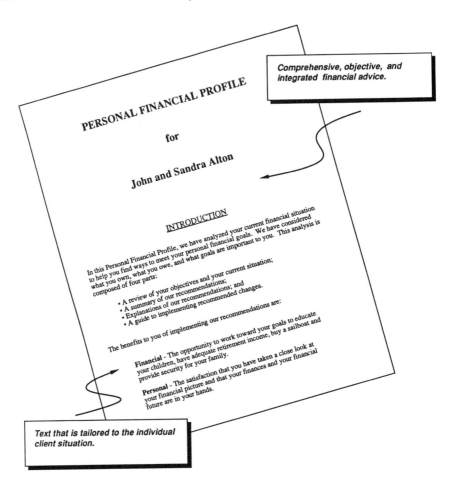

Figure 5   Client report opening page. The opening page of the client report is designed to give a brief overview of the contents of the report and restate the benefits to the client of implementing the recommendations. The benefits statement is constructed from the goals indicated by the client in the questionnaire.

The only section of text in the Alton's client report, as shown in Figure 5, that approaches a boilerplate is on the opening page, which introduces the report and outlines the sections to come. Even here, though, the Altons' individual goals are referenced.

The first page of the body of the report is a review of the Altons' objectives and financial situation (Figure 6). The text plays back the information that they gave in the fact finder and provides the salesperson the opportunity to review the basic facts with the client. This section has been designed to draw the person into reading the report, the idea being that most people enjoy reading about themselves and have a particular interest in their own financial information.

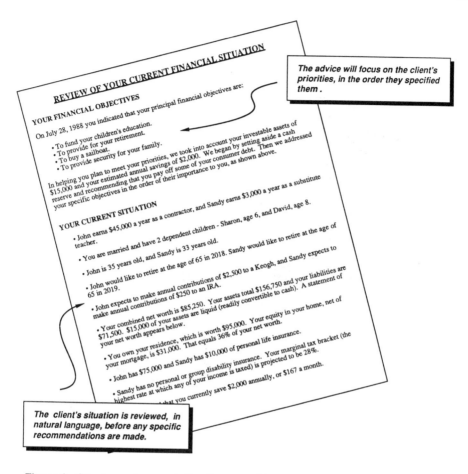

The advice will focus on the client's priorities, in the order they specified them.

The client's situation is reviewed, in natural language, before any specific recommendations are made.

Figure 6 Client report current situation page. The current situation page is designed to replay, in English sentences, the data that was provided on the questionnaire. Major discrepancies in the data can be caught here, although the system includes both verification and validation steps before processing to reduce the likelihood that any report presented to a client is in error. The client is drawn into reading the report by first reading about themselves.

Following a statement of net worth and its distribution over the asset and liability categories, there is an executive summary of the expert recommendations (Figure 7). This section has been designed so that the order of recommendations is determined first by the priorities specified by the client and then in the order that a financial planner would deem important. Note that the recommendations are entirely generic to satisfy the expressed need of consumers for objective and comprehensive advice on meeting their goals.

What follows the summary are detailed explanations of each of the recommendations, again in the preference order of the client. The purposes of the detail range

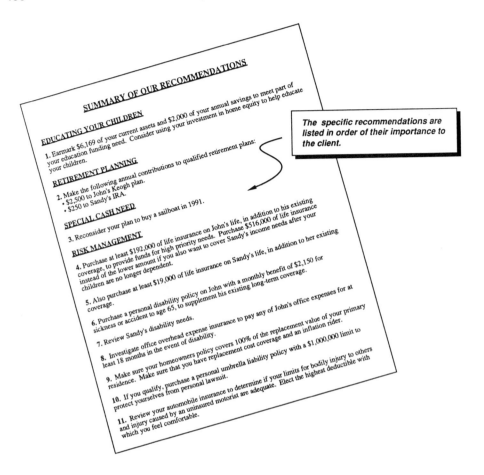

Figure 7   Client report summary of recommendations. The summary of recommendations gives an executive summary of the body of the report text. The recommendations are constructed in the priority order indicated by the client on the questionnaire. The salesperson would use this section to focus on specific recommendations.

from education to elucidation. It is unlikely that this section will be reviewed in a
sales situation. There can be short versions of the report that omit the detailed
explanations.

The last page is perhaps the most important from the salesperson's point of
view. The recommendations are listed, again in client preference order, but this
time with an indication of the corresponding priorities of an expert financial advisor
(Figure 8). There is an area on the last page that is set aside to get the client to
commit to a date for action. The salesperson may even ask the client to initialize a
line if the client has decided not to follow the recommendation, with the express
purpose of providing release from liability. For example, if the report recommended

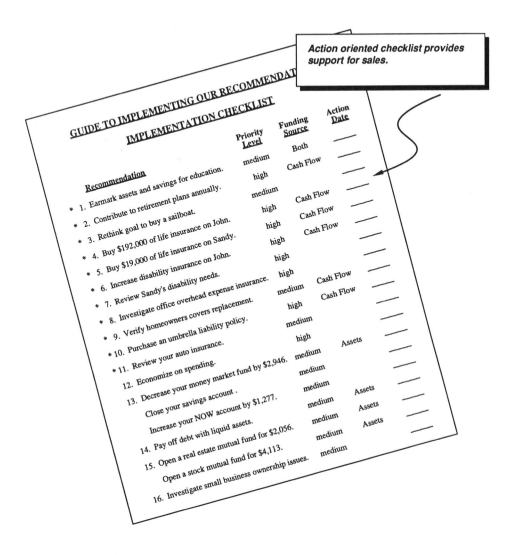

Action oriented checklist provides support for sales.

GUIDE TO IMPLEMENTING OUR RECOMMENDATION

IMPLEMENTATION CHECKLIST

Recommendation	Priority Level	Funding Source	Action Date
* 1. Earmark assets and savings for education.	medium	Both	___
* 2. Contribute to retirement plans annually.	high	Cash Flow	___
* 3. Rethink goal to buy a sailboat.	medium		___
* 4. Buy $192,000 of life insurance on John.	high	Cash Flow	___
* 5. Buy $19,000 of life insurance on Sandy.	high	Cash Flow	___
* 6. Increase disability insurance on John.	high	Cash Flow	___
* 7. Review Sandy's disability needs.	high		___
* 8. Investigate office overhead expense insurance.	high	Cash Flow	___
* 9. Verify homeowners covers replacement.	medium	Cash Flow	___
* 10. Purchase an umbrella liability policy.	high		___
* 11. Review your auto insurance.	medium		___
12. Economize on spending.	high	Assets	___
13. Decrease your money market fund by $2,946.	medium		___
Close your savings account .	medium		___
Increase your NOW account by $1,277.	medium	Assets	___
14. Pay off debt with liquid assets.	medium	Assets	___
15. Open a real estate mutual fund for $2,056.	medium	Assets	___
Open a stock mutual fund for $4,113.	medium		___
16. Investigate small business ownership issues.	medium		___

Figure 8   Client report implementation checklist. The implementation checklist is an action-oriented summary of the recommendations in the report. Recommendations are listed in the priority indicated by the client, and the priority that an expert financial advisor might assign to each area is also indicated. The action date helps the salesperson get action on particular decisions.

disability insurance and the client decides not to buy and was later injured, the agent may be liable for not trying hard enough to sell the coverage.

Sales report.   The sales report is a separate document that is designed to help the salesperson sell into the particular sales opportunity identified by the expert

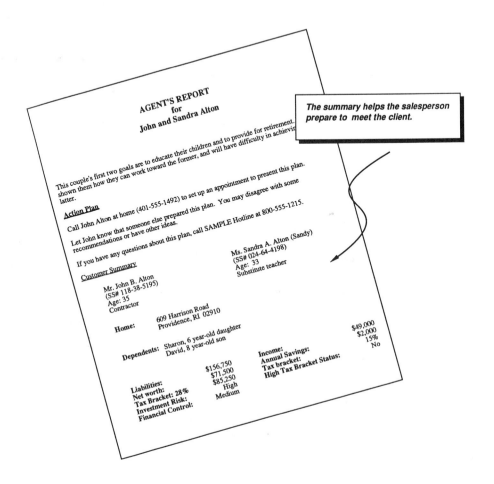

AGENT'S REPORT
for
John and Sandra Alton

The summary helps the salesperson prepare to meet the client.

This couple's first two goals are to educate their children and to provide for retirement. shown them how they can work toward the former, and will have difficulty in achievin latter.

Action Plan

Call John Alton at home (401-555-1492) to set up an appointment to present this plan.

Let John know that someone else prepared this plan. You may disagree with some recommendations or have other ideas.

If you have any questions about this plan, call SAMPLE Hotline at 800-555-1215.

Customer Summary

Mr. John B. Alton
(SS# 118-38-5195)
Age: 35
Contractor

Ms. Sandra A. Alton (Sandy)
(SS# 024-64-4198)
Age: 33
Substitute teacher

Home: 609 Harrison Road
              Providence, RI 02910

Dependents: Sharon, 6 year-old daughter
             David, 8 year-old son

Income: $49,000
Annual Savings: $2,000
Tax bracket: 15%
High Tax Bracket Status: No

Liabilities: $156,750
Net worth: $71,500
Tax Bracket: 28% $85,250
Investment Risk: High
Financial Control: Medium

Figure 9 Sales report cover page, designed to be a very quick summary for the agent and might be reviewed just prior to arranging the presentation meeting with the client.

system (Figure 9). The first page of the report is simply a snapshot of the client—name of client, spouse, children, as well as the basic financial information—and is useful in helping the salesperson prepare for the client meeting. The first page also includes reminders to the salesperson and notes from the expert process.

The second and subsequent pages of the sales report detail, for each of the generic recommendations in the client report, the products that the salesperson might sell (Figure 10). The choice of which products to mention to the client is left up to

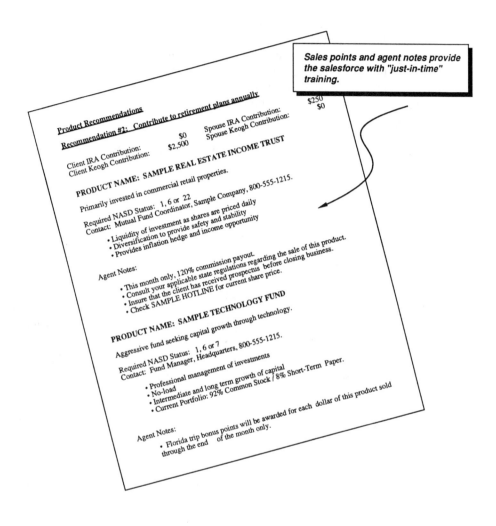

Figure 10 Sales report specific product recommendations. Specific products are mapped to the generic recommendations that are made in the client's report. Product information in the sales report includes sales points from product management and notes to the salesperson from sales management.

the salesperson, who may in fact have more up-to-date information about the client or some personal knowledge about the client's situation that the Expert systems would not have and that may color the specific product recommendations. What is important about the report is that the salesperson is provided with the information he or she needs to know at the time it is needed—"just-in-time training."

The information about each product comes in at least two forms, sales points that might be used in the selling effort and notes to the salesperson. The sales points that are formulated can use knowledge about the clients expressed attitudes and goals so that for products with multiple sales points, those sales points that are client appropriate can be suggested to the salesperson.

Notes to the salesperson include relations to other product suggestions, information concerning the sales promotions that may cover the product, and general sales management information.

An important feature of the system is that the sales points and notes are maintained by the product development, marketing, and sales management functions in a central data base that is accessed by the expert during each run (Product Knowledge-base, or PKB). Multiple product knowledge bases are supported so that the information can be tailored by region or even by individual offices. Separate PKBs may be maintained for test marketing.

Variations on the Theme

The series of reports illustrated in Figures 5–10 and described in the preceding text are but one example of the class of analyses that can be delivered based on expert analysis of individual financial needs. For example, one version of the system produces a report that is best described as a combination of the client and sales reports, but much more brief. This particular report goes to the salesperson only (nothing goes to the client) so that the salesperson can use as much or as little of the analysis as is warranted during the presentation or according to his or her individual comfort or skill levels.

A variation on input via questionnaire uses an intelligent script generation mechanism based on the text generation technology to guide telemarketers. A quite different application produces customized client letters for use in direct marketing campaigns.

The Japanese version, developed by a third party with APEX technology, uses the same reasoning and representation mechanisms but a different text mechanism for output. The fact finder input is screen form oriented with extensive use of menus to overcome the difficulty of using keyboard technology to enter Kanji data. The output reports are very picture and number oriented with little text. The system is deployed in a major bank and a major insurance company in Japan.

Hardware Architectures

The hardware architectures used for delivery of the systems reflect, for the most part, the systems already in place in the client firms.

The simplest configuration uses a PC for data entry. When convenient, a dial-up connection is established to a minicomputer (VAX) at the home office, and client data is transmitted. Once processed, client and sales reports are either printed immediately or transmitted back to the originating PC for local printing. The product knowledge base is maintained on a PC, and product data is transmitted to the VAX where it is stored and used each time a client case is processed.

The system has also been configured so that the data and analysis can be transferred over a wide area network. For example, in one case the data entry is driven from an IMS application on the home office IBM 3090. Data entry is through 3270 terminals in the regional sales office, and client information is stored on the mainframe in an IMS data base. For processing, client data is passed to a minicomputer, and the reports are returned to the mainframe for distribution to the regional offices through the SNA network. In this case, the mainframe is used primarily as a data switch. In another case, the system is built so that PCs on a local area network (LAN) in the regional office can be used for client data entry. Client data is passed up the network to the mainframe, where the expert processing and report generation take place. The results are then passed back down the network for local printing.

While most of the systems APEX has built have been used with (and have made use of) the significant computing resources provided by mainframes and large minicomputers, the software design approach is flexible enough to accommodate less powerful gear where required. Despite the large number of PCs in use and the increasing push to put computers at the point of sale, for both historical and economic reasons computer-based sales and marketing support systems will continue to rely on the large machines.

The sections to follow detail the implementation approach used by APEX for building major computer-based sales and marketing support systems in a number of countries.

There are four major steps that are followed in the development of a new system. The first step is to establish that the product is commercially viable. This certainly needs to be done for each new country but may also be important for each client firm. These kinds of systems link different activities in the firm, and firms in the same industry can have very different organizations. Thus customization of one form or another is inevitable in each installation.

The second step is to understand the technical details of the financial advisory issues as well as the details of issues surrounding the technical infrastructure. It is clear why this must be done for different countries, but it can also be important for different firms. In Canada, for example, interpretation of the relevant laws suggest that banks cannot sell life insurance; what is not clear is whether they can give advice about insurance to their customers (since good financial advice would certainly include advice about risk management).

Third, the knowledge engineering teams together with the system engineers must implement and integrate the new system. Finally, as implementation is completed, the client firms must be supported through the deployment process.

HOW A SYSTEM IS BUILT

Commercial and Technical Feasibility

Building any new system, particularly an expert system with the scope of the sales and marketing systems described in the preceding, begins by identifying the value and proving the commercial feasibility of the system. This applies whether the application is for a new industry or a new country. The commercial feasibility focuses on the system's conditions of use within a particular market.

For instance, a product marketed as a sales support tool in the United States is positioned as a mechanism for compliance in the United Kingdom. Market conditions, regulations, and culture all have to be assessed in order to market, build, and deploy a product that uniquely conforms to the local environment's conditions of use. For example, a fur coat is clearly a luxury item in urban centers but is a necessity of life to all Arctic societies. The application's distribution, manufacturing, its need–want ratio, and its condition of use are governed by the local environment.

Commercial feasibility.   To establish the commercial feasibility of an expert system requires both marketing expertise and in-depth knowledge of the particular industry. This is why expert system application firms like APEX tend to focus on a vertical market, and it is likely the reason that expert system consultants, who concentrate almost exclusively on the technology, build a lot of prototypes yet rarely seem to build a prototype that can be used by anyone. Establishing commercial feasibility for the same expert system outside the home country, as APEX has done, requires both knowledge of the host country's particular industry and international marketing expertise. Expertise of this sort is in short supply in the United States, much less in a small industry based on an emerging technology. At the least it requires international contacts in the appropriate industry sector.

Success in the commercial feasibility work depends most on the need for the application being present and then on the sensitivity of the vendor to the local conditions of use, with a willingness to alter the marketing communications accordingly. Local conditions of use can vary between regions of a country and different markets. The greatest variances occur between countries.

Though worldwide changes in financial services would seem to make every developed nation a suitable market for the sales and marketing systems described in the previous section, in fact some are not and perhaps never will be suitable. In Norway, for example, an individual is taxed on net worth, so Norwegian consumers are very reluctant to disclose what they own. An application that has as a prerequisite the divulgence of comprehensive personal financial information is doomed to failure in this environment no matter what the needs of the individual for financial advice or the needs of the institutions to compete more effectively.

Use of APEX systems in the United Kingdom illustrates changes in marketing communications, where an application that is marketed as a sales support tool in the United States is instead positioned in the United Kingdom as a mechanism for compliance. But even within a firm, the output can be positioned differently; a life insurer might have its sales force use only the product matching and sales scripting capability for sales support and marketing without a report going to the customer; the group business of the firm (employee benefits, affinity groups) may provide the advice in the client report as a service for a fee using the data for the marketing data base but without any direct support for sales.

First, because of the importance of the conditions of use and the marketing communication to the ultimate success of the project, the main objectives of the commercial feasibility work must be to analyze and understand all the customers of the system and carry through a simulation of the process.

Because it is cross-functional, an expert system can have many customers: There are many users of the analysis that the system can produce, and there are many activities that are touched by the system. For example, the customers for APEX's client profiling expert system include consumers (they must get value out of the process if they are to give their valuable financial information), salespeople (they must buy into using the system), and the home office (it needs to achieve targets in revenues, profits, and costs).

Second, it is important to simulate the process. Simulation done on paper, with the human experts doing the work, is often more effective than any machine prototyping effort. While manual simulation is the way we do it, the reason for doing it is to get the vital information that will build the business case.

Manual simulation, with its requirement for working with groups in many levels of the organization, also has the side benefit of helping these groups feel that they have ownership in the resulting system. Too often machine simulation will remove the developer prematurely from contact with the end user. It is very tempting to get tied up with what the machine can do instead of focusing on what is needed.

Another side benefit, particularly when the simulation is very successful, is the creation of some demand that can pull the project through a number of the barriers that can arise during development. For this reason it is important to give careful consideration to the choice of the participants in the simulation. The people involved in the simulated process should preferably be credible salespeople for the system, not only to support the development but also because in preparation for deployment they will be asked to sing the praises of the system to the larger user population.

In order to build the business case at the conclusion of the commercial work, the simulation should be designed with some measurable result in mind (the value!). There are some obvious bottom-line measurables for expert systems applied to sales and marketing support, as there are for systems in securities trading. Less obvious are immediate measures for underwriting or credit analysis applications since for these the impact on the bottom line may only show after several years of operation. Whether showing a direct or indirect impact in the bottom line, the business case needs to strongly demonstrate the value of the application.

For APEX sales and marketing systems, the elapsed time for the commercial work is typically 3–6 months. Staff requirements can be significant on the client side during this phase since, in essence, the client's staff does the prototype work under the direction of the developer. Staffing requirements for the development team include a project manager, someone with industry knowledge and task skills in the application area, and a knowledge engineer–systems analyst.

Technical feasibility.   The technical feasibility work is done either in parallel or following the commercial feasibility work. Technical feasibility entails an understanding of the differences between financial advisory issues as they apply to different segments of an industry (e.g., banking, brokerage, and insurance) or to different countries. These are not always just a matter of a different collection of rules and strategies. For example, in some European countries negotiated taxes and interest rates may completely change the kind of default reasoning that can be employed.

It is also important to understand the technical infrastructures of each firm and the different industries in each country. Attitudes toward departmental computing and the presence and/or prevalence of personal computers in the branch offices can significantly influence deployment.

Similarly, it is important to respect an institution's organization for the delivery of services of this kind (in fact, there may be none). A rule of thumb is that you cannot ask people to do their job too differently from the way they already do it (not if you want the change over any reasonable period of time). If the industry does not do business as if a client's needs matter, then an expert system that focuses on client needs will not fly.

To give some sense of the magnitude of the technical work required to understand the advisory issues between different countries, consider that the APEX systems have about 2,000 rules and use over 400 different classes of objects in the representation, with greater than 1,000 attributes for describing those objects and 1,000 active values attached to the classes.

Lest you doubt that sales and marketing expert system application will be a quite different system in even quite similar countries, consider the following minor rules of personal finance that every consumer is familiar with and that impact financial needs analysis and the strategies for meeting those needs.

- In the United States home mortgage interest is deductible from gross income on a mortgage amount not more than $100,000 above the cost basis of the home. Home equity provides an opportunity for tax advantaged borrowing to fund major needs in the areas of retirement and education.
- In Canada, home mortgage interest is not deductible at all, with the result that the strategies available for funding major needs must be different. Home equity can be used as a funding source but may need to be compared more closely with alternatives like borrowing against life insurance cash values [9].
- In the United Kingdom, home mortgage interest is deductible only on the first £30,000 of the mortgage. This is somewhere in between the U.S. and Canadian situations, which means yet another funding strategy must be formu-

lated. Attitudes toward borrowing and the availability and attributes of financial products (like home equity lines of credit) differ in the United Kingdom and can also affect a funding strategy [10].

- Italians can deduct from gross income only the first 4 million lira of interest paid on a mortgage (7 million for a joint return). The cap on the interest amount that is deductible and the fact that financial institutions limit borrowing (with the result that Italian mortgages are most often under 80 million lira) has a clear impact on funding strategies for other needs.

As already mentioned, advisory issues or approaches may be quite different from group to group in the financial services. This may be cultural or a feature of the legislation, as it is in Canada.

While the financial instruments are somewhat less variable from country to country than tax laws and investment regulations, it is not the case that, for example, a financial product as simple as a mortgage is simply a mortgage. Consider:

- In the United States, mortgages are most often 15- or 30-year repayment contracts based on either a fixed or variable rate of interest. The principal is amortized over the contract term, and payments include both interest and principal.
- In Canada, while the mortgage amount is amortized over 30 years, and the mortgage payments include principal and interest, the mortgage contract is most often only for a maximum of 5 years. Mortgage insurance on the life of the borrower is common and is bundled with the mortgage contract.
- In the United Kingdom there are 25-year repayment-type mortgages with variable interest rates, as in the United States, but very common alternatives are endowment, pension, or unit-linked mortgage contracts. The mortgage payment is interest only; a second payment (premium) is made into an investment/life insurance vehicle that funds the payment of the mortgage principal at the end of the mortgage term.
- Italian mortgages are repayment type with medium terms (10–15 years) and are often under 100 million lira. Approval for a larger mortgage might take nine months.

Similarly, while deregulation has allowed firms to compete in the broader financial services arena, similar financial instruments may acquire a cast from the base business of the firm (witness the nonbank banking products of some U.S. securities firms).

The last piece of the application where there may be significant technical issues to consider is the output. For U.S. life insurance companies, the APEX systems produce a 15–25-page tailored client report and a 10-page sales script for the agent. For other industries the reports produced may be of different lengths or organized in different ways. In most cases 30% of the profiling code is devoted to text production so the text is a major technical consideration.

Of course, a primary consideration for implementation of text output is the language of the target country (some, like Canada, compound the difficulty with two official languages). Language aside, to tailor to the right level, the text expert must know every nuance of expression in the language and be sensitive to cultural expressions. For example:

- In common American usage a *plan* is a method for accomplishing something while a *scheme* is a crafty plot and clearly connotes something slightly underhanded. The British usage is not at all the same, with the result that a pension plan in the United States is properly termed a pension scheme in the United Kingdom.

The main goals of the technical feasibility work therefore are (1) to scope the knowledge base, (2) to understand the system integration issues including the requirements of the technical infrastructure, (3) to identify the major cost factors both for development and operational costs, and (4) to develop an engineering plan to get the system built. The final report should therefore include a scope statement, a cost estimate, and a development schedule.

For the APEX systems, the knowledge base scope statement includes discussion of the joint agreements on advisory and design terminology and includes an agreed upon sequence of planning areas, the basic recommendation and observations that the expert logic is to make, the data required by the system, and the analysis performed. Understanding of the system integration issues includes data entry, archiving of data, and data security. Technical infrastructure includes the hardware and software as well as networks and servers in use.

For the APEX systems, the elapsed time for the technical work is typically 3–6 months. Client staff requirements are not as significant as for the commercial work, and typically the same expert resources are used. Staff requirements for the developer are most often identical to the requirements for the commercial work with the addition of a systems engineer.

The chief benefits of the technical study lie in the identification of the sources of expertise needed to build the system. The preliminary knowledge engineering work of this stage can be used to guide the choice of experts for the full-scale development work. A second benefit is the opportunity to distribute some ownership of the project to the data processing (DP)/management information systems (MIS) group. The end-user group needs to fund the development, but DP/MIS will need to run it eventually.

Implementation

Satisfactory results from the commercial and technical work are prerequisites to implementation of the application. Implementation itself follows at least four phases: specification (which incorporates the bulk of the knowledge engineering), coding, verification, and testing/QA.

The key to success in the implementation stage is to be able to work in a more conventional software development style, with large development teams working from written specifications and facing periodic code review and rigorous testing. At the same time, the development teams should be able to take advantage of the body of artificial intelligence (AI) development technology: rapid prototyping, domain-level programming, and the ability to work on incompletely specified problems at a high level of abstraction.

The reason a conventional approach is key is that there is a good body of knowledge about managing projects that employs 20 and even more knowledge/software engineers. With that number of people, chains of technical communication are long, particularly when they involve overseas communication, and procedures and interactions for organizing and performing the work are complex. Integration of separately produced modules and components is difficult at best and can become totally impossible if careful design and control are not followed at every stage of the work.

This style of development might seem the antithesis of the rapid prototyping approach that has become the model for expert system development. However, the AI development tools are workable (even essential, as claimed) for these projects. The advantages of working in a prototyping style accrue largely to its speed rather than the absence of structure. Not understanding a problem completely at a particular stage of development is a deficiency for which AI technology provides a workaround; it is not a style of development.

The AI style also pays dividends if changes over the knowledge are not totally in the control of the client or development team. Rules and regulations are able to change at the whim of a government; the success of the development project and the ability to provide for ongoing product maintenance can depend on the ability to react quickly to such changes.

To implement a large commercial expert system given the current state of the art in commercial expert system development environment requires significant invention of new technology and development of new project management procedures and methodologies. Largely for this reason, application vendors generally have their own development technology and do not rely on the commercial technology suppliers.

Design phase. The design phase is the period during which the bulk of the knowledge engineering is performed, the specification is produced, and the users sign off on the application functionality.

The APEX view is that there are two basic approaches to expert system design, one based on a theory of expertise and the other based on specification of expertise. Underlying the theory-of-expertise approach is a model of problem solving that in many cases tends to be weak in its own right but relies on powerful heuristics for the end result.

Both OPS5 and Prolog can be viewed from the theory of expertise perspective. The former is derived from work in the cognitive sciences; the latter is a mechanization of formal logic. A common example of a problem-solving model is the three-stage cycle from representation, which guides search, which in turn drives a sampling of the environment for more data, which results in a modification of the representation, guiding further search, and so on [11]. Presumably the cycle eventually terminates with a conclusion.

Many powerful systems have been based on this approach, but the necessary engineering support is lacking. A commercial software firm needs to be able to have as much control as possible over the development process. This is hard enough with conventional applications. Staying in business means staying away from the conventional wisdom on expert system development.

For these reasons APEX has taken the specification-of-expertise approach to develop its products. Specification of expertise simply focuses on what is to be computed, the data required for those computations, and the forms of output to be produced. The only remnant of the theory-of-expertise approach that remains is the focus on *observations* and *recommendations* during the knowledge engineering.

Observations and recommendations can be understood in the context of search. If part of the theory of expertise is that the expert searches some solution space during the problem-solving activity, then one way to understand observations and recommendations is as intermediate and final results, respectively. In applications for the financial services, these observations and recommendations could appear in the written analysis that the system produces, and this is the major reason for focusing on them.

In order to understand the observations and recommendations and generate the rest of the specification, including data requirements, calculations made, rules used, text produced, and so on, the development team undertakes a series of structured interviews over a period of several weeks. Preparation of agendas and questions by participating knowledge engineers (KEs) occurs prior to the interview session. Each KE is responsible for an area of expertise and runs the interviews for that area. Interviews are typically arranged in two 2-hour sessions with two to three KEs and the expert(s). The interviews should be highly focused with stated objectives and goals. In general, all expert interviews should be attended by the lead KE for the particular area and at least one other KE. The lead KE has responsibility for organizing and conducting interviews as well as documenting and designing the area. Experience has shown that optimal KE and expert productivity is derived from interview sessions of 4 hours a day in blocks of 2 hours each. Exceeding these guidelines may impair the participants' abilities to assess and evaluate certain ramifications, document results, or prepare for the next review session.

Recording of the interview is accomplished with structured note taking, and notes are written immediately after the meeting. The experts and other participating KEs should read the notes either by the next session or within an assigned limit of time. Document length and complexity should be accounted for, but rapid turnaround time is essential. This discipline is strictly enforced. The main reason is that it is essential to commit the meeting results to paper while the memory is still fresh; another reason is to get the experts to commit agreements to writing; finally it is important because schedules are tight. Notes are cross referenced and compiled into binders, where they form the basic reference materials for the specification. Communication between areas and review of the overall integrity of the design are achieved through concise, thorough, and clear KE notes, walkthroughs, and the specification. A sample outline for KE notes is given in Appendix A.

Immediately following the initial interview phase, the specification is written, with considerable review by the client. The goal is to have a document that details as much as possible exactly what the expert system will do and have the client agree in writing that this is what they want built. This approach, although conventional, is also quite adaptive. It is as important for an expert system to built right and on time and on budget as it is for conventional applications.

Such specifications are never hard and fast. In particular, expert system specifications have a greater degree of evolution and adaptation than those of conventional systems. Fortunately, the expert system development technology can support some uncertainty in the specification. In all specification processes, no matter the methodology applied, there is a need to put in place a process by which issues can be resolved. Specification and development of an expert system requires KEs to arrange follow-up interview sessions to resolve ambiguities, errors, and inaccuracies in the draft specification. The resulting work product is an updated version of the functional specification. A sample outline for a specification is given in Appendix B.

The duration of the design phase has averaged about two months for the APEX sales and marketing systems. Expert interviewing is generally very short in this phase. However, the earlier commercial and technical feasibility work provides a good foundation for planning the interviewing sessions. The data and text specification are often written separately from the expert logic specification, with the client playing a major role in specifying the text according to their local legislation or conditions of use. The final specification document can run 300–400 pages in length. Figure 11 is a sample project plan for the design phase.

Development phase. The major goals for the development phase are to implement the required expertise, including the calculations and rules that generate the specified observations and recommendations, and build the system interfaces.

One major collaborative effort that takes place in the beginning is the design of the class structure in the representation system. Due to the large number of KEs on the project, it is essential that they all agree on the reference terms for the items about which they will reason. Class names, attributes, and values may be used throughout the system, while the rules and the procedures for each area of expertise may be relatively self-contained. The major result of these design sessions is a style document used by KEs throughout the project.

The knowledge representation system is relatively conventional in features and functionality, with the exception of the capabilities for handling individual cases (data sets) required by high-volume batch processes. One noteworthy aspect of the APEX design approach is the explicit representation of observations and recommenda-

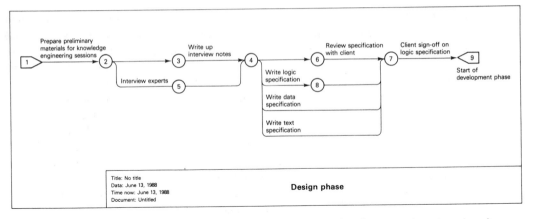

Figure 11 Project plan for the design phase. Planning for expert interviews is quite extensive and makes use of the results of the commercial and technical feasibility work. Teams of KEs interview experts over a relatively short period, after which the specification is written. Separate logic, data, and text specifications are combined in the final report. Engineering will begin while the user reviews and approves the specification. There is allowance for user changes to the specification during the development stage.

tions. Observations and recommendations are instantiated by the expert process during processing and are then used by the text generation system to craft the output reports.

To develop the reasoning in the system, the APEX KEs use a proprietary program description language (PDL) to go from the specification to the program. The language was developed from the pseudo-English that the KEs use in their structured interview notes to capture the expert logic. The fundamental technical strategy behind the APEX development environment is support for the KEs in their work patterns, by contrast with approaches that require a KE to be more programmer than analyst. The PDL approach is related to ideas from CASE technology and is another example of advances through conventional technology used to advantage to build expert systems.

The duration of the development phase for the APEX systems is about three to four months. Some unit testing of the individual modules takes place prior to formal quality assurance activities. Figure 12 is a sample project plan for the development phase.

Quality assurance phase.   The QA phase of the development cycle is designed to verify that the system accurately reflects the specification document. In addition, the validity of the expert analysis is critically examined.

Validation is a much longer process than verification and is usually undertaken by the vendor's QA group in conjunction with the client's experts. Using the framework of O'Keefe et al. [12] as an approach to the validation problem, we have the following questions to answer in designing the validation procedures:

- What to validate.
- What to validate against.
- What to validate with.
- When to validate.
- How to control validation cost.
- How to control bias.

Validation of the APEX sales and marketing systems includes validation of the intermediate results (observations and recommendations), the reasoning of the system, and the final result (documents). Intermediate observations and numerical calculations are validated against the specification, while the reasoning process is validated using the client experts. The text of the final reports is validated against the specification, while the recommendations are validated against the client's experts.

Validation is performed via test cases specifically designed to exercise the system's areas of expertise and against live client cases obtained during the rollout phase. At this early stage of use, feedback from the users and the consumers becomes critical. Ramp up to full deployment is carefully controlled to provide a large collection of real-life consumer cases for testing purposes. By the time of final deployment, a large number of cases have been processed.

Early in the development phase, after the system specification is complete, a test plan is developed that includes a detailed process description, specification of

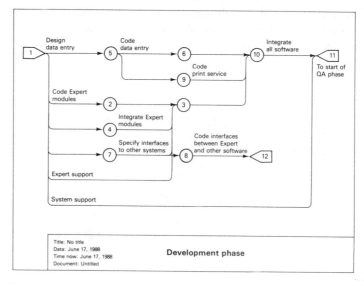

Figure 12   Project plan for the development phase. Development of data entry and interface software is often a separate component of the overall development activity. With the specification approved, code for the expert modules can be developed directly.

particular test tools, and a definition of the acceptance criteria. The results of the expert process must pass a content review as well as a mechanical review (how the documents look). The QA process includes thoroughly testing the communications and the system administration functions, the data entry programs, and the product knowledge base mechanism. Finally, documentation, installation procedures, and performance levels are verified. Once in place, the same QA procedures are followed for each new release.

Typical acceptance criteria will specify acceptable numbers of critical bugs (usually zero), acceptable numbers of noncritical bugs (e.g., formatting or awkward text) per document page, sound basic functionality, and complete test of bug fixes. Performance integrity is also tested and is a critical component of acceptance. A diagram of the activities in the QA phase appears in Figure 13.

Validation occurs in parallel with development and deployment, with the early phases of deployment placing the greatest load on expert resources.

For APEX sales and marketing systems, the elapsed time for the QA work is typically six weeks, although there is unit testing and integration that is an integral part of the development phase. The six-week period is average for a new release. Staff requirements are significant, typically one-half to two-thirds of the resources used for development.

Quality assurance is critical to the successful deployment of the system in large scale. The ability to control the cost of this process is of course one of the skills that APEX has acquired by building several very large expert systems. Knowhow is a large factor, as is the development technology. A flexible development environment coupled with a methodology that leads very directly from the logical to the physical design means that reasons for bugs can be quickly discovered and corrected the first time.

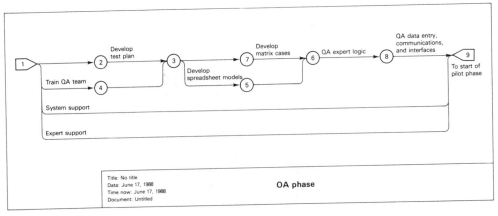

Figure 13 Project plan for the QA phase. Planning for the QA phase and development of the testing tools are significant components of the QA activity. The QA group tests the expert logic at the end of the development phase. The end user must be trained in the QA approaches.

Bias as a factor in the expert-level analysis is either negotiated out of the product (in the process of interviewing the experts) or deliberately included to accommodate a particular client institution. Implementations that provide a report to the consumer tend to try to make the report more objective than might be the case if the analysis were seen by the salesperson only.

Pilot phase.   The pilot phase is the beginning of full-scale deployment. Deployment is generally the longest phase of application development and in many respects the most difficult. Solving the organizational problems that arise during the installation and early use of any large-scale automation project constitutes at least 80% of the work required to ensure the success of the overall program.

The pilot is designed to test the process, identify the major organizational, logistical, and cultural problems, and forge solutions before scaling up to the entire salesforce. The pilot program itself may be phased so that the elapsed time from first use to full use is often months and may be years.

From the developer's point of view, the start of deployment means helping the client firm devise training programs covering the concept and the operation of the system, mechanisms for reinforcing what the program is meant to accomplish, and providing procedures (sales tracks) to facilitate success. In addition to training programs for the end users, there must be technical training for system operators in such tasks as system backup, assignment of user IDs and passwords, and installation of updated versions of software.

The major issues at the start of deployment involve logistics and culture. Logistics, the need for all sorts of supporting materials such as advertising, brochures, and training materials typically bog down the start of any large-scale deployment.

Cultural issues include moving the salesforce from the culture of the one-call close toward the needs-oriented selling supported by the expert system. Needs-oriented selling usually entails two to three customer meetings before any sale. The longer sales process is due to the extra steps involved in understanding the client needs, devising a solution to those needs, and then presenting the recommendations to the client. The one-call close is part and parcel of the single-need or product-push approach. Changing the culture from one-call to needs-oriented selling is no easy task because it means changing the way salespeople work as well as how sales management manages its staff. For example, in the one-call close environment many sales managers manage by the numbers—make 100 phone calls a week, schedule 10 meetings, close 2 sales.

The process of changing the culture in banks does not have the obstacle of the entrenched sales process, but only because a sales culture and a sales process often do not exist in a bank.

Cultural issues may also be just inertial. People have an image of themselves that is resistant to change (can you change a banker to a salesperson, in their own mind?). They also structure their work day and work week in a particular way, and once in the groove, particularly a groove that is successful, they are unwilling to change (how do you explain having to schedule 15 minutes per client for data entry in the new system?). Finally, people will want to know how change will be advantageous to them.

Technical innovation of any sort rarely happens without affecting people. The pilot phase is designed to both introduce the technology and shake out program bugs and gaps in functionality as well as tune the solutions to identified innovation management problems.

CONCLUSION

Ninety-eight percent of all the expert systems built to-date lie forgotten and unused— a stark testament to the importance of choosing the right application domain and following through on deployment. The fact is and will forever be that noone will pay a nickel more for an expert system program that does the same thing as one without the expert system. Organizations pay for the value the application can deliver. Creating value is the essence of domain choice, not the existence of domain experts, nor the use of heuristics in domain problem solving, nor the complexity of the problem, attributes that have become part of the expert system development mythology.

It is also a fact that few successful information systems can attribute their success to the underlying technology. Any expert system developer with a grand vision had better be prepared to deal with a deployment timetable that is three to four times as long as the development timetable. People are the ultimate consumers of expertise, and delivery systems need to be designed to accommodate organizations.

There is now a good deal of evidence that there can be a lot of value in an expert system that can cost-effectively deliver to a life insurance agent both a comprehensive client needs analysis and recommendations for products from the agent's product set (Figure 14). But ensuring the success of the system on full-scale deployment is much more than a matter of putting the necessary analytic and product-matching expertise in a box and handing it to the agent. Expert systems tend to transform the way a job is performed, so deployment of a system that involves change (and few do not) is a massive experiment in organizational behavior.

Figure 14   Benefits of expert systems for sales and marketing support. Expert systems that link the salesforce to the marketing and product development activities of the firm are able to add significant value to the sales process in the retail financial services. The products of expert analysis are a client report that contains comprehensive, objective financial advice to the client, a sales report that provides timely product information and sales points to the salesforce, and a data extract that contains the client information and associated recommendation. The data extract is used by the marketing function to better target market the firm's products and by sales management and product development to understand and manage the sales process.

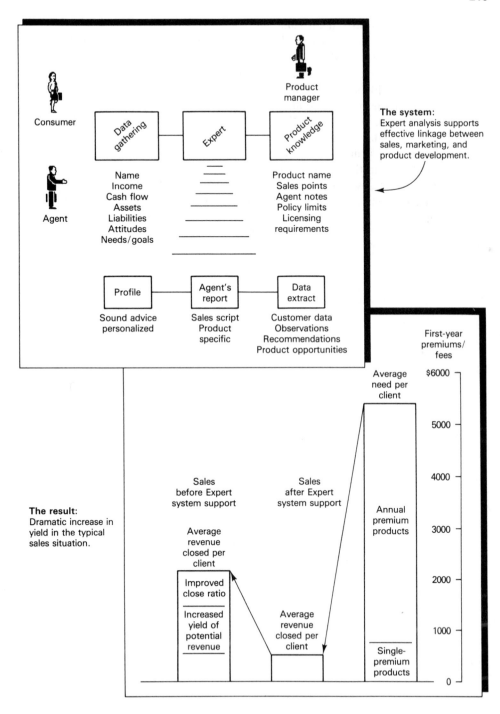

Consumer

Product
manager

Data
gathering — Expert — Product
knowledge

Agent

Name
Income
Cash flow
Assets
Liabilities
Attitudes
Needs/goals

Product name
Sales points
Agent notes
Policy limits
Licensing
requirements

The system:
Expert analysis supports
effective linkage between
sales, marketing, and
product development.

Profile — Agent's report — Data extract

Sound advice
personalized

Sales script
Product
specific

Customer data
Observations
Recommendations
Product opportunities

The result:
Dramatic increase in
yield in the typical
sales situation.

First-year
premiums/
fees

Sales
before Expert
system support

Sales
after Expert
system support

Average
need per
client

$6000

5000

Average
revenue
closed per
client

4000

Annual
premium
products

3000

Improved
close ratio

2000

Increased
yield of
potential
revenue

Average
revenue
closed per
client

1000

Single-
premium
products

0

There is also much value in an expert system that can deliver to the banker a comprehensive customer needs analysis together with recommendations for products from the bank's product set. Here, again, the deployment phase of the expert system is the key to success. Technology is not a substitute for strategy. And the deployment schedule will have to coincide with the slow process of instilling the right sales culture in the bank personnel [13].

These examples from the financial services industry illustrate the points detailed in this chapter. Expert systems must be built in domains that can be shown to deliver significant value to a firm. This means that the development plan must be designed from the beginning to show the value and the results must be measurable. Most expert systems also transform the way people do their jobs, and this implies that any plans for managing the transformation must be well considered from the start.

APPENDIX A: OUTLINE FOR KE EXPERT INTERVIEW SESSION NOTES

**Knowledge Engineering
Example Session Agenda**

Date: _____   Topic area: _____
Documented by: _____   _____
                                        _____
Attendees: _____   _____
           _____
           _____
           _____

Topic area objectives/questions
_____
_____
_____ | List topic area objectives
_____ | and questions. Each
_____ | question is then listed on a
_____ | blank piece of paper where
_____ | all subsequent notes are
                                          | recorded.

Open issues/questions from previous session
_____
_____ | Reference topic and date
_____ | and assign issue to a
_____ | particular person. Give each
_____ | issue a meaningful name
_____ | that may be referenced in
                                          | resolutions in later sessions.

Resolutions to issues from previous session
_____
_____ | Reference topic and date.
_____ | Use the same identifying
_____ | topic area heading as the
_____ | issue resolved.
_____

Summary results of session
_____
_____ | Major decisions, reasons, or
_____ | significant information on
_____ | session topics. Give each
_____ | topic/subtopic a meaningful
_____ | name that may be
                                          | referenced in later sessions.

Rewrite KE notes by: _____
Next scheduled meeting: _____

APPENDIX B: OUTLINE FOR EXPERT SYSTEM SPECIFICATION

Logic Specification Outline

1. Overview
  1. **Introduction:** Brief introduction to document. Probable description of intent of the application; guide to reading the rest of the document. Very brief.
  2. **Top level** (with a different name)
     * Sequencing of modules, fixed and conditional. Processing and text.
     * Concepts important for readers to understand. The objective is to assign a label to and explain each term so that the label can be used without definition throughout the specification: descriptions of terms, as needed.
     * Types of data checks: data entry warnings and stoppers (verification) and data warnings and stoppers (validation).
     * Types and use of parameters: installation level and user level.
     * Out-of-scope stoppers.
     MORE, if needed
     *
     *
     *

II. Expert Logic
 1. Logic Module 1
 2. Logic Module 2
     *
     *
     *
    14. Logic Module *N*

III. List of to-date parameter values
   List of all identified parameterized items and values that are in use during the development/test phase. If this is a complicated set of tables, the source document is referenced and dated.

IV. Data Requirements
   Details include:
   * General definition, if not obvious.
   * Required field?
   * Defaults.
   * Data entry checks, valid values or range.
   * Data validation warning or stopper.
   * Implementation or user parameter?
   * Any pertinent information about use within system.

Tentative Outline for Expert Logic Sections 1 through *N*

Note: any section can be subdivided into multiple related recommendation groups if it makes sense for the report. Each subdivision repeats the outline for the section. Each subdivision can have its own *logic description* and *recommendation text* and also its own *table* and *data requirements*, if appropriate.

Calculation definitions can be included in context the first time they are mentioned. If they are to be referenced again, they should be assigned a label.

Overview

A brief summary of the content and scope of the expertise area.

A synopsis of the recommendations and related text to provide a context for the logic description.

Table(s)

Illustration of any tables with a definition of the fields. Use 9's to show field size limits rather than numbers. Calculations can be included in the definitions. The table section can be prior to or included in any subdivision, as appropriate.

Data Requirements

References the detailed data document, Chapter IV. Focuses, as appropriate, on which section, parts of section, or specific fields are relevant to this expertise area.

Logic Description

Free-form description of the logic—flow, heuristics, calculations, modeling, conditional recommendation, and dot point text—that generates the recommendations. Limit long paragraphs if dot and dash points can be used. Label any calculations that are referred to elsewhere or use labels from tables. Use subheadings if it will contribute to understanding. Reference or quote any text item if it will contribute to understanding.

The target audience is the client experts so the level of detail should be substantial, similar to the KE notes. Since early drafts of the logic descriptions will be sent for review, any outstanding issues should be clearly highlighted. This can be accomplished by either or both including a separate issues section and by imbedding something like ***ISSUE*** within the context of the logic description.

Recommendation Text

This section should contain all possible variations of text identified in the commercial study. Anything conditional should be illustrated as such with conditions, similar to a traditional computed text specification. Embedded conditionality should be avoided for inital releases, where possible.

Design Notes

Anything aside from the logic worth noting or communicating for future phases.

ACKNOWLEDGMENTS

It is a pleasure to acknowledge the help of Beth O'Hara and her timely suggestions on how to improve the manuscript.

REFERENCES

1. Life Insurance Marketing and Research Associates (*LIMRA*), P.O. Box 20X, Hartford CT, 06141.
2. Porter, M. E., *Competitive Advantage: Sustaining Superior Performance*. Free Press, New York, 1985, p. 37.
3. Gourgues, H. W. and Lauterbach, J. R., *Revolution in Financial Services*. BNA Books, Washington DC, 1987, p. 26.
4. Bevington, V. A. and Luconi, F. L., "The Diversification Debate," *Best's Review*, Vol. 88, No. 7, 1987, pp. 29–36.
5. Makelin, M., *A Case Study and Experiences in Financial Expert and Decision Support Systems*, HM&V Research Oy, Finland, 1987.
6. A. Yakata, personal communication, 1988.
7. *Mainichi Daily News*, *Tokyo*, November 17, 1988, p. 1.
8. *Economist*, February 13, 1988, pp. 11–12.
9. Birch, R., *The Family Financial Planning Book*, Key Porter Books, Toronto, Ontario, 1987.
10. Allen, M. *The Hutchinson Money Minder*, Century Hutchinson, Covent Garden, London, 1987.
11. Olson, J. R. and Rueter, H. H., "Extracting Expertise from Experts: Methods for Knowledge Acquisition," *Expert Systems*, Vol. 4, No. 3, pp. 152–168.
12. O'Keefe, R. M., Baki, O., and Smith, E. P., "Validating Expert System Performance," *IEEE Expert*, Vol. 2, No. 4, 1987, pp. 81–90.
13. "Selling Savvy Eludes Banks," *Financial Services Week*, November 21, 1988, p. 1.

An Expert System at the U.S. Energy Information Administration for Quality Assurance and Statistical Survey Support

Jerald L. Feinstein
Howard Magnas
David L. Bailey

INTRODUCTION

This chapter describes an expert system built for the U.S. Energy Information Administration (EIA) to assist in resolving errors and ambiguities in data collected in EIA statistical surveys. The system was built using the LEVEL5 shell interfacing with DBASEIII files of data downloaded from a mainframe and was designed to operate in an IBM PC environment.

The EIA collects massive quantities of data on the production, transportation, and end use of all forms of fossil energy. These data are collected from numerous sources that fall into two broad categories: Federal Energy Regulatory Commission (FERC) forms and EIA surveys. While most filings are mandatory, some surveys such as EIA-627 are voluntary.

Some survey data are reported weekly (e.g., EIA-800-804), some monthly (e.g., EIA-759, FERC-423, EIA-810–814, EIA-816, and EIA-817), and other survey data are reported quarterly (e.g., EIA-400). Still other survey data are reported annually (e.g., FERC-1, EIA-176, EIA-627, and EIA-820).

In checking the survey data, items such as respondent name and ID number, location of data on form (correct line), and general reasonableness of the numbers are examined. For some surveys, data from one respondent are compared to data reported by another. For example, EIA-176 is filed by all natural gas pipeline companies. Checks are made to match deliveries from one company to receipts by other companies. If errors are detected at this stage, either they are resolved by staff (e.g., correct company name or ID number) or the respondent is contacted for corrections. If the survey is mandatory, the respondent is required to file an amended form.

Staff working on EIA's IBM 3084QX computer enter survey data. The data are then passed through programs that scan the data for missing values, out-of-range values, wrong data type (e.g., character data in numeric fields), totals, and internal consistency. Data are also compared to prior reporting periods. This process results in certain data being flagged for further review. These are called edit flags. Staff then attempt to resolve discrepancies and problems with flagged values.

A significant number of flagged values are eventually resolved only after review by EIA professional staff. Because of the complexity of the EIA data collection process, attention by EIA professional staff is often required, and assistance is sought from the respondent. With the massive volume of data handled in this process, it has become a time-consuming and expensive process.

This process also calls for a high level of judgment based on years of experience on the part of the staff. For example, what may appear to be a shifted decimal point or a value reported in the wrong units may in fact not be an error at all. A refinery that normally produces 3 million barrels of crude a month may have reported producing only 300,000 barrels for the current month. There are at least two potential explanations. First, a typographical error could have been made. Second, the refinery operation may have been curtailed for some reason, most likely maintenance. This type of error can readily be resolved by carefully reviewing the level of product produced by the refinery.

Sometimes problem resolution requires significant knowledge of an industry. For example, a situation of this type could arise in reporting variable operating and maintenance (O&M) costs. The distinction between variable and fixed O&M costs is somewhat vague and depends in part on the company's accounting procedures. As a result, when converted to mills/kWh, variable O&M can range from less than 1 mill/kWh to more than 10 mills/kWh. Among the parameters that must be taken into account when evaluating O&M costs are type of unit, emission control equipment used, unit utilization, and values reported for fixed and variable components. Only an individual with considerable expertise would be able to make this type of distinction.

Problems sometimes arise because required data is not defined as clearly as it might be or interpretations of terms may vary from respondent to respondent or from state to state. For example, FERC Form-1 requires that the respondent report all power purchases and sales. For each purchase, the respondent must report quantity (MWh), cost of energy, cost of capacity, demand charges, and type of purchase. Type of purchase is open to interpretation, and sometimes a purchase shared by several utilities under a pooling arrangement is classified differently by each recipient.

THE EXPERT SYSTEM APPROACH

Expert systems are an extension of classical decision support systems that provide enhanced judgmental and justification capabilities and can be linked with statistical and analytical tools offering solutions to problems where algorithm-based software systems fail completely.

The EIA expert system to resolve computer edit flags permits EIA to codify the knowledge and expertise that is involved in a highly knowledge- and labor-intensive process.

In addition to the benefit of codifying valuable knowledge, the system provides consistent resolution of errors. The system is also cost effective because it improves the skill level and the efficiency of staff, provides built-in data quality assurance, and thus reduces the burden of EIA professional staff and respondents.

The data collection and reporting process is time consuming and costly and places a great burden on EIA and its technical staff. The EIA publishes results of its surveys weekly, monthly, quarterly, and annually. The *Petroleum Supply Monthly*, for instance, is based on data filed on EIA-800-804, EIA-810-814, EIA-816, and EIA-817. Several thousand forms from refiners, pipeline companies, importers, terminal operators, and tanker and barge operators must be processed within approximately three weeks in order to produce timely reports. Most monthly forms are due by the 20th of the following month; the *Petroleum Supply Monthly* is then published approximately 30 days later. An expert system would reduce some of this burden by reducing manual processing and improving the accuracy and timeliness of the data collection process.

The EIA expert system mimics human experts. The EIA expert system uses the same methods and information that experts use to solve problems. In addition, the EIA expert system identifies the reason each data element was flagged, makes predictions, and offers explanations just as an expert consultant would. The ability to automate expertise, knowledge, and real-world scenarios is the driving force behind the proliferation of expert systems and the key to achieving tangible benefits for EIA.

Many applications, such as the EIA edit-flag resolution process, are well suited to expert systems. Certain characteristics made this application an ideal candidate for an expert system. These included:

- The task was performed frequently.
- There were only a few experts who could perform the task.
- The current process was labor intensive.
- The accuracy and timeliness of data were critical.

When these situations occur, as in the case of the EIA data collection system postedit application, incorporating error-checking expertise into an expert system is advisable. The process of resolving EIA computer edit flags can thus be preserved within the organization and transferred quickly and easily to new staff.

APPROACH WITH SIGNIFICANT BENEFITS IN RESOLVING COMPUTER EDIT FLAGS

Use of a computer edit-flag resolution expert system would result in large savings in costs, time, and effort as well as increases in accuracy and consistency. An expert system is well suited for this application because there is a well-defined body of knowledge contained in source documents, the minds of the survey managers, as well as the technical staff; the actions are repetitive; and there are significant productivity differences between seasoned survey managers and new staff.

Because the EIA system provides a consistent set of rules and policies, the decision process will become more standardized. Several members of the staff may make different decisions under the same circumstances depending on their experience, understanding of the process, and problem-solving abilities. The edit-flag expert system will standardize the resolution procedure by allowing everyone access to the same body of knowledge.

The edit-flag expert system harvests valuable EIA expertise. The knowledge that the experts draw upon to resolve the computer edit flags would be codified as the rules and facts that the expert system would use to make decisions. This transcription of the experts' knowledge is important for two reasons. First, it allows validation of the knowledge used by the experts, making certain that it is both accurate and complete. Second, the knowledge is protected from loss due to staff relocation and turnover.

The edit-flag expert system can be used as an automated training tool for new staff and a refresher tool for current staff. The edit-flag expert system is designed to provide the rationale for the questions that it poses and ultimately for the recommendation that it gives to the user. By following the expert system's line of reasoning, the data processor can begin to understand the computer edit-flag resolution process for each particular situation. This view of the process provides key insights into the case at hand and potentially many more cases in the future.

Using the expert system will increase all users' awareness of the EIA's policies regarding the localization of error and data imputation. This automated training feature will generate substantial benefits because (1) it improves performance of existing staff, (2) it brings new staff up to speed quickly, and (3) it retains valuable expertise within the EIA in spite of employee promotions and turnover. All of these facts were important to the success of the EIA edit-flag expert system.

SELECTING THE SHELL

Our approach to building the system consisted of several major tasks. First, we reviewed the EIA data collection procedures in order to properly define the domain. We studied the data collection process by reviewing policy and support documentation and then speaking to the survey managers and/or contractors involved in analyzing the computer edit flags. Through this process, we determined the data sources involved, the delivery environment that was necessary, the implementation issues, and the constraints. Then we recommended to the EIA which survey would be a good candidate to automate with a prototype expert system. Because this was the first expert system prototype of its kind, selecting the proper survey was extremely important. The selected survey was of moderate complexity and had experts who currently attacked the problem of data quality assurance.

Next, we evaluated commercially available expert system development tools that met the following EIA requirements:

- Be relatively inexpensive.
- Provide easy-to-use development and delivery interfaces.
- Permit external interfaces with data bases and executable software.
- Compile into a run time version to provide a tamper-proof user copy.
- Have acceptable licensing procedures.
- Provide for end-user maintenance.
- Be an EIA authorized and supported language.
- Have more aspects of a shell than a language.
- Run in both IBM PC and IBM mainframe environments.

We evaluated the available commercial shells to find the most appropriate solution to EIA's situation. The shell selected based on the preceding criteria was LEVEL5, by Information Builders.

In addition to selecting the best expert system shell for the EIA system, we studied the ramifications of integrating the edit-flag expert system into the current EIA data collection system and found that no additional hardware and software were required to integrate the expert system with the existing infrastructure.

After purchasing the EIA-approved shell, we familiarized ourselves with the expert system software product. This allowed us to proceed directly to the coding of the experts' knowledge during the development phase.

KNOWLEDGE ENGINEERING AT EIA

The Triton/Phase Linear Systems knowledge engineers worked closely with the EIA survey manager and other experts to design and build the initial prototype of the expert system. Close contact was essential throughout the development process to ensure that the resulting expert system was on target both in terms of usability and knowledge validity. In addition, one or two Triton/Phase Linear Systems staff members with expertise in the energy survey area and in data quality assurance worked closely with the knowledge engineer.

Our knowledge acquisition effort was the vital link between the design and development stages. Knowledge acquisition is one of the most complex and arduous tasks of expert systems development. Several knowledge acquisition methods were employed by Triton/Phase Linear Systems to ensure effective, efficient identification and encoding of the expert's knowledge:

- Familiar tasks.
- Structured interviews.
- Limited information tasks.
- Tough-case method.

The decision process of the expert usually involves significant observable behavior. By working through several familiar tasks, the expert demonstrated key aspects of their selective classification process. In addition, the resolution process performed by the technical staff was documented. We observed their behavior, questioned their actions and their rationale, and interviewed them to gain valuable insights into the edit-flag resolution process. Because knowledge engineering is an inductive process, we refined our analysis by studying a large number of computer edit-flag resolutions. We taped several sessions using microcassette recorders so that the knowledge engineers could later review the tapes and repeat specific examples as the system was being developed.

Structured interviews formed the core of our knowledge acquisition process. The team was highly trained and experienced in conducting such interviews, which saved the experts much valuable time, and recorded the information for later translation into rules, frames, decision trees, and other knowledge representation schemes as applicable.

Knowledge engineers provided structure to the decision-making process of the experts. The tough-case method allowed the extraction of refined reasoning procedures that otherwise might have taken days to document. By reviewing an extremely difficult case, the rules and relationships that an expert uses may be applied to other cases as well as yielding a wealth of insight.

BUILDING THE EIA PROTOTYPE SYSTEM

During the course of knowledge acquisition, we partitioned the problem domain into subproblems as appropriate. This process assisted us in more narrowly defining the task, thereby accelerating the completion of the expert system prototype. For example, the various survey-specific postedit activities and decisions of the data processors decomposed into logical units that could then be placed into modules in the prototype system.

We worked closely with the survey manager in developing the design of the computer edit-flag resolution expert system. The design began as a one-page overview of the problem and evolved into a more sophisticated development guide. The one-page overview contained a logical breakdown of the problem, a list of data sources, external interfaces, and a set of outputs that the system was required to produce. Potential outputs included such recommendations as "Confirm data with respondent," "Check original data," or "See survey manager." As the design process continued, we selected the types of knowledge representation to be used, identified the location and format of external data, and designed the appropriate user interfaces.

After the design was completed, we began to enter the results of the knowledge acquisition into the expert system shell. Implementation started with one of the logical design subproblems in a rapid prototyping fashion. Rapid prototyping provided a presentable expert system application early in the project. As implementation proceeded from one completed subproblem to another, the initial prototype exhibited more of the capabilities of the finished expert system prototype and thus resembled the computer edit-flag resolution process of the survey managers.

Rapid prototyping coupled with a high degree of interaction with the survey manager helped ensure that the expert system evolved properly in terms of both its knowledge and its user interface. All of the survey-specific postedit analysis activities were incorporated into the appropriate logical subdivisions of the expert system. Interfaces were artistically designed using menus, windows, and simple text commands along with extensive help and explanation facilities. This made the expert system prototype suitable for use by data technicians with a high school education.

EXPERT SYSTEMS LIFE-CYCLE MANAGEMENT AND QUALITY ASSURANCE

At specified stages during the development process we evaluated the expert system in terms of specified performance goals as well as the ergonomics of the user interface. Evaluation during initial stages validated the experts' knowledge, filled in gaps in the information, and guided development of the system. The testing used simulated data for the initial prototype developed by our energy staff. The Triton/Phase Linear Systems energy staff assisted in prototype testing. Final testing evaluated the following areas:

- System scope adequacy.
- System logic validity.
- External data base integration.
- User friendliness.
- System security and integrity.

- Help feature quality.
- System complexity level.

USER EVALUATION

After the prototype was developed and tested, we delivered it to the EIA. The staff used for evaluation included a mix of experts, users, and managers. This was necessary in order to obtain comprehensive feedback.

After receiving EIA approval, Triton/Phase Linear Systems completed the computer edit-flag resolution expert system. Using evaluation results, we identified additional functions and features that we included in the final prototype.

In building and delivering the final prototype, we focused on:

- Further developing the knowledge base.
- Incorporating additional functions and features.
- Polishing the user interfaces.
- Finalizing the explanation facilities.
- Integrating it with the actual EIA data collection system.
- Developing interfaces to data bases and other external sources.

We tested the system in three phases. First, we used test cases provided by external experts to validate the knowledge base. Second, we had a select group of users test the system using typical cases. Finally, we had the data-processing staff use the expert system under actual operating conditions.

Our quality assurance team reviewed the design, development, and implementation of the edit-flag resolution system throughout this process. By designing quality into the system in the first place, we could ensure smooth operation and implementation of the final prototype. A sample user session of the edit-flag expert system follows.

Upon entering the EIA Edit Flag Resolution System, the user sees this introductory screen:

```
┌─────────────────────────────────────────────────────────────────────┐
│              Edit Flag Resolution System Prototype Version 1.0        │
│                                                                       │
│   E I A   E D I T   F L A G   R E S O L U T I O N   S Y S T E M       │
│                      Prototype Version 1.0                            │
│                                                                       │
│              Developed for the Energy Information Administration      │
│                   by Phase Linear Systems Incorporated               │
│                                                                       │
│                 Expert system to assist in the resolution of edit     │
│                 flags raised in the processing of the EIA-759         │
│                       Monthly Power Plant Report                      │
│                                                                       │
│               Press F1 for instructions on the use of the system, or  │
│                 Press F3 (STRT) to start the knowledge base . . .     │
│                                                                       │
│   1 PAGE      3 STRT         6 S/R    7 PRNT    8 MENU    9 HELP    10 EXIT │
└─────────────────────────────────────────────────────────────────────┘
```

The user then presses F3 to start a session with the expert system. The first screen requests the user's ID number. A number is assigned to each user by the project manager and is used for record-keeping purposes.

```
┌─────────────────────────────────────────────────────────────────────┐
│                     Edit Flag Resolution System                       │
│                                                                       │
│   Enter your user ID number.                                          │
│                                                                       │
│                                                                :100   │
│                                                                       │
│                                                                       │
│                                                                       │
│                                                                       │
│                                                                       │
│                                                                       │
│                                                                       │
│   1 PAGE      3 STRT         6 S/R    7 PRNT    8 MENU    9 HELP    10 EXIT │
└─────────────────────────────────────────────────────────────────────┘
```

The next screen requests the transaction number of the flag that the user is currently resolving.

Edit Flag Resolution System Prototype Version 1.0

Enter the transaction number shown on the printout.

:40045

1 PAGE   3 STRT   6 S/R   7 PRNT   8 MENU   9 HELP   10 EXIT

This screen lists the eight different types of flags produced by the statistical program. The user points the arrow to the flag currently being resolved. The questions following this screen vary based upon the selected flag and the information that the expert system requires to reach a recommendation.

Edit Flag Resolution System Prototype Version 1.0

The current transaction number is   40045.
Which edit flag has been raised?

$\Rightarrow$ Stocks value flagged by statistical tests
   Key does not exist
   Calculated generation differs from given
   Month on transaction is not current month
   Total generation for plant or prime mover exceeds maximum
   Generation value flagged by statistical tests
   Efficiency flagged by statistical tests
   Efficiency outside range

1 PAGE   3 STRT   6 S/R   7 PRNT   8 MENU   9 HELP   10 EXIT

After selecting the flag "Stocks value flagged by statistical tests," the user sees the following screen, requesting the type of fuel used at the plant:

```
              Edit Flag Resolution System Prototype Version 1.0

  The current transaction number is    40045.
  The current flag is Stocks value flagged by statistical tests.
  What fuel type is used at this plant?
   (Press F1 for more choices)
  ⇒ Light Oil
     Heavy Oil
     Anthracite
     Bituminous Coal
     Natural Gas
     Coke
     Sub Bituminous Coal



  1 PAGE     3 STRT      5 EXPL    7 PRNT    8 MENU    9 HELP    10 EXIT
```

The next screen asks the user for the value for stocks found on the printout.

```
              Edit Flag Resolution System Prototype Version 1.0

  The current transaction number is    40045.
  The current flag is Stocks value flagged by statistical tests.
  The type of fuel is Light Oil.
  Enter the value for stocks.

                              :10293




  1 PAGE     3 STRT      6 S/R     7 PRNT    8 MENU    9 HELP    10 EXIT
```

Next, the user is asked to select the type of prime mover used at the plant.

Edit Flag Resolution System Prototype Version 1.0

The current transaction number is   40045.
The current flag is Stocks value flagged by statistical tests.
What is the prime mover for this plant?
    Steam
    Internal Combustion
    Gas Turbine
    Combined Cycle Steam
⇒ Combined Cycle Gas Turbine
    Wind Turbine
    Solar
    Hydro

1 PAGE   3 STRT   5 EXPL   7 PRNT   8 MENU   9 HELP   10 EXIT

At this point, the expert system accesses a data base of historical information on the plants. The information for the plant that is currently being checked is located by entering the code number for the plant found on the printout.

Edit Flag Resolution System Prototype Version 1.0

What is the code number of the plant?

:377

1 PAGE   3 STRT   6 S/R   7 PRNT   8 MENU   9 HELP   10 EXIT

After accessing the data base and retrieving historical data, the system asks the following question regarding notes on the original form sent in by the company.

```
┌─────────────────────────────────────────────────────────────────────────────┐
│                  Edit Flag Resolution System Prototype Version 1.0            │
│                                                                               │
│  The current transaction number is      40045.                               │
│  The current flag is Stocks value flagged by statistical tests.              │
│  Are there any notes on the form explaining that there has been a change in   │
│  the amount of stocks in the past month?                                      │
│                                                                               │
│                                                                               │
│     Yes                                                                       │
│  ⇒ No                                                                         │
│                                                                               │
│                                                                               │
│                                                                               │
│                                                                               │
│                                                                               │
│  1 PAGE    3 STRT       5 EXPL    7 PRNT    8 MENU    9 HELP    10 EXIT       │
└─────────────────────────────────────────────────────────────────────────────┘
```

Using all of the information that it has acquired, the expert system then provides the user with the following summary of responses and a recommendation for action.

```
┌─────────────────────────────────────────────────────────────────────────────┐
│                  Edit Flag Resolution System Prototype Version 1.0            │
│                                                                               │
│   User ID: 100 Transaction number:      40045                                │
│   Edit Flag: Stocks value flagged by statistical tests                       │
│   Fuel Type: Light Oil                                                        │
│   Stocks this month: 10293                                                    │
│   Stocks last month: 0                                                        │
│   Are there explanatory notes regarding stocks? No                           │
│   The recommendation is: Call the respondent.                                │
│   Confirm with the respondent why there were no stocks last month but there   │
│   are stocks this month. Fill out an RCR and change the record on the system  │
│   if necessary.                                                               │
│                                                                               │
│                                                                               │
│   1 PAGE    3 STRT       6 S/R    7 PRNT    8 MENU    9 HELP    10 EXIT       │
└─────────────────────────────────────────────────────────────────────────────┘
```

Throughout the session, explanatory screens are also available for more detailed information on a question. For example, if the user is on the screen that asks about notes on the form, the F5 key (EXPL) can be pressed to see the following information:

Explanatory Information

Look on the form for this company and see if there
are any notes regarding stocks. The notes could
account for a discrepancy in the change in stocks
from last month to this month.

- Press the Space Bar to Return to Questions -

1 PAGE   3 STRT   6 S/R   7 PRNT   8 MENU   9 HELP   10 EXIT

USER TRAINING

We provided 40 hours of in-depth training in the use of the final prototype of the
computer edit-flag resolution expert system for the users and managers of the system.
The training included:

- Operation of the expert system.
- Test results and known limitations.
- Assumptions built into the system.
- Limitation of the system.
- Maintenance of the knowledge base.

SUMMARY

The EIA survey support expert system is important because it opens new areas for
expert system applications in statistical support for large surveys. By integrating
powerful statistical packages with applications similar to the one at the EIA, new
economies of scale will be possible through decreasing costs at the same time improving accuracy and consistency. Thus, large federal and state agencies will be able
to provide higher quality at less cost to taxpayers while the private sector will
accrue better return on investment and a better competitive position within an increasingly selective global marketplace.

11

Expert Systems for Crisis Management: The HIT Project

Richard G. Vedder

INTRODUCTION

Crisis management problems can be good candidates for expert system (ES) applications. This chapter examines some of the principal aspects of crisis management and discusses an ES application for one type of crisis management, namely hostage-taking situations. The Hostage-taking Information and Tactics (HIT) system exists only as a prototype. Nevertheless, it highlights one of the strengths of ES technology: its ability to support the decision-making process in stress-laden circumstances.

SOME ASPECTS OF CRISIS MANAGEMENT

There is a growing sense of urgency within both the public and private sectors that we as a Nation . . . remain inadequately postured to cope with the spate of natural and technological crises of these complex times. [1]

Fink [2] defines a crisis as "an unstable time or state of affairs in which a decisive change is impending" for good or ill, "a fluid, unstable, dynamic situation." An incident does not have to be life threatening to be a crisis, but all crisis events do have some things in common. During a crisis the normal "rules of the game" for solving problems do not apply. Moreover, time pressures often magnify the emotional stress caused by a crisis. The risk of decision-making error increases. Most importantly crises need not be life threatening to endanger the finances, reputation, or other valued assets of organizations and people.

The term *crisis management* often refers to handling human-caused disasters, while *emergency management* often applies to natural disasters. Since ESs can provide support in both problem areas, this chapter will not distinguish between the terms. Therefore, crisis management is defined herein as the process of employing organizational and external resources to first control and then resolve a crisis.

Crisis management, of course, is not a new phenomenon. Many decision makers confront and resolve crises on a daily basis. For instance, newspaper editors must reconcile publication deadlines with late-breaking stories and advertising changes. Indeed, a number of organizations predicate their existence on the management of crises (e.g., the Red Cross and the armed forces).

What is new is the spread of dangerous crises to organizations that thought themselves immune. The Tylenol, Bophal, Chernobyl, *Challenger* and Exxon *Valdez* disasters are recent examples of different sorts of crises that jolted the organizations involved (to say nothing of their impact on people). Moreover, in today's world it is increasingly likely for dangerous crises to spread from one geographic area (be it the inner cities of America or the Middle East) to other places where the traditional crisis-handling organizations (e.g., police and fire departments) often lack the expertise required to deal with them. A case in point is the recent journey throughout much of the eastern United States of a Japanese Red Army terrorist allegedly intent on assembling bomb components for use in New York. In short, a major catastrophe can today strike anyone, anywhere, anytime.

The managerial disarray often caused by the appearance of a crisis makes it all the easier for critical events to assume a life of their own. Until controlled or exhausted of their energy, crises may endanger not only involved organizations but also individuals and society in general. Achieving control means reducing risk and uncertainty, often under conditions of time pressure and emotional stress.

Moreover, rarely does one have the luxury of dealing with only one crisis at a time. There are several distinct phases in the evolution of a crisis [2]. A decision maker may simultaneously have to deal with the resolution of an "old" crisis, the explosion of a "new" crisis, and the buildup for a "forthcoming" crisis.

Crisis management, to be effective, is not only a process but also an attitude and a state of mind. Briefly stated, what are some of its essential requirements? Foremost, perhaps, is a willingness to admit that serious crises can strike one's organization just as easily as someone else's. From this willingness flows the energy to make preparations and to confront a crisis forthrightly when it happens. Second is a clearly defined chain of command that assigns unambiguous responsibilities to every person affected by a crisis situation. Third is the need to uncover and supply all available data on the crisis to decision makers as fast as possible (preferably at rates speedier than normally experienced). Fourth is making every effort to evaluate the problem dispassionately and calmly (obviously difficult as the pressures of time, poor communications, and human emotions often intervene). Last is providing effective communications with all parties (including the media) so as to encourage cooperation and disseminate vital information in a timely manner and without confusion.

Organizational policies can meet some of these requirements, such as creating a special crisis command post and provision for appropriate training in crisis response. However, it is also possible to support effective crisis management by using computer resources. This support can take many forms. For example, electronic data base systems can help identify and manage human and material resources during a crisis. Another form makes use of ES technology. Expert systems can help identify and respond to crises as well as train humans in the concepts of good crisis management. One type of crisis suitable for this type of artificial intelligence (AI) support is hostage taking.

HOSTAGE-TAKING INCIDENTS AS AN ES DOMAIN PROBLEM

Hostage-taking incidents certainly qualify as examples of crises. Contrary to popular expectations, most hostage-taking incidents in the United States are not the result of terrorism. Disrupted bank robberies and family disputes are instead the leading causes [3]. These sorts of incidents can happen in any community at any time. They are tension-filled, life-threatening situations where the slightest mistake could have tragic consequences.

Local law enforcement agencies need trained personnel who can manage this type of life-threatening crisis. Unfortunately, this type of training is expensive and must be repeated on a regular basis to be effective. Local governments cannot always afford these costs. If a community is near a major metropolitan area, it may be able to take advantage of "big city" expertise and resources on a time-delayed basis. However, legal liability issues and other problems may intervene, and in any event what are the tens of thousands of rural communities to do? The bottom line is that although police expertise with hostage taking and other forms of terror incidents is needed at many places, that expertise is in scarce supply.

Yet there is available a common body of knowledge about responding to hostage-taking incidents. Genuine experts in hostage-taking response and counter-terrorism exist. Many are willing to share their experiences and articulate their methods with other law enforcement officials. The challenge is how to deliver this knowledge and expertise for training and field purposes. Expert system technology can help answer this problem.

INITIAL DEVELOPMENT OF HIT

The HIT expert systems project began out of a concern for a major social problem of our times and from a desire to see how AI technology in the form of ESs could help. The HIT project has two principal investigators, the author and Dr. Richard O. Mason of Southern Methodist University. The project's goal is to explore how an ES could support (not replace) the decision-making process in this type of crisis situation [4]. The ES has evolved through several versions, and this process is instructive.

Research began while both investigators were working at the University of Arizona and focused on trying to prove the soundness of taking an ES approach to the problem. Development of the first two versions of HIT were on a VAX 11/785 system at the University of Arizona. The toolkit used was Ruler, a simple backward-chaining, rule-based shell written in C and patterned after EMYCIN. Ruler is an example of a "university shell," that is, a noncommercial shell tool created for academic research purposes. The absence of project funding and the ready availability of Ruler combined to make it the tool of choice for the initial work.

We did not recruit a human expert right away, as it was important to acquire first a basic knowledge of the problem domain. The author devoted six weeks to background reading about hostage-taking incidents and police procedures. This study identified a number of key situational attributes, such as the type of hijacking, the weapon used (if any), the number, age, sex, and social status of the hostage(s), the number of hostage takers, and whether or not the hostage taker was politically motivated. These attributes were then correlated with the actions taken by the responding law enforcement units and the outcome of the incidents.

The next step was to build the first version of HIT using as a knowledge base this collection of incident descriptions, situational attributes, actions taken, and their outcomes. The underlying assumption here was that when faced with a hostage-taking incident, police negotiators searched their minds for analogous situations and used those past incidents to develop their responses to the present crisis.

HIT version alpha's mode of operation was to have the user describe the situation he or she faced by answering a series of questions designed to identify the relevant attributes of the incident. Then the system retrieved and presented all cases that matched on all or most attributes. Prominently highlighted were the actions taken and outcomes realized. Finally, a short conclusion helped the user associate actions with outcomes so that a more informed decision could be made.

Although encouraged by the performance of the version alpha prototype, we knew we had to get away from using a knowledge base heavily dependent on secondary sources. To supply the essential heuristic knowledge, we recruited as our human expert Police Captain Ronald Zuniga, Commander of the Hostage Negotiation Unit for the City of Tucson Police Department.

We first asked Zuniga to evaluate HIT version alpha. His reactions were mixed. Zuniga was impressed by the amount of work already accomplished and by the informativeness of the software. The fact that we "had done our homework" (his words) was important, perhaps vital, in obtaining his enthusiastic support for the project. Experience has shown that human experts are understandably skeptical of the claims made for ES technology. Moreover, if their field is a good candidate for an ES application, their expertise will likely be in high demand. They may view assisting with an ES project as a waste of their time, especially if the expert has to "nurse-maid" a knowledge engineer who is naive with respect to the problem domain. An important reason for building HIT version alpha was to stimulate our learning about police procedures and theories of hostage taker motivations. "Doing our homework" paid off in convincing our chosen (and skeptical) human expert that we were competent to undertake the project. This experience forms an important lesson for any knowledge engineer.

On the other hand, Zuniga emphasized that HIT version alpha would never work effectively in a real, ongoing, and emotionally charged hostage-taking situation. These were the major problems he cited:

1. Law enforcement officials responding to a hostage-taking incident must act initially on the basis of very little information. They only gain information as the case unfolds, partly as the result of the actions they take. By the time they would have collected enough information to use HIT version alpha, many of their options for action would no longer be valid. In fact, the entire incident might be over. HIT must be able to provide assistance even when police have little concrete information at hand.

2. Zuniga reacted to the long paragraphs of advisory text supplied by HIT version alpha as being "too academic." Decision makers dealing with a dynamic, emotionally charged crisis have no time for reading verbose screens regardless of how informative or helpful the information might be.

3. Tucson police procedures identified not one but four decision makers among whom responsibility shifts as a hostage-taking incident unfolds. These are the initial responding officer(s), the On-Scene Commander, the SWAT or Emergency Response Team Commander, and the Hostage Negotiation Unit Commander. These parties share data and specialized expertise. They must coordinate their activities at all times. Their individual needs for information and advice, while often distinct, sometimes overlap.

4. Captain Zuniga wanted the ES to also help police develop psychological profiles of both the hostage taker(s) and the hostage(s). With this information negotiators could estimate better the degree of possible rapport achievable between them and the hostage taker(s) as well as between the hostage taker(s) and the hostage(s).

5. Finally, Zuniga believed that the system must continue to provide needed advice irrespective of how officers responded to its earlier recommendations.

The next step in the project was constructing HIT version beta. Interviews with Captain Zuniga formed the basis of the knowledge acquisition process. We soon discovered that police officers make use of scenario models in both training for and responding to hostage-taking situations. These scenarios sparked plenty of "what-if" questioning and provided an excellent structure for eliciting heuristic knowledge. They illustrated the truism that humans are much more informative when using their expertise to answer specific questions than when asked to provide a "memory dump" of their knowledge.

Consequently, a general scenario model of a hostage-taking incident provides the underlying structure for version beta's knowledge base. The scenario begins with the arrival of the first responding officer(s) and tracks each possible situation as it unfolds until the incident terminates. Ideally this happens when all hostages are released unharmed and the hostage taker is arrested. The advice provided by HIT tries to maximize the likelihood of achieving this outcome.

Zuniga's discussion of the various situation states within the scenario model was often expressed in an *if–then* format. That is, if X was the given situation state, then Y was the recommended action for handling it. This use of procedural and judgmental knowledge is well suited for incorporation as rules, so we continued to use Ruler as the toolkit for building HIT version beta. The resulting ES is diagnostic in function, identifying the current situation state and recommending the appropriate response for that state.

Zuniga's contributions altered the development of HIT in several ways:

1. The underlying assumption of the scenario model allows HIT to make conditional responses based on incomplete data. The questioning by HIT discovers the particular state of events within the scenario in which users find themselves. The system then provides information and advice keyed to that event state.

2. Short, succinct "bullet" texts became HIT's primary format for giving advice. If the officer has time to consider further, an "Additional Information" section offers more information in paragraph form.

3. HIT uses an introductory menu to determine which of the four possible decision makers is using the system and then tailors both questions and advice accordingly. The system permits redundancies when information needs overlap. For example, HIT will ask both the On-Scene Commander and the SWAT Commander if the inner security perimeter is established. System dialogue also encourages communication among the four decision makers as needed.

4. HIT version beta contains two other demonstration knowledge bases in addition to the one devoted to incident response. One provides simple advice in developing the psychological profile of a hostage taker. The other incorporates the version alpha incident data for exploring analogies.

5. Version beta's use of the scenario model keys HIT's responses much more to situation states rather than to specific police actions or inactions. This improves the availability of good advice at any point during an incident.

Figure 1 illustrates a representative screen from HIT version beta constructed using Ruler. The pattern of questioning determines the situation state. Based on the incorporated scenario model, recommended actions follow. The body of knowledge structured by the scenario model indicates that the responding officer, as the first police officer at the scene, must determine the need for help, contain the incident, and report fully to dispatch. Having satisfied these requirements, HIT then inquires about the command post and reminds the officer of the correct procedure for locating the post.

About three months of effort went into the development of HIT version beta. The new prototype had 64 rules dispersed over three different knowledge bases. In a public forum, we used HIT in a simulation of an actual hostage-taking incident that occurred at a Valley National Bank office in Tucson, Arizona. Representatives of the Tucson Police Department (including Captain Zuniga), the Valley National Bank (including the hostage who was a Bank employee), the press, and the general public were in attendance. Volunteers from the audience assumed the roles of various decision makers and operated HIT. They had to respond to such events as a bomb

Please answer my questions with *y (yes), n (no), u (unknown), or w (why)* unless asked for a value, in which case you should respond with *w (why)* or an appropriate value.

Are you the responding officer? *y*
Do you need help for initial police response? *n*
Has a containment perimeter been established? *n*
Has police dispatch been advised of the total situation? *y*
Has a command post been established? *n*

ACTION: → site command post
    1. Identify location for command post.
    2. Consider:
        a. Cover and concealment from incident point;
        b. Ease of access by responding personnel;
        c. Space for staging area.
    3. Advise other personnel of location.

Figure 1 Sample HIT version beta dialogue.

threat, the request for a SWAT team, and finally the coordination of the method of surrender with all officers, including snipers, to ensure the hostage taker's safety. Although a very modest test, it served to validate both version beta's design and the utility of the basic concept.

LATER DEVELOPMENT

As noted earlier, the Ruler toolkit stored Captain Zuniga's knowledge and expertise in rule form. This format seemed appropriate for the procedural and judgmental types of knowledge involved. Therefore, a search began for a commercial rule-based toolkit with more power and functionality as well as better documentation and support than Ruler.

Another factor influencing the tool selection process was the importance of being able to deliver HIT to police patrol cars, SWAT staging areas, hostage negotiation posts, and other highly mobile sites. Consequently, we needed to transfer HIT from the VAX environment to that of IBM-type PC/XTs, ATs, and especially laptops. By this time both investigators had relocated to the Dallas area. The author obtained a copy of Texas Instruments' Personal Consultant Plus as part of TI's University Expert Systems Development Program. He used this toolkit to build the current PC-based version of HIT.

Personal Consultant (PC) Plus is an example of a structured rule-based expert system shell. According to the taxonomy found in Harmon, Maus, and Morrissey [5], structured rule-based tools allow knowledge engineers to partition a single knowledge base into rule sets arranged hierarchically. In addition to providing better control for the use of large knowledge bases, this arrangement allows an expert system to use a given rule set more than once during the same consultation (a process called multiple instantiation). Moreover, this structuring allows one rule set to inherit information produced by another.

PC Plus calls its rule set structures "frames," each of which contains a subset of the rules and data required to address part of the overall problem. (It is important to note, however, that this concept of frames is not the same as the classical definition of frame-based systems.) PC Plus frames communicate with each other using a hierarchical frame tree that records their interrelationships. Figure 2 provides a sample display of the PC Plus frame tree structure as used in HIT. Only when a problem requires a given frame is it "instantiated," or loaded into main memory. This reduces wasted space and improves performance. It is easy to copy parts of frames or even entire frames and move them around the knowledge base.

Figure 3 shows a sample rule from HIT's knowledge base formatted in ARL (Abbreviated Rule Language), a highly structured form of English. A knowledge engineer builds rules using ARL. PC Plus then translates the ARL into Scheme, the dialect of LISP used to create PC Plus. Since the shell translates ARL into Scheme incrementally, the knowledge engineer can test a new or revised rule at once. To assist with debugging, PC Plus can output the contents of its knowledge bases in either ARL, Scheme, or English (using the English descriptions of the rules supplied by the knowledge engineer) or in all three formats. This particular rule says in its laconic fashion that IF the user is the Hostage Negotiation Unit Commander and there is a demand for alcohol or other drugs, THEN police should refrain from meeting this demand and display this recommendation to the user.

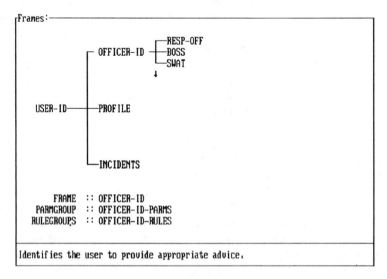

Figure 2 Sample frame tree from HIT.

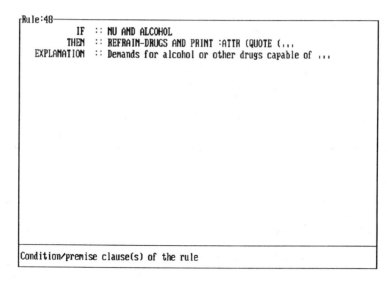

Figure 3 Sample rule from HIT.

Normally all rules in PC Plus have at least three associated properties: IF, THEN, and EXPLANATION (which stores a description of the rule). One may use a variety of components to write the IF and THEN clauses. This rule uses three parameters and a text string. The parameters NU, ALCOHOL, and REFRAIN-DRUGS are data structures used by PC Plus to store specific information or facts in a knowledge base. In this case, all three parameters simply record the existence or absence of the situation states they represent.

Figure 4 shows the parameter ALCOHOL and its associated properties. As with EXPLANATION, TRANSLATION records the knowledge engineer's description of the property. PROMPT indicates that the ES must ask the user for the value of ALCOHOL. TYPE shows what that value must be a yes (true) or no (false). Any parameter can have more properties than these if required.

The search control strategy of PC Plus's inference engine defaults to backward chaining, but it can forward chain if specified by the rules. Since HIT employs an incident scenario model, it is important to keep the number of search possibilities under tight control. Therefore, HIT uses the default backward-chaining paradigm.

PC Plus has a "snapshot" utility that can convert graphic images, such as a color-coded floorplan of a bank, for display within a consultation. This made the ES toolkit attractive for providing needed visual support for police. Also, PC operates in an IBM XT/AT hardware environment, meeting another important requirement. The remaining system illustrations in this chapter are screen displays generated by PC Plus.

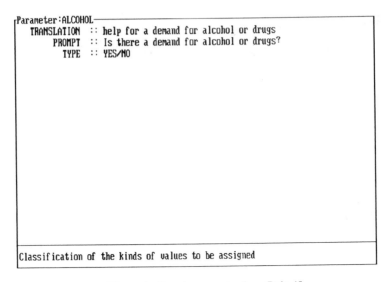

```
┌Parameter:ALCOHOL─────────────────────────────────────────────────┐
│    TRANSLATION  :: help for a demand for alcohol or drugs          │
│        PROMPT   :: Is there a demand for alcohol or drugs?         │
│         TYPE    :: YES/NO                                          │
│                                                                   │
│                                                                   │
│                                                                   │
│                                                                   │
│                                                                   │
│                                                                   │
│                                                                   │
│                                                                   │
│                                                                   │
│                                                                   │
│                                                                   │
│Classification of the kinds of values to be assigned               │
└───────────────────────────────────────────────────────────────────┘
```

Figure 4   Sample parameter from Rule 48.

EVALUATION

Presently HIT remains in prototype form, suitable only for demonstration purposes. All work to date has been done without any research funding support. Further work on the project will depend on identifying and securing research and development funding. Nevertheless, the project has been beneficial.

One of the most important findings from developing HIT is that some of the expert's advice on what to do in specific circumstances is counterintuitive. This means that the typical police officer (who, remember, does not have extensive training in hostage-taking incidents) may in the stress of the moment easily overlook his or her best course of action. Figures 5–7 provide some examples. Figure 5 assumes an offer to exchange hostages. HIT urges refusal of exchanges of policemen or others for existing hostages. Experience shows that such an exchange lessens the situational advantage of the police because it introduces new elements of uncertainty into the crisis. (Recall that reducing uncertainty and increasing control is basic to effective crisis management.)

HIT's advice in Figure 6 assumes existence of a demand for food. The intuitive response would be to deliver hamburgers or whatever other "fast food" the hostage taker wants. Instead, HIT recommends sending in materials for on-site food preparation. Experience here suggests that the activity of food preparation refocuses the hostage taker's attention, is a calming influence, and helps bind the hostage taker(s) to the hostages in a common communal activity.

The situation state in Figure 7 assumes that the hostage taker wants to surrender and that the hostages include men, women, and children. Again, the intuitive response

```
ACTION:

1. Negotiate.
2. Consider:
       a. Sending in materials for food preparation;
       b. Medical and nutritional issues;
       c. Do not send in everything that might be needed as this will
          encourage further negotiation.
       d. If possible, do not place food next to a door; instead put it
          away from doors so that someone must come out and get it.


ADDITIONAL INFORMATION:

In order to encourage the growth of personal relationships between the
hostage taker/s and the hostage/s it would be better to send in materials
for food preparation than ready-to-eat food.

** End - RETURN/ENTER to continue
```

Figure 5   HIT's advice for exchanging hostages.

```
ACTION:

1. Demand should be put off.
2. Ultimately should be refused.
3. Consider:
       a. Ruins the value of any rapport established between hostage/s
          and hostage taker/s;
       b. Lessens police control of situation (new element of uncertainty
          introduced);
       c. Exchanging with police volunteers also lessens control of the
          situation.

** End - RETURN/ENTER to continue
```

Figure 6   HIT's advice for responding to a demand for food.

```
ACTION:

1. Arrange for transfer.
2. If possible, negotiate for release of hostages in this order: male,
   female, child.
3. Advise on-scene commander and SWAT commander.
4. Prepare for debriefing of hostages.


ADDITIONAL INFORMATION:

It is situationally important to follow the release order given above.
Children are the least threatening to the hostage taker/s and therefore are
in the least amount of danger. Male hostages, on the other hand, can easily
feel pressured by social values and their own self-image to do something
brave. Consequently they are in the greatest danger from the hostage
taker/s and should be released first.

** End - RETURN/ENTER to continue
```

Figure 7   HIT's advice for organizing the surrender of hostages.

would be to negotiate for the release of first the children, then the women, and finally the men. Note that HIT advises the release of male hostages before women or children. Experience shows that this course of action can deescalate the intensity and emotionality of the situation: male hostages tend to put more pressure on the hostage taker(s) because they may dare some "macho" act. The need to reduce uncertainty and gain control over the crisis necessitates their removal as soon as possible. Children, in contrast, pose little or no threat and in fact may be a stabilizing influence.

All three of these situations represent points in the unfolding of an incident where an untrained or forgetful officer under great stress might instinctively make the wrong decision. In each case HIT cautions against intuitive actions and explains why. This is one of the strongest advantages of using an ES like HIT to help manage a crisis.

Besides improving the general problem-solving robustness of the system, HIT needs a number of additional improvements. Among these are the following:

1. Only one, very general scenario model provides the underlying structure for HIT's knowledge base. In reality terrorism experts have many different scenario models to choose from in responding to a hostage-taking incident. To improve robustness, HIT must incorporate these additional models into the structure of its knowledge base.

2. The system requires expertise from a number of different human experts. Beyond an expert in hostage negotiations, the project needs to tap the knowledge of a SWAT commander, an on-scene commander, and a psychologist familiar with hostage taker and hostage behaviors.

3. HIT requires access to external law enforcement data bases such as those available at the National Crime Information Center. In addition to producing data on known felons from these sources, it remains useful for the system to cull out prior hostage-taking incidents that would be similar to the situation currently being dealt with.

4. Similarly, the system ought to provide the four decision makers with information drawn from other kinds of external data bases, such as color-coded floorplans of banks, convenience markets, and other high-risk sites. As matters now stand, if a public or commercial building is the site of a hostage-taking incident, the security firm for that building has to locate, gather up and deliver to police a set of the latest blueprints for that structure.

5. The need mentioned in the preceding for various types of external information support raises the issue of encryption and other data communications problems. Hostage takers and other kinds of terrorists are by no means ignorant of the potential benefits gained from monitoring police communications. It might even be necessary for security reasons to keep the ES software centralized at police headquarters instead of residing in patrol car PCs.

6. Tucson Police procedures are not the same everywhere. For instance, the distinct team approach (i.e., SWAT, a negotiation unit) does not apply in Dallas, which uses a centralized emergency response team in which every team member trains for all possible decisional roles. Therefore, local community or organizational differences would demand different versions of HIT.

Our present human expert, James Garrett of the Dallas-based St. James Group, an international risk analysis and protection firm, believes the technology may have more benefit for training than for real-time use. Dallas police officials echo this opinion. Applying the HIT technology to the needs of training law enforcement officials is clearly an option worth exploring. Instructors might select a lesson from a number of incident scenarios stored in the knowledge base. Moreover, with modifications to the knowledge base, HIT could help improve the response of those people at high risk of becoming hostages (e.g., bank employees and foreign service personnel).

At any rate, HIT's technology has yet to prove itself in the field. It is certainly unrealistic to expect a lone officer faced with a hostage-taking incident to suspend action in order to consult with any computer system. We envision HIT being used in the field as part of a team effort and believe that the HIT prototypes demonstrate good potential for this type of decision support.

The HIT project illustrates the opportunities presented by crisis management for ES development. Both training and field applications are possible. Other crisis domains include bomb detection and disposal, responding to chemical fires or spills of unknown origin, poison control response, 911 response, and allocating resources after a natural disaster such as a tornado or earthquake.

REFERENCES

1. Chartrand, R. L., "Optimum Emergency Management: The Effective Use of Information Technology," in *Theory and Application of Expert Systems in Emergency Management Situations*, S. I. Gass and R. E. Chapman (eds.), Department of Commerce, National Bureau of Standards Special Publication 717, U.S. Government Printing Office, Washington, D.C., 1986, pp. 109–123.

2. Fink, S., *Crisis Management: Planning for the Inevitable*, American Management Association, New York, 1986.

3. Strentz, T., "The Inadequate Personality as a Hostage Taker," *Journal of Police Science and Administration*, Vol. 11, No. 3, 1983, pp. 363–368.

4. Vedder, R. G. and R. O. Mason, "An Expert System Application for Decision Support in Law Enforcement," *Decision Sciences*, Vol. 18, No. 3, 1987, pp. 400–414.

5. Harmon, P., R. Maus, and W. Morrissey, *Expert Systems Tools and Applications*, Wiley, New York, 1988.

An Expert System Development Methodology as Applied to Project Management

William Casey Mattimore
Robert T. Plant

INTRODUCTION

Project management is an attempt to effectively represent, efficiently plan, and schedule a complex undertaking composed of diverse activities and requirements. These activities are integrated so as to maximize the prescribed objectives.

To solve the problems of planning, scheduling, and controlling a project, many techniques have been developed to assist the manager, including heuristic and deterministic approaches. Among them are mathematical formulations such as linear or integer programming. These techniques are used where optimality and resource constraints are of importance, but their large computational requirements all but eliminate them from consideration in anything more than a modest project. Promising work such as that of Patterson and Roth [1] solve the multiresource zero-one integer programming problem with a significant decrease in computation time. Doersch and Patterson [2] have an integer programming formulation of the project-scheduling problem of cash flows in a project when progress payments and cash outflows are made upon completion of activities.

Of the other methods that offer promise and are computationally more appealing include: Hildelang and Muth [3], who have developed DCPM [Dynamic Programming for Decision Critical Path Method (CPM)], an effective and general way of handling discrete time/cost trade-off problems that can perform sensitivity analysis; a multilevel network system by Kapur [4] that permits the development of independent but related networks at different levels of the project hierarchy and should be particularly useful when the flow of information is complex; Willis and Hastings' ''Branch and Bound'' [5] method, which minimizes overall duration subject to availability of resources; Cooper's sampling method, which generates a set of schedules using statistical techniques and selects the best schedule among them [6]; BPERT by Britney [7], which uses Bayesian point estimates for beta activity duration times to minimize the potential losses of misestimation; and Monte Carlo Simulation by Cook and Jennings [8], which shows that the intelligent simulation of Program Evaluation and Review Technique (PERT) networks are not too costly and are considerably more accurate than standard PERT analysis.

As a tractable alternative, network algorithms were developed. Recent advancements in this area have produced heuristics of stochastic orientation such as GERT (Graphical Evaluation and Review Technique), which considers time, cost, and risk, and VERT (Venture Evaluation and Review Technique), which has the ability to model decisions in the network in terms of time, cost, risk, and performance. While these provide valuable information, by far the most accepted and practiced approaches are PERT/CPM. PERT's power is in the planning, scheduling, and controlling of the one-time development project. While it is an effective tool for the management of time, other parameters of importance, such as performance, are not addressed sufficiently. Algorithms such as PERT/COST are difficult to prepare, require appreciable amounts of information, and are difficult to update. Many times the analysis is augmented by other techniques such as LOB (Line-of-Balance), GERT, and VERT. The project manager who applies these procedures must weigh and consolidate the information on time, cost, performance, and risk and produce a coherent plan for progress. Even if the manager is experienced, he or she may be inundated and overwhelmed by the multitude of information required and produced by the system. This coupled with the need to integrate the information properly may result in ineffective or costly decisions in the projects. The project manager needs to blend and appropriately interpret this information, which is our goal in developing an expert assistant for network planning and scheduling.

This chapter has two major objectives, which are addressed in the following sections. The first objective is the development of an intelligent knowledge-based system that assists project managers in creating their scheduling networks. However, the creation of such a system needs to be done in a rigorous manner in order to have user confidence in the results. We therefore develop and present a methodology for expert system construction, our second objective, and discuss how our approach makes the system complete, consistent, and rigorous.

INTRODUCTION TO EXPERT SYSTEM DESIGN METHODS

Knowledge-based systems (KBSs) have often been criticized for the limited theoretical base upon which they are constructed. The partially valid view held by many is that systems are often constructed in an ad hoc individual way that leads to unmaintainable, unreliable, and unrigorous systems. This holds even though there have been several attempts at producing development methodologies to assist the knowledge engineer in the construction process [e.g., 9–11]. A large contributing reason for the limited applicability of these methodologies is that they aim to produce an implementation directly from the knowledge elicitation process. This path is however not necessarily the best, and in this section of our chapter a new alternative approach is introduced that shows the benefits of taking a software engineering philosophy toward the development of KBSs. The methodology breaks down the process of creating a KBS into constituent parts and discusses ways of creating formal specifications for those parts, as is applicable. This includes specifying the knowledge base, the representation, the control architecture, and other important components/issues.

Our aim is to show that even though the total formal specification of a KBS is as yet not feasible, it is possible to be formal at certain parts of the system development and rigorous for the remainder, and the specifications created can ultimately be combined to form a specification from which the system can be implemented.

The very nature of the problems that KBSs typically attempt to solve (e.g., complex, yet poorly structured problems within a large domain) prevents in all but trivial cases a total formal specification from being constructed (i.e., the full specification of the problem for all cases). However, we can produce a partial formal specification for a system in that it is possible to specify several key points in the development process and link these together in a rigorous manner.

We first consider what are the points that need specifying for a total specification, as shown in Figure 1.

The full specification consists of five parts. The first is the specification of the problem definition, which as we have already mentioned is not a specification that can be precise for domains that are nontrivial or nonfinite in size. The second specification is that of the user in which a model is created. This details, usually in English or some pseudocode, the user interface needs and operating parameters.

Thus, we have two parts for which formal specifications other than in a limited form are not yet feasible on complex problems and are areas of active research by both knowledge and software engineers. However, the remaining three parts can be specified more formally.

The third part is the specification of the knowledge base. This is possible in the sense that the knowledge elicited from the domain expert/knowledge source is

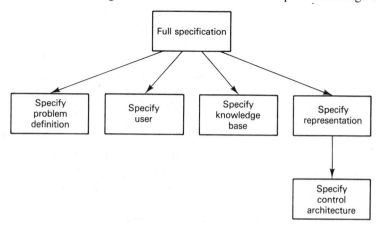

Figure 1

finite, and by utilizing transformational processes, this can be specified formally. The specification of the knowledge base is vital if the system is to be maintained and the representational independence of the specification allows clarity and flexibility.

Fourth, it is vital that a suitable representation is selected, and this is done by analyzing the representational needs of the knowledge base. Once selected, the syntax and semantics of the representation can be specified. Having specified the representation, it is then possible to select an appropriate control architecture, the operation of which can also be specified.

We can therefore formally specify three aspects of an expert system each of which are fundamental to its construction, and in this chapter we show how these points can be rigorously reached from an initial specification of the problem definition. We also describe how they can then be combined with the specification of the user to form a concrete specification from which the system can be implemented.

The methodology as a whole can be introduced by considering Figure 2. The development commences with an initial specification, the aim of which is to act as an informal software requirements document. This gives a broad outline of the systems parameters and boundaries to be used by the knowledge engineer as the basis of both the knowledge elicitation phase and the creation of the user model. In the knowledge elicitation phase the most suitable knowledge elicitation technique is selected with which to extract knowledge from the domain expert. The knowledge engineer then uses this extracted knowledge as the basis of the elicited representation, an unprocessed representation that usually has a textual form. The elicited representation, however, is too coarse in nature to act as the specification for an implementation, and so it is necessary for their presentation to undergo a refinement process. The result of this is a more adequate representation, termed the primary representation. It is adequate in the sense that an adequate level of completeness and consistency has been reached to allow major knowledge processing of the representation to be performed. The first process is to transform the primary representation into a formal representation, a mathematical specification written in the "Z" specification language. The second process is an analysis that examines the constituent characteristics present in the primary representation before attempting to match these with the characteristics of "classical" representations such as frames, production rules, and semantic networks. From this matching process a specification of a suitable representation language can be produced. This is known as the representation specification. Following this the domain specification and representation are drawn together to form the secondary representation, in which the domain knowledge from the domain specification is represented in the form advocated by the representation specification; this plus the specification of the control architecture forms the concrete specification. This then acts as a specification for the implementation of the knowledge base, which when combined with the user specification (which allows the human computer interaction considerations to be understood) provides the basis for implementing the whole system.

The remainder of this chapter will be used to examine these stages in greater detail.

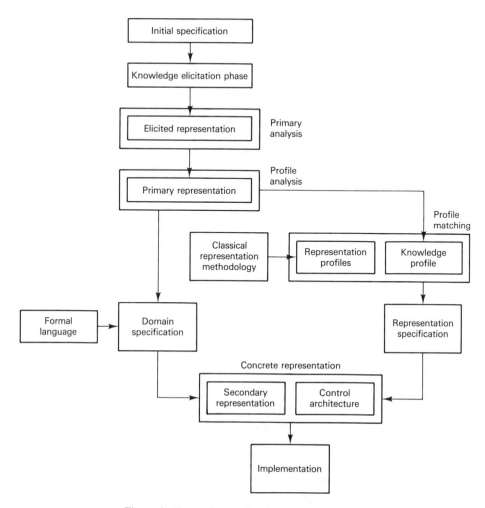

Figure 2 Expert System Development Methodology

THE INITIAL SPECIFICATION

An expert system can be viewed as a type of computer system, and as such the development constraints that software engineers place on conventional software systems can also be applied to the expert system life cycle. The first stage in this life cycle, which we call initial specification, is often termed "requirements analysis and definition" by software engineers.

The aim of the initial specification is to establish boundaries on the solution space of the problem. This is very important in a software system such as this, for expert system domains lack much of the definition associated with their more traditional counterparts. This lack of definition does not mean that producing an initial specification is impossible but merely that more effort is required with perhaps a change of emphasis.

THE KNOWLEDGE ELICITATION PHASE

The first major stage to be encountered is the knowledge elicitation phase. The term *knowledge elicitation* is used intentionally here as opposed to *knowledge acquisition*. The literature at present gives a confused view of these terms. It mainly uses the terms interchangeably to mean the whole process of constructing a KBS, commencing with extracting the knowledge from the domain expert to the implementation of this knowledge. In this chapter knowledge elicitation and knowledge acquisition are used to mean two different things. Knowledge elicitation is the process whereby the knowledge is extracted purely from the domain expert without any analysis of that knowledge by the knowledge engineer. The term knowledge acquisition is used in relation to the analysis of that knowledge extracted during the knowledge elicitation phase.

CHOICE OF ELICITATION TECHNIQUE

Some of the major knowledge elicitation techniques currently available to the knowledge engineer are:

1. Verbal transfer via the knowledge engineer.
2. Expert use of intelligent intermediary program.
3. Induction program to extract knowledge from a body of available data.
4. An investigation of the literature.
5. Machine learning.

One of the aims of the methodology is that the knowledge elicitation phase should result in a textual form of elicited representation. Thus, the first technique will generally be used. Some of the more specialized methods in this area are:

1. The domain expert talks out loud as he or she solves a problem, which is taped and then transcribed. This process is known as concurrent verbalization.
2. The domain expert talks about a problem he or she has solved; this is taped and transcribed. The process is known as retrospective verbalization.
3. The knowledge engineer asks the domain expert questions as the domain expert solves a problem. The interaction is taped and then transcribed. This process is known as concurrent probing.

THE ELICITED REPRESENTATION

The result of the knowledge elicitation phase is the elicited representation, the form of which is intended to be textually based. For example, a transcript of an interview between a domain expert and a knowledge engineer could act as an elicited representation.

THE KNOWLEDGE ACQUISITION PHASE

The next stage in the methodology is that of knowledge acquisition. As stated earlier, knowledge acquisition is the process of analyzing the knowledge extracted during the knowledge elicitation phase.

The aim of this phase is to produce a representation (the primary representation) of the elicited knowledge that is rigorous enough to allow several demanding analyses to take place upon it. One of these ultimately produces a formal specification of the domain and another acts as the basis for the selection of the high-level "classical" representation, which ultimately will be used to represent the domain knowledge held in the formal specification.

The reason that the elicited representation is not used directly as the basis of these analyses is that the elicited representation is in the form of English text, which is far too ambiguous in nature. Also the text may be noisy, suffer from problems of continuity and high modularity, or have poor linkage between areas of knowledge, problem areas that are not always apparent in unanalyzed English text.

PRIMARY REPRESENTATIONS

As stated, the aim of this phase is to produce from the elicited knowledge a more rigorous, primary representation. The characteristics of a primary representation are that it has very simple syntax and semantics and is weakly typed. The reasoning behind this is to make the best compromise between rigor and flexibility. Rigor is used in the sense that the language and/or form used for the primary representation should encourage unambiguity along with highlighting any lack of consistency or completeness while flexible enough to mold the primary representation around a variety of elicited representations. The aim of having only a simple syntax and semantics is that due to their simplicity, they will cover a large range of textual situations, while because they have some formal basis, the freestyle text of the elicited representation can be transformed into a more rigorous form with which to reason about the domain. The weak typing is also an attempt to capture and categorize as much freestyle text as possible and instill some formality upon it. The elicited representations purposely do not have complex syntax and semantics or strong data types as the philosophy of the approach is one of representation refinement where only small changes are made at each stage, enabling justifications to be made, which also helps prevent information loss or change of semantic meaning. It is not possible to adhere to this philosophy if large jumps in the representation are made.

Further characteristics of the primary representation are that (i) it is amenable to the transformation of large quantities of textual information and (ii) it possesses little or no basis for inference. The reasoning behind the first of these considerations is due to the sizable transcripts and texts that are obtained during the knowledge elicitation phase. The reasoning behind the need for little inference capacity in the primary representation is that the representation will not be required to act as a basis for inference and the inclusion of these facilities would only add to the complexity of the language or form. Features that prevent information loss or change are to be encouraged as translations between representations can sometimes influence a change in semantic meaning.

Having compiled this set of characteristics describing the form a primary representation should take, several representations that adhere to them have been created. Two are the flow diagram and the contour diagram.

The Flow Diagram

The flow diagram is based on the flowchart idea, but instead of detailing the flow of control for a program, we try to establish the knowledge flow contained within the elicited representation.

The Contour Diagram

The contour diagram is used generally for elicited representations that have a finer grain size of textual information than that used by the flow diagram. The basis for the contour diagram is the structured decomposition of the elicited representation.

THE TRANSFORMATIONAL CHARACTERISTICS

One set of characteristics that could be used to indicate a suitable primary representation is the following:

1. Noise.
2. Modularity of knowledge.
3. Linkage of knowledge.
4. Operational types.
5. Sequencing.
6. Justifications.
7. Explanations.

These characteristics are sequenced specifically, commencing with what could be termed low-level characteristics and progressing to higher level ones. The lowest level of all the characteristics is noise, which is defined as words or segments of text within the elicited representation that are undefined or unrecognizable.

The second two characteristics are highly interrelated. However, before describing this interrelationship, definitions of each will be given. Modularity refers to a module of knowledge that can be described as a collection of knowledge statements with the following characteristics.

1. The knowledge statements are related in subject, this being a subset of the domain.
2. The knowledge statements are physically in close proximity to each other on the transcript or other form of elicited representation.

In relation to the primary representation, modularity has to have a slightly different definition.

Modularity is the ability of the primary representation to allow statements that are conceptually related and in close physical proximity to each other within the elicited representation to keep this relationship. Linkage can broadly be defined as the relationships among modules and is a measure of their independence.

We can now discuss the role of modularity and linkage within the elicited representation. Elicited representations that have highly modular knowledge are easier to represent in any of the primary representations than nonmodular ones, for the knowledge is focused and the context of that knowledge is then clearer for the knowledge engineer to understand.

The linkage of knowledge is important with respect to justification and explanations. If the elicited representation is highly modular and has high linkage, then this makes explanations and justifications easier to accomplish. If there is a little linkage, modularity, or sequencing, then explanations and justifications are harder to achieve.

The operational-type characteristic is based upon the different types of operations that are performed within the elicited representation. The more operational types there are, the more complex the primary representation will need to be.

Sequencing refers to the relationship that individual items of knowledge have with each other. The sequencing of information and knowledge within an elicited representation can also be regarded as a complexity indicator for that representation.

The justification and explanation characteristics present within an elicited representation may be either explicit or implicit. Explicit ones are justifications and explanations included in the text by the domain expert.

Thus, each of these characteristics must be taken into consideration before deciding upon a primary representation. This is because each of the primary representations have a different capability to accommodate different characteristics. For example, the flow diagram cannot represent any elicited knowledge that has a low linkage of knowledge because this is against one of the basic principles that the representation is founded upon. Contour diagrams, on the other hand, do not prohibit small amounts of linkage, and so if everything else were equal, the contour diagram would be the best primary representation for an elicited representation with low linkage.

In order to aid the decision of which primary representation to select for a given elicited representation, bandwidth and trace diagrams have been introduced. Traces are diagrams that outline the amount of each characteristic within the elicited representation while bandwidth diagrams show what range of values is most sensitive to a primary representation. The aim is to select the primary representation that best encloses a trace.

For example, the trace

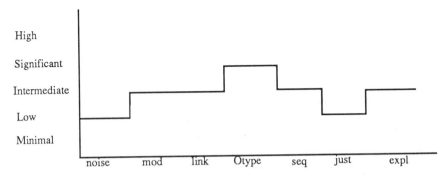

would be better represented in bandwidth *A* than *B*,

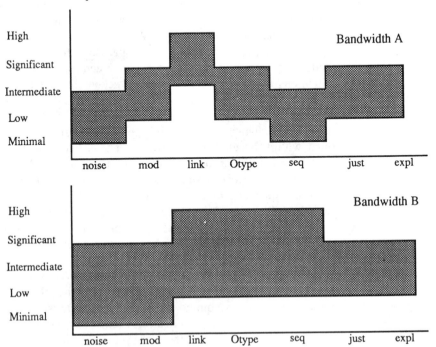

because the closer the fit of the bandwidth, the more suitable the constructs in the primary representation will be for representing the elicited representation.

The second bandwidth does enclose the trace but not as closely as the first. This implies that the constructs of the elicited representation are more generalized and thus not as useful as those in *A*.

SUMMARY OF KNOWLEDGE ACQUISITION PHASE

The following diagram can be used to help us summarize the process of selecting a primary representation:

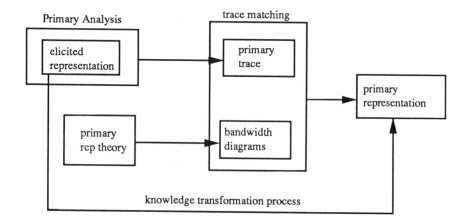

1. The knowledge elicitation phase produces the elicited representation.
2. The elicited representation is then examined for the transformational characteristics, and a trace of these characteristics is produced. This process is known as primary analysis.
3. The primary trace is then compared to the bandwidth diagrams of the primary representation. This is known as trace matching.
4. The trace-matching procedure will suggest the most suitable primary representation to use.
5. The elicited representation is transformed into the primary representation formalism.

USING THE PRIMARY REPRESENTATION

The creation of the primary representation is a significant point in the development process. It is the first point at which a position of adequacy has been reached even if the level of adequacy is quite restrictive. To reach a higher level of adequacy, it is necessary to develop from the primary representation a more rigorous representation. This is one of the aims behind the production of a "domain specification," a formal specification of the elicited domain knowledge.

The adequacy of the primary representation also enables it to act as the basis of analysis techniques that indicate the most suitable classical representation in which to carry forward the design of the system.

DOMAIN SPECIFICATIONS

The primary representation provides us with a more rigorous form than the elicited representation with which to reason about the domain. However, this representation has several drawbacks. The primary representation itself is still far too ambiguous and may contain inconsistencies and incompleteness that cannot be spotted due to the structures used. It is the aim of the domain specification to help reduce these problems.

The domain specification therefore will have to have mathematics as its basis, and this leads to the adoption of the "Z" notation, a formal specification language developed at the Programming Research Group, Oxford [12, 13].

Specifications in "Z" consist of formal text and natural-language text. The former provides a precise specification while the latter is used to introduce and explain the formal parts. Specifications are developed via small pieces of mathematics that are built up using the schema language to allow specifications to be structured. This leads to formal specifications that are more readable than a specification presented in mathematics.

The domain specification plays several roles. First, it acts as a rigorous specification of the elicited knowledge. Second, the specification can act as a basis for the future maintenance of the knowledge base. The role of correct maintenance is very important, and the procedures for updating the knowledge base can themselves be formally specified. Third, the "Z" specification can act as a medium for communication between the knowledge engineer and the domain expert as well as between the knowledge engineer and the implementer of the system.

Thus, it can be seen that the use of a formal language in the development of a knowledge base is very advantageous.

TOWARD THE REPRESENTATION SPECIFICATION

The next step in the development methodology is to identify which (if any) classical or hybrid representation is the most suitable form around which to base the representation specification, where the classical representations are "frames," "production rules," and "semantic networks."

In order to find the most suitable form, several stages have to be accomplished:

1. Creation of a knowledge profile for the elicited knowledge contained within the primary representation. This is known as profile analysis.
2. Comparison of the domain's knowledge profile (created in stage 1) with profiles for the classical representations. This is the profile-matching process.
3. Selection of the most suitable form around which to base the representation specification.

These stages will now be described in more detail.

Profile Analysis

Profile analysis is the process of producing a knowledge profile for the elicited knowledge contained within the primary representation, where a knowledge profile is a graph that indicates the amounts of certain knowledge types within the domain.

The graph structure.   The graph structure around which the profiles are constructed is the following:

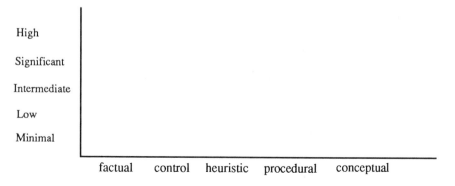

The knowledge engineer uses such a graph to plot the amount of each knowledge type present within the primary knowledge.

The vertical axis is not numeric as giving numeric values to the amount of a knowledge type in a domain is felt to be unrealistic. This process is far more subjective—hence the vertical scale. The horizontal axis is based upon a set of knowledge types that compose the majority of knowledge within any given elicited representation.

The knowledge profile.   By considering definitions for the knowledge types and by following guidelines for constructing a profile from a given primary representational form [14], a profile can be created: for example,

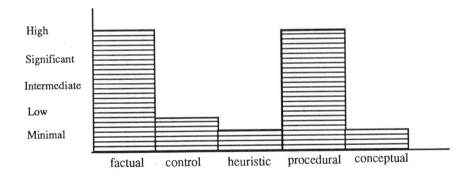

This is the profile of a primary representation that contained high factual knowledge, significant amounts of procedural knowledge, and intermediate amounts of control knowledge but only minimal amounts of heuristic and conceptual knowledge.

Profile Matching

The aim of this stage is to compare the knowledge profile for the domain with profiles of classical representations. These representational profiles are created by first having a standard representation of a given classical form, such as frames, and then examining it for the ability to represent the five knowledge types. From these analyses, profiles are drawn.

The representation that has a profile closest to that of the domain is chosen.

In order to make the selection, the domain and representation profiles are overlaid and the differences are examined. For example, if the representation profile were selected and overlaid with the domain profile, we get

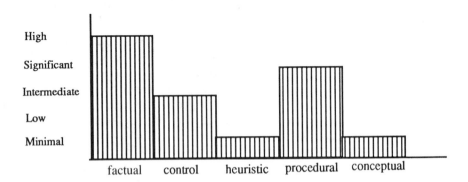

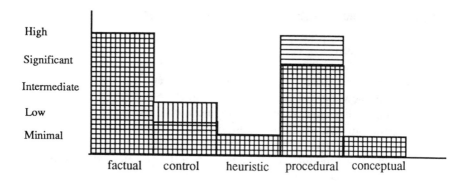

which informs us that the representation is deficient (negative deviance) in the representation of control knowledge and that when the representation specification is constructed, this should be taken into account. The representation has more representational power in representing procedural knowledge (positive deviance) than is needed in this particular case, but this is not a problem.

The Representation Specification

Having performed the matching process, the knowledge engineer can assess the results to produce a formal syntax and a denotational semantics for a representation suggested in the matching process.

THE CONCRETE SPECIFICATION

The concrete specification has two parts: a secondary representation and a formal specification of the control architecture in ''Z'' to be used in conjunction with the selected classical representation. The secondary representation attempts to bring together both the domain and representation specifications in that the correct knowledge should map into the most suitable representation. This is not directly implementable as the representation will be a cross between a high-level version of what will be implemented (i.e., minus the syntactic sugar of the implementation language) and a formal specification in the style suggested by the syntax and semantics of the representation specification. Having created the concrete specification, this is then used as the basis of the knowledge base implementation and augmented by the user specification to build the human computer interface.

THE APPLICATION OF KBS TO PERT DEVELOPMENT

Introduction

In the previous sections, we outlined a theoretical framework for developing KBSs. The framework was based upon the creation of five specifications, each of which defined a key area in the development process, these being linked together in a rigorous manner to form a partial formal specification. We now attempt to show how this development philosophy and style was used in the creation of a knowledge-based help system to assist the nonexpert user create and maintain a network model for project management.

Problem Definition

The first of the five specifications to be produced was that of problem definition, and in order to create it, the following five stages were undertaken:

1. Outline area from the domain expert.
2. Research area.
3. Prepare a preliminary project proposal.
4. Clarify project proposal.
5. Produce the initial specification.

In step 1 a report was created that outlined (i) the proposed project area, (ii) the reasons behind the need for the system, and (iii) references that introduced the literature. After this report had been produced, the literature was surveyed. The major aim of the second stage was that of familiarization, the result being a feasibility report. This was then used in the third stage, where discussions were undertaken between the knowledge engineer and the domain expert in order to further focus on the areas of the domain that were to be investigated. The first step in the process was to clarify the knowledge engineer's understanding of the domain and the domain expert's understanding of the KBS problem-solving process. At the end of this stage the parties involved were in a position to produce a report detailing the domain definition and problem description. This is termed the initial specification.

A section of the initial specification is given: The domain for this system is that of project management networks, and the aim of the project is to create a KBS that can assist in the creation and maintainance of these networks.

The KBS approach that is to be utilized is that of Plant [14]. This approach utilizes a series of formal specifications connected by rigorous steps in order to maximize the integrity of the system and to produce a system that matches the intent of the knowledge used by the domain expert.

The aim of the system is to enable proficient developers of networks to create systems that previously could only have been built by experts. A second aim is to enable these users to maintain and change systems created by others, this being an undertaking of a significant enough magnitude that it requires expert advice when developing manual systems.

The Knowledge Elicitation Phase

The role of the initial specification stage and the specification itself is to enable the knowledge engineer to approach the problem of eliciting knowledge from the domain expert with a firm understanding of the problem and its associated domain. The initial specification allows the knowledge engineer to gain a feel for the domain and a basic view of the way the problem area is composed.

The first task that had to be tackled was that of selecting an elicitation technique. The initial choice is of a technique area: verbal transfer, intermediary program, inductive program, literature-based investigation, or machine learning. Of these it was decided to use the first, verbal transfer via the knowledge engineer. This elicitation area has the following subcategories:

1. *Interview*: structured, unstructured, focused.
2. *Reporting*: on-line, off-line, hybrid.
3. *Formalized*: repertory grid, inference structure.

All of these are discussed by Plant [14].

For several reasons, the decision was made by both the knowledge engineer and domain expert to use an unstructured interview in the initial stages. First, the domain expert would not be forced in the early stages to focus on any particular aspect as the aim early on is to obtain an introductory overview of the domain. Second, the form of the unstructured interviews was that of the knowledge engineer giving a few seed questions before allowing the domain expert to develop his or her own discussion path. From time to time the knowledge engineer redirected the domain expert to ensure that he or she did not digress too far from the boundaries of the initial specification.

After a series of unstructured interviews had been performed, it was decided to undertake a series of more focused interviews in which the knowledge engineer took more of a leading role. These interviews were an attempt to focus upon individual topics in a regulatory way in which the knowledge engineer introduces the new material and tries to exert more control over the direction the interview takes. The aim is to obtain a finer grain size of information over a small subset of the domain.

The interviews were taped and then transcribed to form the elicited representation. An example section of an initial unstructured interview between the knowledge engineer (KE) and the domain expert (DE) is given:

KE: How would I as a novice in the area of project management prepare a bar chart or network to help me undertake a project?

DE: Well, there are three basic methods that one could use—there is the original method developed by Henry Gantt at the turn of the century, but that's no longer used as it was superseded by CPM and, of course, PERT.

KE: CPM?

DE: The critical path method.

KE: PERT?

DE: Sorry, PERT stands for Project Evaluation and Review Technique; stop me if I use any jargon.

KE: Ok, so all of these are networking techniques or methods?

DE: Yes.

KE: And you say that the bar chart is no longer used.

DE: Well, not for anything significant. CPM and PERT are far superior theoretically and practically. They build upon Gantt's original ideas where he had a graph and represented the activities that composed a project with bars upon it. The beginning of the bar represented the start of the activity and the end of the bar, the finish or termination of that activity.

KE: Is it worth looking at the bar chart or shall we go straight to PERT and CPM?

DE: Well, it is easier to start with the bar chart and build upon it.

KE: Ok, so what are the basic steps in creating a bar chart?

DE: Well, first of all the project should be analyzed and the basic approach considered. Once this has been done the project can be broken down into a reasonable number of activities. These can then be scheduled; you see you don't want, at least at the outset, too few or too many activities as this clouds the picture.

KE: So what is actually involved in scheduling the activities?

DE: Well, after you have listed all the jobs—activities—that have to be performed and put them in order, each activity needs to have an estimated time associated with it, the time needed to perform that activity.

KE: A start and finish time?

DE: Yes, or a duration period, to be more accurate.

KE: What's an event?

DE: Events are points in time that are said to occur when all activities leading to that event are complete.

KE: Then what?

DE: Well, once you have your activities and their durations, they need to be placed in sequence of time, ensuring that the ordering is accurate. You have to remember that some have to be performed in a specific sequence while others can be performed simultaneously.

KE: Do you have to ensure that they can all be fitted in before the final deadline for the project.

DE: Sure, that's the whole idea; you have to adjust the events until the completion date constraint is satisfied, and that's one of the reasons bar charts are unsatisfactory, in that the bars do not show explicitly enough the dependence relationships among the activities; also slippage of schedules on activities can easily become a problem, as can lack of detail, and so on.

KE: What's the "and so on"?

DE: Well basically these are events that are poor at showing interdependencies and not generally detailed enough to detect project slippage early enough.

KE: So, bar charts got superseded by CPM and PERT.

DE: Yes, these are network-based methods, graphical in nature.

KE: So, how would we create a project network and how are they different from the bar chart approach.

DE: The difference primarily stems from the ability to show the interdependencies of activities and show greater details of time constraints; it's this greater detail that enables greater control over the project to be achieved.

The Knowledge Acquisition Phase

Having performed the knowledge elicitation phase, the next stage of the development that was undertaken was the process of analyzing the knowledge elicited from the domain expert.

The aim of this phase was to produce a representation (the primary representation) of the elicited knowledge that highlights the organizational structure of the knowledge in order to allow it to be analyzed in a more rigorous manner.

The Primary Representation Phase

The five steps discussed earlier were followed.

> **Step 1.** {The knowledge elicitation phase produces the elicited representation.}

This has already been performed and is given in the preceding section.

> **Step 2.** {The elicited representation is examined for transformational characteristics, and a trace of these characteristics is produced; this is the primary representation phase.}

Having examined the elicited representation for the characteristics (discussed earlier), the following trace was drawn:

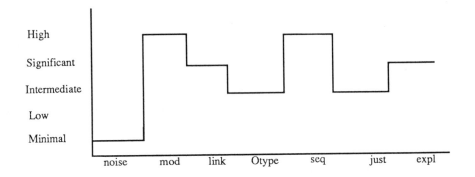

Steps 3, 4. {The primary trace is compared to the bandwidth diagrams of the primary representations in order to decide which is the most suitable; this is known as trace matching.}

The bandwidth diagram for the flow diagram is

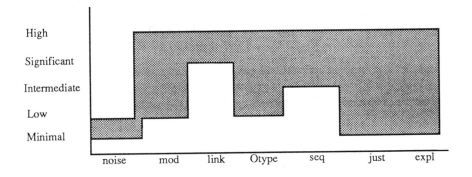

The bandwidth diagram for the contour diagram is

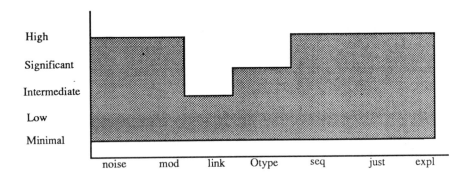

The bandwidth diagram for the decision tables is

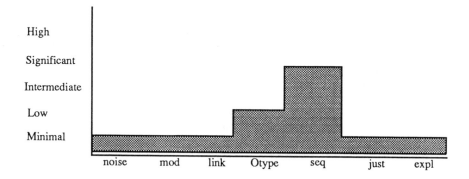

The reasons for the shape of these bandwidths is based upon the given representation's ability to capture the individual characteristics (noise, modularity, etc.) to a greater or lesser degree. Detailed information is given by Plant [14].

Step 4. {The trace-matching procedure will suggest the most suitable primary representation to use.}

It is clear from the trace and bandwidth diagrams that the flow diagram is the most suitable representation with which to re-represent the elicited representation, the bandwidth of the flow diagram being a better fit than that of the contour diagram or the decision table. The area of the contour diagram bandwidth is larger and therefore covers more cases and is consequently more general.

Step 5. {The elicited representation is transformed into the primary representation formalism.}

The flow diagram will be created from the elicited representation by the following guidelines:

1. Take a small segment of text and break this down into the components of the flow diagrams: actions, decisions, processes, and so on.
2. Construct a separate flow diagram for each of the textual points.
3. Unify the separate flow diagrams into one large diagram.
4. Examine the structure for repetitions and redundancies.
5. Examine the structure for deficiencies, that is, undefined paths from decision boxes and incomplete actions upon diagnosis of problems.
6. Recheck initial representations to improve the deficiencies.

Domain Specifications

Having created a primary representation, we are in a stronger position from which to analyze the elicited knowledge in that a higher degree of adequacy has been reached (adequacy is a measure of a representation's ability to reflect: completeness, consistency, versatility, accuracy, correctness, sensitivity, and unambiguity). However, a more formal representation is still preferred, and this is found in the domain specification.

The creation of the "Z" specification follows an analysis of the primary representation. The approach taken is to examine each of the operational types in the flow diagram taking each item in turn and using it as the basis for the predicate part of the "Z" box. This predicate then has suitable data types created for it if none have already been created. The specification is then built up trying to ensure consistency through cross checking the "Z" statements and enforcing strict, consistent data typing.

The following is a section of the primary representation specified in "Z" forming the domain specification.

CPM ──

i,E,t,L,S,D,ES,EF,LS:N
expected project duration, last-event-occurrence-time,
scheduled-completion-time, earliest-occurrence-of-event,
earliest-activity-start, earliest-activity-finish,
latest-activity-start, activity-duration,
event-last-occurrence-time, activity-total-slack,
free-slack, earliest-event-occurrence:N

---

initial event ─────────────────────

CPM ──────────

i = 1

---

terminal event ─────────────────────

CPM ──────────

i = t

---

project duration ─────────────────────

CPM ──────────

expected-project-duration = Et

last event occurrence —————————

CPM
———————

last-event-occurrence-time = Lt

project terminal event —————————

CPM
———————

Et = Lt

completion time —————————

CPM
———————

scheduled-completion-time = Ts

earliest event occurrence —————————

CPM
———————

earliest-occurrence-of-event = Ej

event occurrence —————————

CPM
———————

Ej = max(Ei + Dij)

activity start time —————————

CPM
———————

earliest-activity-start = ESiJ

earliest activity start —————————

CPM
———————

ESij = Ei

earliest activity finish —————————

CPM
———————

earliest-activity-finish = EFij

activity finish time _____

CPM

$EFij = Ei + Dij$

latest activity start _____

CPM

latest-activity-start = LSij

activity slack total _____

CPM

$LSij = Lj - Dij$

estimates mean duration _____

CPM

$Sij = Lj - EFij$

event last occurrence _____

CPM

activity-duration = Ej

activity slack total _____

CPM

event-last-occurrence-time = Li

free slack _____

CPM

activity-total-slack = Sij

earliest event occurrence _____

| CPM

| free-slack = FSij

earliest activity start _____

| CPM

| earliest-event-occurrence = j(Ej)

earliest activity finish _____

| CPM

| i − j(LSij)

Representation Specification

Having taken our primary representation and produced the domain specification from it, the next phase was to perform a second analysis of the primary representation in order to identify which classical representation (frames, semantic network, rules, etc.) would be most suitable to utilize in our development.

The stages that were necessary in order to produce the representation specification were profile analysis and profile matching.

Profile analysis (Stage 1). The following knowledge profile was constructed for the elicited knowledge by following the guidelines given by Plant [14, 15]:

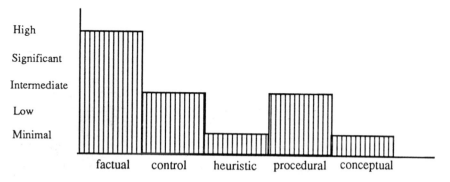

Profile matching (Stage 2). Having drawn the domain profile, the process of selecting a suitable classical representation was performed based upon the following steps:

Step 1

Comparison 1: Frame representation profile and domain profile.

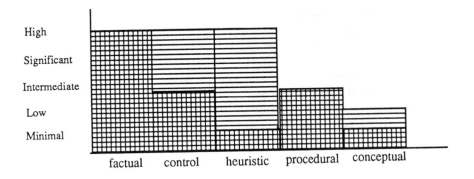

Comparison 2: Rules profile and domain profile.

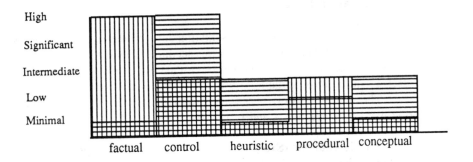

Comparison 3: Semantic network profile and domain profile.

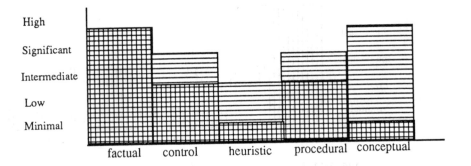

Step 2. {Count the divergencies and place them in a table.}

Step 3. {Summate all the positive divergencies (P.D.) and give them a nonnumeric value.}

Step 4. {Summate all the negative divergencies (N.D.) and give them a nonnumeric value.}

Frame match:

N.D.	0	0	0	0	0	0	match
P.D.	0	2	4	0	1	7	high

Rules match:

N.D.	4	0	0	1	0	5	high
P.D.	0	2	2	0	2	6	high

Semantic network match:

N.D.	0	0	0	0	0	0	match
P.D.	0	1	2	1	4	8	high

Step 5. {Select the representation with the lowest number of negative divergencies.}

This reduces the representations to select from frames and semantic networks.

Step 6. {Examine the negative divergencies in the matches.}

They are both total matches.

Step 7. {Examine the positive divergencies.}

Even though they both have high values of positive divergence, frames have a lower deviation over all knowledge types while also having two matches against the semantic network type.

We therefore selected frames as the representation to use in the development of this domain.

The language used as the representation specification was specified in B.N.F. as follows:

```
-----<section-name>------------------------------------------------

    <desc-spec>
    _____

    <section-body>
    _____


    <para-type>
    _____

    <body-type>
    _____


    ==================================================

    <text-name>
    ------------------------------------------------------------------

    <text>
    _____
```

\<section-spec\>:: = \<section-name\> \<desc-spec\> \<section-body\>
\<section-name\> :: = \<simple-string\>
\<section-body\> :: = \<pred\> ⇒ ref \<section-spec\> |
                \<pred\> ⇒ \<text-gen\>
\<pred\>:: = (\<paragraph-spec\>)? |
       (\<paragraph-spec\> \<operator\> \<action\>)? |
       {(\<paragraph-spec\>)? \<operator\> \<pred\>}*
\<paragraph-spec\>:: = \<para-type\> \<body-type\>
\<action\>:: = \<pred\> | \<const\>
\<const\>:: = \<simple-string\>
\<para-type\>:: = \<para-name\> \<type\> | \<xor\> \<xor-para\>
\<xor-para\>:: = \<para-name\> | \<para-name\> \<xor-para\>
\<text-gen\>:: = \<text-name\> \<text\>
\<para-name\>:: = \<simple-string\>
\<text-name\>:: = \<simple-string\> \<text-no\>
\<type\>:: = [\<type-body\>] | \<type-double-body\>
\<type-body\>:: = fact | rule | category | number | phrase
\<type-double-body\>:: [category] [rule] | [fact] [rule]
\<body-type\>:: = \<fact-body\> | \<rule-body\> | \<category\>
             \<number-body\> | \<phrase-body\> | \<category-body\>
             \<fact-rule-body\>
\<fact-body\>:: = \<desc-spec\> \<expl-spec\> \<query-spec\>
\<rule-body\>:: = \<desc-spec\> \<expl-spec\> \<rule-spec\> \<query-spec\>
\<category-body\>:: = \<desc-spec\> \<expl-spec\> \<options-spec\> \<query-spec\>
\<number-body\>:: = \<desc-spec\> \<expl-spec\> \<options-spec\> \<query-spec\>
\<phrase-body\>:: = \<desc-spec\> \<expl-spec\> \<query-spec\>
\<category-rule-body\>:: = \<desc-spec\> \<expl-spec\> \<options-spec\> \<rule-spec\>
             \<query-spec\>
\<fact-rule-body\>:: = \<desc-spec\> \<expl-spec\> \<rule-spec\> \<query-spec\>
\<string-item\>:: = @\<para-name\> | #\<para-name\> | \<simple-string\>

```
<simple-string>:: = <name> | <char-sequence>
<name>:: = <lowercase> | <name> <letter< | <name> <digit>
<lowercase>:: = a..z
<letter>:: = <lowercase> | A..Z
<digit>:: = 0..9
<text>:: = <string> {<string>}*
<string>:: = <string-item> {<string-item>}*
<desc-spec>:: = desc: <string>
<expl-spec>:: = expl: <string>
<options-spec>:: = options: option {,option}*
<number-spec>:: = range: <number>..<number>
<rule-spec>:: = rule <rule> {,<rule>}* |
               rules: <rule> {,<rule>}*
<query-spec>:: = query: <text>
<option>:: = <name> – <string> | <name>
<rule>:: = <expression> [if <pattern>] | <pattern> [If <pattern>] | use <goal> [if <pattern>]
<pattern>:: = <p1> {or <p1>}*
<p1>:: = <p2> {and <p2>}
<p2>:: = not p2 | <valuespec> <relation> <valuespec> | <name>=<name> | (<pattern>)
           | <true> | <false> | <name>
<value-spec>:: = <name> | <number>
<operator>:: = <relational> | <boolean-op>
<relation>:: = = | < > | <|>|< =|>=
<expression>:: = <e1> {<addop> <e1>}*
<addop>:: = + | –
<multop>:: = * | /
<boolean-op>:: = .AND. | .OR. | .NOT.
<e2>:: = ( <expression> ) | <value-spec>
<value-spec>:: = <name> <number>
<text-no>:: = <digit> | <text-no> <digit>
<number>:: = <unsigned-number> | <sign> <unsigned-number>
<sign>:: = + | –
<unsigned-number>:: = <digit-sequence> | <decimal-number> | <exp-number>
<char-sequence>:: = <letter> | <char-sequence> <letter>
<digit-sequence>:: = <digit> | <digit-sequence> <digit>
<decimal-number>:: = <digit-sequence> · <digit-sequence>
<exp-number>:: = <digit-sequence> <mantissa-number> | <decimal-number>
                <mantissa-number>
<mantissa-number>:: = E <sign> <digit-sequence>
```

The Concrete Specification

Having produced a domain specification and a representation specification, we brought the two together. This produced the secondary representation part of the concrete specification. This then had a specification for a control architecture added to it, and the total formed a base from which the implementation could be developed.

A segment of this concrete specification is given:

title _____

Project Management Development System

(not beginner)? ⇒ ref introduction-system
(beginner)? ⇒ ref introduction-help

introduction-system _____
Desc: This section enables users to consider the
prerequirements to the creation of a network

(bar)? ⇒ ref bar-info
(not bar) ⇒ ref network-info

network-info _____

Desc: To direct users through CMP/PERT

(CPM)? ⇒ ref CPM-network
(PERT)? ⇒ ref PERT-network
(not CPM) ? AND (not PERT) ? ⇒ Text 1

CPM-network _____

Desc: To assist the user to develop a CPM network

(not analyzed)? ⇒ ref start-analyze
(analyzed)? ⇒ ref problem-breakdown

start-analyze _____

Desc: To initiate the analysis

(start-analysis)? ⇒ ref problem

problem-breakdown _____

Desc: Step 1 in creation of CPM

(start-time)? ⇒ ref step2
(not start-time)? ⇒ ref get-start-time

Implementation

The final step in our development was to take the concrete specification and map this onto an implementation. The chosen vehicle for implementation was that of the ESP Advisor Shell. The representation specification language is a close match to the Knowledge Representation Language (KRL) used in ESP and the mapping was straightforward. Then ESP compiles the KRL into Prolog.

CONCLUSION

The aim of this chapter was to show how an expert system can be developed to address the problem of project management scheduling. The problem is one that has a wide-ranging applicability, but due to the complexities of the task, it is underutilized. However, our approach demonstrates a unique flexibility among methodologies and is computationally feasible. These factors will allow our system, when fully developed, to be used by a larger spectrum of management than those currently available.

REFERENCES

1. Patterson and Roth, "Scheduling a Project under Multiple Resource Constraints: A Zero-One Programming Approach," *AIIE Transactions, 8,* 449–455 (1976).
2. Doersch and Patterson, "Scheduling a Project to Maximize Its Present Value: A Zero-One Programming Approach," *Management Science, 23,* 882–889 (1977).
3. Hindelang and Muth, "Dynamic Programming Algorithm for Decision CPM Networks," *Operations Research, 27,* 225–241 (1979).
4. Kapur, "Designing a Multi-level Network System," *Journal of the Operations Research Society, 29,* 1121–1125 (1978).
5. Willis and Hastings, "Project Scheduling with Resource Constraints Using Branch and Bound Methods," *Journal of the Operations Research Society, 27*(2), 341–349 (1976).
6. Cooper, "Heuristics for Scheduling Resource Constrained Projects: An Experimental Investigation," *Management Science, 22,* 1186–1194 (1979).
7. Britney, "Project Management in Costly Environments," *Project Management Quarterly, 9,* 31–42 (1978).
8. Cook and Jennings, "Estimating a Project's Completion Time Distribution Using an Intelligent Simulation Method," *Journal of the Operations Research Society, 30,* 1103–1108 (1979).
9. Hayes-Roth, F., Waterman, D. A., and Lenat, D. B., *Building Expert Systems,* Addison-Wesley, Reading, MA, 1983.
10. Davis, R., "Expert Systems: Where Are We and Where Do We Go From Here?" MIT-AIM-665, MIT Technical Report, Boston, MA, 1982.

11. Weiss, S. M. and Kulikowski, C. A., *A Practical Guide to Designing Expert Systems*, Chapman & Hall, London, 1984.

12. Sufrin, B., *Mathematics for System Specification*, Programming Research Group, Oxford University, Oxford, 1985.

13. Morgan, C., *The Schema Language*, Programming Research Group, Oxford University, Oxford, 1984.

14. Plant, R. T., "A Methodology for Knowledge Acquisition in the Development of Expert Systems," Ph.D. Thesis, University of Liverpool, Liverpool, 1987.

15. Plant, R. T., "A Case Study in Expert System Development," paper presented at the Second International Symposium On Methodologies For Intelligent Systems, Charlotte, NC, 1987.

13

CESA: An Expert System Prototype for Aiding U.S. Department of Defense Research Contracting

Jay Liebowitz
Laura C. Davis and Wilson F. Harris

INTRODUCTION

The contracting area is a ripe application for expert system development. In the U.S. Department of Defense (DOD) research contracting business, there are two major phases of a contract: a preaward phase and postaward stage. The contract preaward phase involves the packaging of necessary forms and information to generate an acceptable procurement request package. The procurement request package typically serves as the vehicle for generating proposals in response to the government's advertised need. Once proposals are received, reviewed, and evaluated by an evaluation team within the sponsoring government activity, the successful bidder (i.e., contractor) is informed of his or her selection and some negotiations may follow to iron out the details. Once the contract is in place, it is monitored by a government representative. The monitoring of the contract and the reviewing of the work performed under the contract are part of the contract postaward phase.

Expert systems could play valuable roles in assisting in the contracting process. For example, expert systems could be used to help train new contracts specialists, help to assemble a "complete" procurement request package, and assist in tracking the processing of that package. Expert systems could also aid in monitoring a contract and providing advice if a deliverable is late or inferior to what was promised. An expert system might also act as an advisory system to explain such areas as how to exercise an option, how to terminate a contract, or how to select appropriate remedies short of termination. Additionally, an expert system could help flag discrepancies or inconsistencies in contractor monthly progress reports.

This chapter discusses the development of an expert system prototype called CESA (COTR Expert System Aid), constructed at the Navy Center for Applied Research in Artificial Intelligence (NCARAI) at the Naval Research Laboratory

(NRL). Currently, CESA concentrates on providing advice on the contract preaward area. Before describing CESA, we look briefly at some of the automated techniques being employed to support the contracting process and discuss the need for a system such as CESA at the NRL. We explain the development of CESA in detail, highlighting the various steps of the knowledge engineering process.

BRIEF SURVEY OF SOME AUTOMATED TECHNIQUES USED IN CONTRACTING

To date, little work has been performed in developing expert systems to help in the contracting area [1, 2]. Many management information systems (MISs) and data base management systems (DBMSs) are being used to assist with the tracking of procurements and the storing of procurement forms and sample completed forms. Decision support systems (DSSs) are also being used in the contracting area to help implement project management techniques for better managing the contracting process. Within the defense community, these automated aids are also being used to help in "acquisition management" activities. However, unlike the wide deployment and use of these MISs, DBMSs, and DSSs in the contracting arena, few expert systems have been developed for assisting in the contracting business.

There has been some work in applying operations research and information systems techniques to improving the defense contracting process. The Air Force has developed a system called ACQUIRE, which through keyword matching provides assistance in locating defense contracting regulations housed on a compact disk [3]. There has also been work in applying game theory to contracting science. For example, a sequence of bids on a competitive defense contract has been modeled as a dynamic game [4]. Another system called PRISM, by Compusearch, is a full-function purchase request information system that is a helpful aid in the contracting arena [5].

While these techniques have greatly helped improve the contracting process, expert systems could further aid and provide direct support for individuals involved

TABLE 1. Examples of Expert Systems in Program/Acquisition Management and Law

Program/acquisition management
Expert System Acquisition Strategy (Defense Systems
Management College)
Program Impact Advisor (Analytics)
Logistics Planning and Requirements Simplification
System (Army Material Command)
Law
Legal Decisionmaking System (Rand Corporation)
Legal Analysis Program (Gardner)
Taxman (Rutgers University)
LRS (Hafner)
DSCAS (Kruppenbacher)

in contracting. Some expert systems under development for program and/or acquisition management are given in Table 1. It is interesting to note that a number of expert systems have been developed for legal applications, as also shown in Table 1, which deal with rules and regulations akin to the contracting domain [6].

The expert system prototype, CESA, which will be described in this chapter, serves as an advisory system to help the ARO/COTR (Acquisition Request Originator/ Contracting Officer Technical Representative) perform his or her duties and responsibilities more effectively. The next section will look at the need for such a system, and then the building steps of CESA will be explained.

NEED FOR CESA

An important advantage of expert systems technology is its ability to aid in the training function of a particular application. Before an expert retires or leaves an organization, an expert system can serve in capturing the expert's knowledge and experiential learning to help train others in performing a specific task. In this manner, individuals in the organization, especially neophytes, can learn from the successes and failures of their predecessors in order to improve their effectiveness and productivity.

At the NRL, as in most government contracting, there is a myriad of skills involved in the contracting process [7]. These skills range from the knowledge required in handling procurement request generation and execution to monitoring and evaluating contractor performance. The front end of the process is the preaward phase of the contract in which the appropriate materials are packaged to support the proposed acquisition. The back end is the postaward phase, which involves the monitoring of contractor performance and inspection and acceptance of goods and services received. At the NRL, the individual who is responsible for providing all technical requirements, specifications, justifications, and statements necessary to support the proposed acquisition and who usually helps evaluate the technical aspects of all proposals, bids, or quotations is designated the ARO. Thus, the ARO is concerned with the contract preaward phase. The person in direct support of the contract postaward phase is the COTR. The COTR's duties include assuring quality, providing technical direction as necessary with respect to the specifications or statement of work, monitoring the progress, cost, and quality of contractor performance, and certifying invoices. At the NRL, the individual who is certified as the COTR on a particular contract most likely also serves as the ARO.

There are two major reasons for developing an expert system to help the ARO/COTR [8]. First, the nature of contracting involves many complex and often changing rules and regulations. It is difficult for the ARO/COTR to remember and to keep up to date with these new rules and procedures, particularly since he or she is principally a scientist or engineer and not a contract specialist and may be called upon to perform contract-related duties only on an irregular basis. Even though the COTR at the NRL takes a formal course and passes a test to become eligible for certification, an expert system can act as a supplemental trainer and also can refresh the COTR on specific aspects of this material as necessary. A second reason for developing an ARO/COTR expert system aid is to provide an interactive, interesting way for the ARO/COTR to reference and learn the contract information needed as well as to furnish a convenient vehicle for assisting in ARO/COTR problem solving. It should be noted that the need for a system such as CESA at the NRL was first raised by a member of its COTR community.

The next session will discuss the development process of CESA.

DEVELOPMENT OF THE CESA PROTOTYPE

CESA's development followed the rapid prototyping approach using the following knowledge engineering steps: problem selection, knowledge acquisition, knowledge representation, knowledge encoding, and knowledge testing and evaluation [9]. Each of these steps will be discussed in turn.

Problem Selection

In response to a suggestion by a COTR at the NRL that expert systems technology might be applied to help the COTR better perform his or her functions, the NCARAI conducted a feasibility study that identified four possible alternatives for system development within the COTR environment. These were [10]:

- An expert system prototype for procurement request generation and routing.
- An expert system prototype to act as a training aid.
- An expert system prototype for specific problem-solving activities relating to the performance of a contract.
- An expert system prototype for monitoring the progress of a contract.

Analysis using the analytic hierarchy process revealed that the areas of (1) COTR problem-solving activities relating to contract performance and (2) procurement request generation and routing appeared particularly amenable to expert system development at the NRL [7].

The top-ranked COTR problem-solving alternative had to be scoped much further to select a well-bounded task for developing a proof-of-concept expert system prototype. After discussions with numerous individuals, especially our contract expert, who had over 26 years of contracting experience, it was decided that the contract preaward phase (i.e., procurement request generation) would be a better task area for developing the proof-of-concept prototype than the postaward phase. The main reason for selecting the preaward area as our focus was that it seems to be particularly troublesome to the ARO community at the NRL; experience shows that contracting specialists often receive incomplete or inaccurate procurement request packages that have to be returned to the ARO before processing, thus delaying the procurement process. Based on the strong need for such a system in the preaward area and the structuredness and specificity of the preaward domain, it was decided that the preaward phase would be a high-interest, high-payoff area for near-term expert systems development. If the proof-of-concept version of CESA was successful, tasks within the postaward area could later be incorporated into CESA.

The preaward area also met the criteria for selecting an appropriate problem for expert system development. Namely, it was mostly symbolic in nature; there was a general consensus on the correct solution; the problem took a few minutes to a few hours to solve; it was performed frequently; it dealt mainly with cognitive skills as opposed to motor skills; and an expert existed who would be able to participate in the project. For these reasons the preaward area, procurement request generation and routing, was selected as an appropriate task for the CESA prototype.

The next step in CESA's development involved knowledge acquisition. To prepare for this step, the CESA development team obtained various NRL contracting instructions and manuals to become more familiar with the preaward domain before meeting with a contract expert. By reviewing this documentation, the CESA development team felt more comfortable in conversing with the expert and asking the right questions.

Knowledge Acquisition

After selecting a well-bounded task, the next major step in developing CESA was performing the knowledge acquisition process. Knowledge was acquired through two major sources. The first source was the many NRL instructions and manuals that address the preaward contract phase. The second major method of acquiring knowledge was through interviewing a contract expert.

The expert was a retired annuitant who had over 26 years of contracting experience. Tasked by the head of NRL's contracts division to take part in CESA's development, she was very enthusiastic about helping in this project because she felt there was a great need for developing such a system to assist ARO/COTRs at the NRL. She also was excited that her expertise would be "preserved" and used to help others at the laboratory. The knowledge acquisition sessions were conducted with the expert once a week, 2–3 hours per meeting, for two months, in order to build the CESA prototype.

In acquiring knowledge from the expert, various forms of interviewing methods were used. Structured interviews were effective because once the major preaward areas were mapped out, the knowledge engineering team would acquire knowledge from the expert in each of these areas one at a time. The technique of using "constrained information tasks" forced the expert to use her thinking within a short period of time in order for the knowledge engineering team to determine the important heuristics involved. The technique of using "limited information" during parts of the interview required the expert to determine what was important in terms of information being omitted and material that was used. Another useful interviewing technique used in acquiring knowledge for CESA was the scenario approach. In this method, the knowledge engineering team posed sample scenarios to the expert, and the expert would then "think aloud" during the process of solving these cases.

A sample excerpt from a knowledge acquisition transcript with the expert follows [1]:

Knowledge engineer (KE): At first, maybe we could take a look to see what are some general categories of problems that COTRs run into. Then within one of those categories, perhaps, we can go into more specific problems.

Expert (E): Do you want to discuss initiation, delivery, or monitoring through the process first? Which one?

KE: Well, what would be the area that is causing the most problems for COTRs?

E: Now, we are presuming that a COTR is an ARO also. An ARO will be the initiator of a requirement and then after become the COTR. That is usually the case at the laboratory, but they do have two different designators. So we are going to consider that the COTR covers the whole span, as far as our discussions are concerned.

The main problem is getting the project off the ground—not having adequate packages with which to work. Because if you don't have an adequate package, you can't get started. And if you can't get started, you can't get a contract awarded. And so on.

There were several factors that made the knowledge acquisition process an effective and enjoyable task. First, the expert allowed the knowledge engineering team to tape the knowledge engineering sessions. This was useful in obtaining a better, more complete record of discussions with the expert than simply jotting down some notes. Also, the expression and intonation of the expert, which had some significance in the phrasing of certain information, could be captured. Second, using the different interviewing techniques previously mentioned helped uncover a variety of knowledge needed to be incorporated in CESA. Third, documentation such as the NRL instructions and contracting handbooks was extremely useful in providing additional information for the knowledge base as well as familiarizing the knowledge engineering team with the domain, as noted earlier, prior to interviewing the expert. Fourth, each knowledge acquisition session usually ran about 2 hours, which seemed to be an appropriate length of time for not tiring the expert. Fifth, as the knowledge engineering team climbed the learning curve in understanding the contract area, the expert became more and more enthusiastic about the project. When the expert obtained hands-on experience early on in running versions of the CESA prototype, the expert really felt that CESA was "her baby."

After acquiring the knowledge for CESA, the next major step involved representing the acquired knowledge. This will be explained next.

Knowledge Representation

Knowledge in expert systems should be represented in the most natural way that the expert employs his or her knowledge. From the knowledge acquisition sessions with the expert, it became apparent that the expert's knowledge could be easily represented as condition–action, or if–then, rules. This notion was further confirmed by reviewing the documentation on contracting, which typically consisted as a series of if–then clauses. For example, an excerpt from the NRL *COTR Handbook* reads [12]:

> If the COTR finds that the contractor is not complying with a specific requirement contained in the contract, the COTR should call the contractor's attention to the discrepancy and seek voluntary commitment to remedy the failure. If the contractor makes such a commitment, the COTR should follow up to see if the action is taken.

The proof-of-concept version of CESA consisted of 146 rules. Two examples of rules from CESA are shown in what follows. Rule 77 indicates one of the forms needed for a procurement request (PR) package, and rule 10 indicates the type of contract preferred for a particular situation:

RULE NUMBER: 77

IF: (1) Your questions involve the preaward phase
       and (2) You need to explore adequacy of PR package items
       and (3) You want to know about what is needed in the PR
                package
       and (4) Procurement is a major procurement costing $25,000
                or more
       and (5) PR involves a new contract or a modification to
                the contract in excess of $100,000
THEN: (1) NDW-NRL 4200/1304 (5–87)—Format for Additional
                Resources Required for New and Existing Contracts
REFERENCE: NRLINST 4205.3A (April 19, 1988)

RULE NUMBER: 10

IF: (1) Your questions involve the preaward phase
       and (2) You have specific preaward questions on adequacy
                of the PR package
       and (3) You want to know about what type of contract is
                desired
       and (4) The Contract deals with hardware items when the item
                has not been developed previously or is in the
                research-and-development stages of development or study
                contracts when the NRL cannot define explicitly the
                requirements but can provide general work statements

THEN: (1)   Type of contract desired is cost-plus-fixed fee
        and (2)   Stay away from cost-plus-fixed fee level-of-effort
                contracts because once the level of effort is
                consumed, the contract is finished
REFERENCE: *COTR Handbook* (March 1987) and discussions with
                Virginia Dean, Contracts

After representing the knowledge as rules, the next step was to encode the knowledge in the knowledge base. This step will be explained next.

Knowledge Encoding

To help in the prototyping process, an expert system shell was used for developing a proof-of-concept version of CESA within a short period of time (two months). Exsys [13] was the shell selected for CESA's development because:

- Exsys can handle rules, and it can use backward or forward chaining (backward chaining was needed for CESA's application).
- Exsys runs on the IBM PC, which was the recommended hardware for CESA since most ARO/COTRs have access to a PC.
- Exsys has a fairly easy-to-use text editor for creating the knowledge base; this feature was important because CESA eventually will need to be maintained by someone in Contracts who is not a computer specialist.
- Exsys can handle uncertainty in its rules.
- Exsys has a single-fee run time license available so that unlimited copies of CESA can be distributed and used laboratorywide.
- Exsys allows for free-text comments to provide definitions and descriptions of qualifiers and their values.
- Exsys is a fairly inexpensive expert system shell.

The major drawback in using Exsys is the user interface; although adequate, it could certainly be improved in flexibility of displays. However, the documentation for Exsys is well written, and generally speaking, the advantages of using Exsys far outweigh the disadvantages.

Encoding the knowledge for CESA using Exsys was an iterative process. After acquiring and representing the knowledge for each preaward area, the knowledge was subsequently encoded into the system, one preaward area at a time. By quickly encoding prototypical cases into CESA, the expert could see some tangible results occurring from the knowledge acquisition sessions. Also, by encoding this knowledge early on, the expert could more easily identify omissions in the knowledge or incorrect knowledge being applied. By seeing how the chaining in CESA took place, the expert could easily identify if the proper conclusions were reached from the combinations of the input provided. When weaknesses in the knowledge base were identified, the knowledge was reacquired, represented, and encoded into CESA.

To help develop and eventually maintain CESA, the knowledge base was set up in a modular fashion. Sections in the knowledge base relate to each preaward area, and within each preaward area, further subdivisions are made. Thus, each preaward area is fairly autonomous from the other preaward areas; this means that there is little, if any, "interlinking" between preaward areas, and knowledge revisions relating to one preaward section can be made without affecting the knowledge in the other preaward sections. Although this approach may add a seemingly redundant qualifier or two to some rules, it ultimately will help in the maintenance of CESA by contracts personnel. Figure 1 shows a sample user session of CESA.

The next step after encoding the knowledge was testing the knowledge and evaluating the proof-of-concept version of CESA. This will be explained next.

Knowledge Testing and Evaluation

The last major step in developing the CESA prototype was knowledge testing and evaluation. Knowledge testing involved verification and validation of the knowledge [14]. This relates to "developing the expert system right" and "developing the right expert system." Evaluation entails obtaining user feedback on the human factors design of the expert system as well as commenting on the accuracy and quality of the decisions reached.

For the proof-of-concept version of CESA, verification and validation were performed in a variety of ways. First, CESA's knowledge was verified by tracing paths for logical consistency. When combinations of answers led to incorrect or incomplete conclusions, the knowledge base was modified or augmented to rectify these situations. Second, historical test cases were run against CESA to see if the expert-system-generated results were the same as the results from the documented cases. Specifically, completed (and successfully processed) PR packages were used to see if CESA generated the same list of forms to be included in the PR package as were found in the successful PR packages. Generally speaking, CESA was very accurate in its judgments and/or conclusions. Third, the expert and other test users ran CESA with hypothetical cases to test the quality and accuracy of CESA's decisions. This greatly helped during the knowledge refinement process.

In terms of evaluating the "user friendliness" of CESA, both naive users (those individuals who just completed the COTR course) and knowledgeable users (those persons who have been COTRs for a few years) were generally pleased with CESA but suggested that additional free-text comments be added to better define some qualifiers and values used in the system. Also, some of the wording used in questions asked of the user needed to be improved since some of the wording was contract specialist oriented as opposed to ARO/COTR oriented. Additionally, some of the users would like to have seen a more graphically oriented user interface.

CESA has been well received by NRL Contracts management, who considers the proof-of-concept prototype a success. They favor continued near-term development of the system, field testing, and then distribution to ARO/COTRs in the laboratory. A discussion of future work appears in the last section.

The next section identifies some factors instrumental to CESA's successful development.

CESA (COTR Expert System Aid)

by: Jay Liebowitz, Laura Davis, and Wilson Harris
Expert consultant: Virginia Dean

Press any key to start:

Welcome to CESA–COTR Expert System Aid. This expert system prototype will help you answer questions pertinent to problems you might be having as an ARO/COTR. To operate CESA, respond to questions with the number of the appropriate response. For multiple answers, put the number of the answers and separate them with a comma (e.g., 1,2). If you are not sure why a question is being asked, then type the word why. If you would like a description of the terms used in the question, then type a question mark (?). At the end of your session, the conclusions will be displayed ranked in importance by a value from 1 (least often applies) to 10 (most often applies). Have fun!

Press any key to start:

Your questions involve the
 1 preaward phase
 2 postaward phase
 3 advice on how to complete preaward forms
1

Enter the number(s) of the value(s)   WHY to display rule being used <?> for details   QUIT
to save data   <H> for help

You have specific preaward questions on
 1 adequacy of the procurement request (PR) package
 2 routing of either the duplicate original (advance copy) of the procurement-planning document (PPD) or PR package, or routing of the original PPD, or routing of the original PR
 3 use of the PPD
?

Enter the number(s) of the value(s)   WHY to display rule being used <?> for details   QUIT
to save data   <H> for help   <Ctrl-U> to undo

The PPD is a major PR in support of an NRL work unit for processing up to but not including actual contract award in advance of receipt of the sponsor funds that will finance the procurement. "Adequacy of the PR package" refers to such items as what is needed in a PR package, Justification and Approval information, Statement of Work questions, what type of contract is desired, synopsis requirements, evaluation procedures, and others.

Figure 1 Sample user session with CESA.

TO RETURN TO PROGRAM PRESS <SPACE>

You have specific preaward questions on
    1   adequacy of the PR package
    2   routing of either the duplicate original (advance copy) of the PPD or PR package, or
        routing of the original PPD, or routing of the original PR
    3   use of the PPD
1

Enter the number(s) of the value(s)   WHY to display rule being used <?> for details   QUIT
to save data   <H> for help   <Ctrl-U> to undo

You want to know about
    1   what is needed in a PR package
    2   Justification and Approval (J&A) if requirement to be specified is sole source
    3   the statement of work (SOW)
    4   evaluation procedures
    5   synopsis procedures
    6   the ADP Procurement Checklist
1

Enter the number(s) of the value(s)   WHY to display rule being used <?> for details   QUIT
to save data   <H> for help   <Ctrl-U> to undo

Your procurement is a
    1   major procurement costing $25,000 or more
    2   procurement under $25,000
1

Enter the number(s) of the value(s)   WHY to display rule being used <?> for details   QUIT
to save data   <H> for help   <Ctrl-U> to undo

Your procurement is
    1   competitive
    2   sole source (noncompetitive)
    3   for an 8a small disadvantaged business
1

Enter the number(s) of the value(s)   WHY to display rule being used <?> for details   QUIT
to save data   <H> for help   <Ctrl-U> to undo

contract
    1   involves access to, receipt of, or generation of classified material and/or access to classified
        areas
    2   does NOT involve access to, receipt of, or generation of classified material and/or access
        to classified areas
2

Enter the number(s) of the value(s)   WHY to display rule being used <?> for details   QUIT
to save data   <H> for help   <Ctrl-U> to undo

Figure 1 (*continued*)

Procurement request is for
  1   capital equipment
  2   sponsor-funded equipment
  3   neither capital equipment nor sponsor-funded equipment
3

Enter the number(s) of the value(s)   WHY to display rule being used <?> for details   QUIT
to save data   <H> for help   <Ctrl-U> to undo

Your procurement request deals with
  1   acquisition of commercially available hardware/software, services/maintenance, or materials where the vendor can quote a price that will not change during the life of the contract and can deliver at that price (vendor assumes risk)
  2   minor modification to hardware/software to suit government needs (vendor assumes risk)
  3   major R&D modification to hardware/software to suit government needs (government assumes risk)
  4   research and development of hardware/software (government assumes risk)
  5   R&D studies/services where NRL cannot define explicitly the requirements but can provide general work statements (government assumes risk)
  6   university research and development (government assumes risk)
5

Enter the number(s) of the value(s)   WHY to display rule being used <?> for details   QUIT
to save data   <H> for help   <Ctrl-U> to undo

PR involves a(n)
  1   new research effort at NRL
  2   existing research effort at NRL
why

Enter the number(s) of the value(s)   WHY to display rule being used <?> for details   QUIT
to save data   <H> for help   <Ctrl-U> to undo

Rule Number: 68
IF: (1) Your questions involve the preaward phase
      and (2) You need to explore adequacy of PR package items
      and (3) You want to know about what is needed in a PR package
      and (4) Your procurement is a major procurement costing $25,000 or more
      and (5) Your procurement request deals with R&D of hardware/software (government assumes risk) OR R&D studies/services where NRL cannot define explicitly the requirements but can provide general work statements (government assumes risk)
      and (6) PR involves a new research effort at NRL
THEN: NDW-NRL 3900/1002 (Rev 11–84)—Work Unit Assignment Summary (DD Form 1498), required by Code 1005—Confidence = 10/10

Figure 1   (*continued*)

IF line # for derivation, <K>-known data, <C>-choices, <R>-reference, or previous or next rule, <J>-jump, <H>-help or <ENTER> to continue:

PR involves a(n)
    1   new research effort at NRL
    2   existing research effort at NRL
1

Enter the number(s) of the value(s)   WHY to display rule being used <?> for details   QUIT
to save data   <H> for help   <Ctrl-U> to undo

Your procurement involves
    1   nonpersonal services (e.g., research study, maintenance)
    2   personal services (e.g., data entry, secretarial)
    3   products rather than services (e.g., hardware, software)
1

Enter the number(s) of the value(s)   WHY to display rule being used <?> for details   QUIT
to save data   <H> for help   <Ctrl-U> to undo

acquired services are
    1   being funded with RDT&E (research, development, testing, and evaluation) dollars
    2   NOT being funded with RDT&E dollars
1

Enter the number(s) of the value(s)   WHY to display rule being used <?> for details   QUIT
to save data   <H> for help   <Ctrl-U> to undo

contract is (PLEASE HIT ? FOR DESCRIPTION OF ADP BEFORE ENTERING YOUR RESPONSE)
    1   ADP (automatic data processing)
    2   non-ADP
1

Enter the number(s) of the value(s)   WHY to display rule being used <?> for details   QUIT
to save data   <H> for help   <Ctrl-U> to undo

PR involves a new contract or a modification to the contract
    1   in excess of $100,000
    2   NOT in excess of $100,000
1

Enter the number(s) of the value(s)   WHY to display rule being used <?> for details   QUIT
to save data   <H> for help   <Ctrl-U> to undo

Company/product/service relating to the PR is
    1   on the GSA schedule
    2   NOT on the GSA schedule
1

Figure 1   (*continued*)

Enter the number(s) of the value(s)   WHY to display rule being used <?> for details   QUIT
to save data   <H> for help   <Ctrl-U> to undo

Product relating to the PR is
   1   competitive on the GSA schedule (i.e., product or similar item available from at least
       two offerors on the GSA schedule)
   2   NOT competitive on the GSA schedule
1

Enter the number(s) of the value(s)   WHY to display rule being used <?> for details   QUIT
to save data   <H> for help   <Ctrl-U> to undo
Thank you for using CESA. Please hit any key to display the conclusions.

                         Press any key to display results:
                         Values based on 0–10 system   VALUE

   1   Procurement request (NDW-NRL 4235/2404 (Rev 8–86)—WHITE FORM   10
   2   Statement of work (SOW)   10
   3   NDW-NRL 3900/1002 (Rev 11–84)—Work Unit Assignment Summary (DD Form
       1498), required by Code 1005   10
   4   ADP Approval Checklist with supporting documentation and ADP System
       Accreditation Report if purchasing or leasing ADP equipment or services   10
   5   NDW-NRL 4200/1304 (5–87)—Format for Additional Resources Required for New
       and Existing Contracts   10
   6   Evaluation criteria and weights; evaluation plan, including list of recommended
       evaluation panel members   10
   7   NPSQ (Nonpersonal Services Questionnaire)   10
   8   Proposal requirements documentation for insertion in Section L of the contract   10
   9   Contract Data Requirements List (Form DD1423)   10
  10   Complete the MENS (Mission Element Needs) form   10
  11   You need to synopsize intent to purchase the specific products/services,
       highlighting critical elements   10
  12   Provide a source list of competitive bidders   10

Press any key for more:
                         Values based on 0–10 system   VALUE

  13   You do NOT need NDW-NRL 4200/1293 (2-86)—Contractor Advisory Assistant
       Services (CAAS) documentation   9
  14   You do NOT need a Security Checklist; DD Form 254 (Rev 1-78)—DOD Contract
       Security Classification Spec and Attachments; SCI Contract Support Information
       Sheet (NIC Form 5540/1 (Rev 10-85); NDW-NRL 4200/1209 (9-86)—Procurement
       Request/Contract Information Sheet   9
  15   Appropriate type of contract is cost-plus-fixed-fee (CPFF) AND normally level-of-effort CPFF
       since government is buying hours of effort resulting in research reports

All choices <A> only if value>1 <G> Print <P> Change and rerun <C> Rules
used <line #> Quit/save <Q> Help <H> Done <D>

Figure 1   (*continued*)

SUMMARY

Expert System Success Factors

A number of factors contributed to the success of the proof-of-concept version of CESA. These success factors might serve as helpful hints to future knowledge engineers involved in expert systems projects.

One very important factor in the success of the CESA project was the support and financial backing of top management to the CESA concept. The head of the contracts division as well as the chief of its encompassing directorate were very encouraging and enthusiastic about the prospects and payoffs of CESA. They approved the necessary resources, both people and dollars, to build the proof-of-concept prototype.

A second critically important criterion for the success of any expert system is the availability and cooperation of a domain expert. In the case of CESA, the time of the expert was dedicated to the project, and she became more and more enthusiastic about CESA as each iteration of CESA was shown to her. The CESA team found that it was important to start encoding the prototypical cases as soon as possible in order for the expert to see some substantive, tangible results from the knowledge acquisition sessions. The project would not have been successful without the helpfulness and eagerness of the expert.

A third lesson learned from the CESA experience was the importance of using an expert system shell for developing the proof-of-concept CESA prototype. Otherwise, the demonstration system would not have been ready in two months. A shell allowed the knowledge engineering team to concentrate on the development of the knowledge base since the supporting system structures were provided. Of course, the expert system requirements had to be determined first, and then a suitable shell was selected to meet those requirements. The knowledge engineering team was aware of the motto "Every shell has a perfect task; but every task does not have a perfect shell!"

The fourth factor that played a large role in the successful development of CESA was good project management [15]. The CESA team had established a reasonable schedule of deliverables and milestones and then used a systematic approach in developing CESA. The knowledge acquisition sessions were structured to carve out a piece of the knowledge base at a time. That knowledge was then represented, encoded, and shown to the expert for her validation. The CESA team had a reasonable schedule to follow even though most expert system demonstration prototypes take three to six months to complete.

A fifth success factor in the CESA case was the elicitation and incorporation of comments from the test users and the expert. The suggestions from a diversity of users were helpful in the iterative refining of the CESA prototype.

A final success factor in CESA's development was the participation of two (rather than one) knowledge engineers during the knowledge acquisition sessions. One knowledge engineer took the lead in asking the questions, whereas the other knowledge engineer provided follow-up or supplemental queries. Also, note taking was easier with two persons present even though a tape recorder might be used (as in CESA's case) during the knowledge acquisition sessions.

Next Steps for CESA

After analyzing the best approaches for the next stage of development of CESA, it was determined that (1) CESA's knowledge of the preaward area would be refined further; (2) advice on completing selected PR forms would be provided within CESA; and (3) sample completions of selected PR forms would be included within CESA via access to dBase III. Prior to field testing, documentation would be provided on how to use CESA, and training sessions would be given to a selected group of potential users of CESA at the NRL. Following field testing of the CESA prototype at selected NRL sites, a formal evaluation of the users' comments and experiences would be made and used as a basis for further refinement of the CESA prototype.

There are several other avenues along which CESA could be expanded, if desired later. One avenue is to include postaward knowledge in CESA, which relates to the contract-monitoring and problem-solving processes that the COTR undertakes. A second expansion could be to include actual procurement request forms in CESA. A third approach is to develop CESA into an intelligent tutoring system for training ARO/COTRs and possibly new contract specialists. The intelligent tutoring system approach is a more time-consuming avenue than the other alternatives mentioned previously, but it contains many interesting research issues.

Even though a great deal of work is needed to develop CESA into a production system, the CESA project has made a good beginning on this road to full production and implementation. With the continued cooperation of all parties involved, CESA could eventually become a most-needed tool to help the ARO/COTRs conduct their contracting activities.

ACKNOWLEDGMENTS

The CESA knowledge engineering team is grateful to many key individuals who helped make this project a success. Virginia Dean, our NRL Contracting Specialist, served superbly and enthusiastically as our expert. We are grateful to Jack Brown and John Ablard, who sponsored the project and had the foresight to see the potential value of such a system. Appreciation also goes to Randall Shumaker, who gave us the go-ahead to work on CESA. Ensign Patricia Morgan, USN and key individuals at Exsys also are thanked for their help.

REFERENCES

1. Liebowitz, J., "Expert Systems for Business Applications," *Applied Artificial Intelligence Journal*, Vol. 1, No. 4, 1987.

2. Feinstein, J., J. Liebowitz, H. Look, and B. Silverman (eds.), *Expert Systems in Business Conference Proceedings*, Learned Information, Medford, NJ, 1987.

3. Air Force Institute of Technology, *ACQUIRE Marketing Literature*, Wright-Patterson Air Force Base, Ohio, 1988.

4. Womer, N. K., "Contracting Science and Game Theory," Contracting Science Workshop, *TIMS/ORSA Bulletin*, No. 25, The Institute of Management Sciences and Operations Research Society of America, Washington, DC, April 1988.

5. Compusearch, *PRISM Marketing Literature*, Compusearch Corp., Falls Church, VA, 1988.

6. Liebowitz, J., "Expert Systems in Law: A Survey and Case Study," *Telematics and Informatics: An International Journal*, Vol. 3, No. 4, 1986.

7. Liebowitz, J., L. C. Davis, and W. F. Harris, "Using Expert Systems to Help the Contracting Officer Technical Representative: A Feasibility Study and Selection Methodology," *Educational Technology*, Educational Technology Publications, Englewood Cliffs, NJ, in press.

8. Liebowitz, J., L. C. Davis, and W. F. Harris, "Expert Systems in Business and Information Systems Management: Developing CESA," *Expert Systems for Information Management*, Taylor Graham, London, in press.

9. Liebowitz, J., *Introduction to Expert Systems*, Mitchell, Watsonville, CA, 1988.

10. Davis, L. C., J. Liebowitz, and W. F. Harris, "Feasibility of Developing an Expert System to Aid the COTR in Contract Administration," NRL Technical Memorandum, Navy Center for Applied Research in Artificial Intelligence, Naval Research Laboratory, Washington, DC, January 1988.

11. V. Dean, L. C. Davis, and J. Liebowitz, Personal Communications, Naval Research Laboratory, Contracts Division, June 1988.

12. Naval Research Laboratory, *COTR Handbook*, NRL Publication 0066–1200, Washington, DC, March 1987.

13. Exsys, *Exsys: Expert System Development Package*, Albuquerque, NM, 1988.

14. Liebowitz, J. and D. A. DeSalvo (eds.), *Structuring Expert Systems: Domain, Design, and Development*, Yourdon, New York, 1989.

15. DeSalvo, D. A. and J. Liebowitz (eds.), *Managing AI and Expert Systems*, Prentice-Hall, Englewood Cliffs, NJ, 1990.

Index